The Man Who Would Be Perfect

John Humphrey Noyes, about 1850

The Man Who Would Be Perfect

John Humphrey Noyes and the Utopian Impulse

ROBERT DAVID THOMAS

University of Pennsylvania Press/1977

Library of Congress Cataloging in Publication Data

Thomas, Robert, 1939-
    The man who would be perfect.

    Bibliography: p.
    Includes index.
    1. Noyes, John Humphrey, 1811-1886. 2. Oneida
Community. 3. Social reformers--United States--
Biography. I. Title.
HX656.05N697   335'.9'74764 [B]   76-53198
ISBN 0-8122-7724-4

Frontispiece photograph courtesy of Imogen Noyes Stone.

To Becky: Amy, Kristen, and Megan

Contents

Introduction

The life and thought of John Humphrey Noyes have continually attracted the attention of journalists, historians, sociologists, psychologists, and popular writers. The tempo of this interest has increased over the past decade or so, and no wonder, since Noyes would undoubtedly have found a niche in the welter of reform and communal movements that emerged out of the tumultuous decade of the 1960s. The debates over sex roles and family life, the proliferation of urban and rural utopian visions and experiments, and the emergence of a secularized Perfectionism would have seemed familiar enough to him. Some writers have treated Noyes leniently, praising him for his prescience, idolizing him as a "Yankee Saint." Others have been less charitable, branding him a Vermont Casanova, a mentally unbalanced sexual misfit. These categorical versions of Noyes's life and work, however, do not encompass the complexity of the man, and because he is both interesting and important, his life and work are worthy of further consideration.

The present work is psychoanalytically oriented. Noyes's mind and motivations have been the subject of prior investigation. But either the insights offered were not pursued far enough, or the effort was systematic in a psychoanalytic sense but reductionist in thrust, viewing Noyes in terms of fixed energies and displaced symbols of a personal past.[1] In either case the dynamic view of Noyes was not tied securely to his time or society; Noyes was not seen as an actor in a particular situation that he could define in consistent and sensible

1. See Maren Lockwood Carden, *Oneida: Utopian Community to Modern Corporation* (Baltimore, 1969), pp. 26–35, and Ernest R. Sandeen, "John Humphrey Noyes as the New Adam," *Church History* 40 (1971): 82–90.

terms *for some people*, or in terms that would have made sense to those people.

To argue therefore that Noyes was not normal, that he was "a man deranged, beseiged with sexual fantasies and terrified of physical relationships with women," is not very illuminating since we cannot tell in these terms how Noyes became a leader, a person with considerable insight into theological problems and one who could and did provide consolation for different people over time.[2] By the same token, it is not helpful to argue that Noyes was normal, or sane and sensible, because in truth Noyes was riven by conflict, a man full of contradictions: radical yet conservative; shy yet arrogant and demanding; retiring and passive in his ultimate quest yet active, forceful, and even destructive in his leadership. The problem is rather to see how this man, who did suffer but who was also quite capable, reconciled these contradictions and made a life for himself in a particular historical context—indeed, became a man of some prominence. Given the internal conflict and the historical epoch, Noyes was able to act as teacher and healer under some conditions just as he could be the source of pain and discouragement under other conditions.

In short, we must see the whole man, his conflicts and capabilities, the capacity to contribute and to disturb, to be insightful and childishly fretful—and always in terms of the environment in which he lived. We must see Noyes, for example, against the background of American activism that constituted a social norm, against the social tensions that made it very difficult for many people of his region, age, and class to maintain a sense of balance by living up to their own and society's expectations of success.[3] We must also see Noyes against the background of religious enthusiasm, since America was still a society in which religious choices or the choice of a religious vocation was legitimate and even honored.

What I am suggesting, then, is that it is just as important to see Noyes as an actor in his antebellum world, faced by daily exigencies to which he had to respond, as it is to see him in terms of genetic development. To be sure, the past counts, but, as Peter Blos has argued, there is no linear development between childhood and adult

2. Robert S. Fogarty, "Onedia: A Utopian Search for Religious Security," *Labor History* 14 (1973): 202–27, briefly discusses the emotional consolations Noyes provided his followers.

3. Two good articles here are Maxwell Gitelson, "Therapeutic Problems in the Analysis of the 'Normal' Candidate," *International Journal of Psychoanalysis* 35 (1954): 176 (hereafter cited as *Int. J. Psa.*); Helen H. Tartakoff, "The Normal Personality in Our Culture and the Nobel Prize Complex," *Psychoanalysis—A General Psychology: Essays in Honor of Heinz Hartmann,* ed. Rudolph M. Loewenstein, *et al.* (New York, 1966), pp. 222–49.

years because ego development and social factors intervene.[4] Thus, while there is a paucity of data on Noyes's early childhood, it is not that affecting; besides, there is enough evidence on his adolescent and adult years to legitimately draw certain inferences. In fact, by paying close attention to Noyes's adolescent conflicts we will be able to see how he marshaled his internal resources, related to others, as he attempted to master a confusing and rapidly changing social world.

I should note that since psychoanalytic terms distract and often confuse readers, I have restricted the use of these terms in the text itself, reserving more detailed psychoanalytic expositions for the notes. These constitute, therefore, a significant and integral substructure of the work.

Finally, a word on sources: much of the later correspondence was edited by George Wallingford Noyes in his *Religious Experience of John Humphrey Noyes* and *John Humphrey Noyes, The Putney Community*. In the preface to his first collection, G. W. Noyes admitted that many of the documents "consisted of imperfect reports of extemporaneous talks," and so "some condensing and rearranging" were necessary. Yet, he also told his readers that he had "scrupulously avoided any alteration of the sense."[5] Are the edited letters therefore reliable? I think they are; for when placed alongside independent sources, the letters do have a degree of internal consistency and integrity. In cases where G. W. Noyes's tampering substantially altered the meaning of a letter, one can sometimes find it reprinted in one of the Community periodicals. Through a process of checking and cross-checking documents, one can catch many of G. W. Noyes's alterations and make judgments accordingly.

John Humphrey Noyes's own *Confessions of Religious Experience* is an invaluable source for understanding his feelings and responses to events, but this document must also be approached with caution. Like so many other eighteenth- and nineteenth-century spiritual autobiographies, the *Confessions* was written for a specific purpose.[6] In his opening statement, Noyes said that he wished to retrace the steps

4. Peter Blos, "The Epigenesis of the Adult Neurosis," *Psychoanalytic Study of the Child* 27 (1972): 106–34 (hereafter cited as *Psa. St. Chi.*). Also see Samuel Ritvo. "Current Status of the Concept of Infantile Neurosis," Ibid. 29 (1974): 159–79; Marian Tolpin, "The Infantile Neurosis," Ibid. 25 (1970): 273–305.

5. "Preface," *Religious Experience of John Humphrey Noyes, Founder of the Oneida Community* (New York, 1923), p. v.

6. Daniel B. Shea, Jr., *Spiritual Autobiography in Early America* (Princeton, N.J., 1968). Other useful studies on autobiography are William G. Spengemann and L. R. Lundquist, "Autobiography and the American Myth," *American Quarterly* 17 (1965): 501–19; Robert F. Sayre, *The Examined Self: Benjamin Franklin, Henry Adams, Henry James* (Princeton, N.J., 1964).

that had led to his Perfectionism, and for the seventy pages that followed, he was not above exaggerating the emotional strain and obstacles that he had to overcome to reach his goal. Noyes's *Confessions* was thus partly propaganda; he was telling others that they too could find peace and security in life if they were willing to follow his beliefs, if not his exact course. His assertions and depictions of events, though, can also be checked against his other letters and the observations of outsiders. So, even when taking Noyes's hyperbole into consideration, I think that the *Confessions* stands as a reliable indicator of Noyes's response to the society around him.

In the years it has taken to research and write this book, I have accumulated innumerable intellectual and emotional debts that most likely cannot be repaid. Fred Weinstein patiently read every revision of the manuscript. His probing, trenchant criticisms—and certainly there were enough of them—forced me to rethink and rewrite countless passages. Fred is a teacher in the best sense of that word. William R. Taylor suggested that I write on Noyes, and he provided his usual perceptive comments on organization and style. William J. Gilmore, Barbara Finkelstein and David F. Allmendinger, Jr., all provided, at one time or another, critical comments and/or encouragement in the writing.

In the process of my research, several libraries were generous in their assistance, and none more so than the Newberry Library. As a Fellow there from 1972 to 1974, I had the freedom to do further research and writing unencumbered by the responsibilities of the classroom. My special thanks go to William Towner, Director, and his highly competent staff. The staffs of the following libraries also provided ample cooperation: Lena A. Arendts Rare Book Room of the Syracuse University Library, Rare Book Room of the University of Michigan Library, The New York Public Library, The Garrett-Evangelical Theological Seminary Library, and the University of Chicago Library.

Constance Noyes Robertson shared her knowledge of the Oneida Community with me, and Stephen R. Leonard, Jr., graciously allowed me to examine his father's manuscripts.

A final word of appreciation. Anyone who has written a book knows about the emotional strain placed upon the writer and those closest to him. With this in mind I realize that the dedication of this book to my wife and children is hardly recompense for what they have had to endure.

1 A Time of Turmoil:

John Humphrey Noyes's Youth

and His Religious Conversion

Rural New England in the nineteenth century brings to mind a picture of gently-sloping hills, small well-kept towns—hardly static yet somehow still close to nature—and close-knit families with their emotional warmth and security. This picture may have reflected reality in some small way at the time of John Humphrey Noyes's birth in 1811, but far closer to the truth was the fact that the rural dweller was no more impervious to the impact of social change than his city cousin in Boston or New York.[1]

This picture of tranquillity does not even reflect the life of Noyes's father, also named John, whose own career during the late eighteenth and early nineteenth centuries was one of constant change and movement. In 1791, at the age of twenty-seven, the older Noyes quit his job as a peripatetic teacher and entered Dartmouth College. After graduating with honors in 1795, and within a five year span, he had taught in a private academy, tutored at Dartmouth, and had a brief fling as a minister. By 1800, his interests had turned from the spiritual to the material, and he set out for Battleboro, Vermont, where business opportunities beckoned. From that time to his retirement seventeen years later, his business and political success was mercurial. It was common knowledge that his trading deals earned him a good sum of money during the war of 1812, and that he shrewdly knew how to make that money work to his benefit.[2]

By 1815 his reputation for honesty and business acumen had gained him a seat in the House of Representatives. Since he believed it im-

1. Richard D. Brown, "The Emergence of Urban Society in Rural Massachusetts, 1760–1820," *Journal of American History* 61 (1974): 29–51.
2. Robert Allerton Parker, *A Yankee Saint: John Humphrey Noyes and the Oneida Community* (New York, 1935), p. 9.

1

possible to transport his growing family to Washington, the elder Noyes was separated from them for much of the time during his two-year stint. In many ways this physical separation simply reflected and intensified an already existing emotional separation from his wife and children. Conservative in dress as well as politics, he carried himself with "an extraordinary self-control and reserve." While he expressed his feelings to his wife and children "in many practical ways," he never "lavished on them those little endearments by which most fathers express their affection." Although nominally a religious man, his spiritual fervor was at best lukewarm, in marked contrast to his wife's.[3]

Some sixteen years younger than her husband, Polly Noyes was strong-willed and deeply religious. Above all else she taught her children "to fear the Lord," and was "more anxious that they should please God than that they should attain any earthly applause." In the selection of the family residence, the choice of schools for the children, and other important family matters, she was primarily concerned with the religious consequences, and her voice carried considerable weight in deciding the issues.[4]

Polly had ample time to mull over her emotional separation from a taciturn husband, given his frequent absences from home for political or business reasons. The more she contemplated, the more distressed she became until one night, alone, "God infused her spirit" urging her to "separate from her husband's world for fulfillment in a spiritual one." From that time on she always treated her husband cordially and usually with deference, but she kept a distance between her spiritual and his secular world.[5]

Shortly after the birth of their third child, a daughter, Polly lapsed into a depression that at times was quite severe. What the exact causes of her gloom were we do not know, but she suffered from "an active conscience and sleepless nights." This mental state continued unabated for several months, reducing her to "quite near a state of insanity." One day while watching her three daughters at play, she

3. "One of the Four—A Memoir of Charlotte A. Miller, I," *Oneida Circular* 12 (8 March 1875): 75.

4. Ibid.; "One of the Four, A Memoir of Charlotte A. Miller, II," *Oneida Circular* 12 (15 March 1875): 83.

5. "Memorial of Mrs. P. Noyes, V," *Circular* 3 n. s. (16 July 1866): 138. Noyes was given the middle name Humphrey in honor of his father's father and eldest brother. Noyes had three older sisters of whom Joanna was later to play a significant role. After John Humphrey came George, who was born when Noyes was two and died when John was eleven. Next came Horatio, who was born when John was four. Then there was Harriet (1817), Charlotte (1819), and George (1822), who was named after the dead brother. The last three were to play important roles in Noyes's communities at Putney and Oneida. Parker, *Yankee Saint*, p. 8.

was struck by the feeling that she was going to die and would have to leave the children with someone else. Terrified, she turned to God, and while deep in prayer, He assured her that she would live because she had too many other tasks to accomplish.[6]

God seemed to have kept his promise by endowing her with another child. She was continually in "a state of high religious joy" during her pregnancy, and on one occasion she remembered walking into a garden and receiving "a baptism that was indescribable." With the birth of their fourth child, Polly prayed to God that this first-born son, John Humphrey, might one day become a devoted minister of the gospel. And this was no idle prayer of the moment; Polly had a great emotional investment in her son. In all his subsequent growth and education, she recalled clearly "that prayer was before my mind and I could never think of anything short of that for him."[7]

John Humphrey Noyes possessed a good mind and showed promise as a student, but hesitations and doubts about his capabilities led him to belittle his own intelligence and achievements. Nevertheless, he successfully negotiated the academic rigors of several private schools and at the age of fifteen was ready to enter college. His father thought he was "well-fitted and a superior scholar," and wanted him to go to Yale. Polly, however, felt that Dartmouth, closer to home and "not in the midst of a city's temptations," was better suited to her son's morals. The elder Noyes was at first displeased with his wife's interference, but in the end she won out. In 1826 young John went to Dartmouth.[8]

In a letter home during his first year, Noyes gave an indication that Dartmouth's school day left little time for idle minds.

> Up at five. Go to prayers at a quarter after. Then immediately go to recitation. Then have breakfast. Then study till eleven, when we recite in Graeca Majora, which takes up an hour. Then until one we employ ourselves as we please. At one we take dinner, then study till four, when we recite in the grammar, which takes an hour also. At a quarter before six we go to prayers, which with supper takes up the time till dark, leaving us only three-fourths of an hour in the evening to get our lessons in Livy for the next morning.[9]

This terse, staccato-like description of the daily routine hardly does justice to the physical hardships Noyes and the other students had

6. "Memorial of Mrs. P. Noyes, V," p. 139.
7. Ibid.
8. "Memorial of Mrs. P. Noyes, VI," *Circular* 3 n. s. (23 July 1866): 147. On Noyes's lack of confidence in his scholastic abilities see G. W. Noyes, ed., *Religious Experience*, p. 10.
9. G. W. Noyes, ed., *Religious Experience*, p. 14.

to endure, particularly in the winter months. One student recorded in his diary that during the dark, winter mornings he went to chapel, "sat there freezing a few minutes and then went to the recitation room, no fire, bitter cold . . . like to froze both my ears and my nose."[10]

A strict regimen and spartan living, set within Hanover's woods, seemed to guarantee Polly Noyes's wish that her son's morals would be protected. They were, but not to the extent that Polly would have liked. While most of the Dartmouth student body came from rural New England, as did Noyes, many of the students, unlike Noyes, were boisterous and often difficult to control. The college soon gained the reputation for being "a difficult place in which to teach" and for turning out graduates characterized by "enterprise and sturdiness of character" rather than social refinement.[11]

Student intoxication was not unknown, and the spring thaw was usually accompanied by the smashing of dormitory windows and the breaking of furniture. In 1829 a student attack on the store of an unpopular villager was narrowly averted, but the homes of villagers often fell prey to students' breaking and entering. When many of the students arrived at Dartmouth, they had brought their guns with them, and during a night of revelry, shots could be heard ringing in the air.[12] Thus, during the 1820s and 1830s, Dartmouth, like so many other colleges, did not qualify as a sanctuary for the timid and shy.[13]

Noyes received continued support from his parents while struggling with the school's academic and social life, and their letters testify to the basic dichotomy in temperament and emotional relationship to him. From his mother he received caring, nurturing concern along with gentle prods that he continue to study diligently and improve himself both spiritually and intellectually. She once more reminded Noyes of her earnest hope that he become a minister. From his father came terse reminders of his duties as a man, and no mention of spiritual matters. The elder Noyes admonished his son to aim for a high level of achievement and success, hoping that he would shun "every notion and habit" that might impede that climb.[14]

Despite this encouragement from home, Noyes had to contend with multiple inner tensions during his college years. Although the turbulent period of adolescence as we know it today did not exist in the

10. Leon Burr Richardson, *History of Dartmouth College* (Hanover, N.H., 1932), 2: 479.
11. Ibid.
12. Ibid., pp. 482–89; Wilder Dwight Quint, *The Story of Dartmouth* (Boston, 1914), pp. 130–32.
13. David F. Allmendinger, Jr., *Paupers and Scholars: The Transformation of Student Life in Nineteenth-Century New England* (New York, 1975), pp. 97–110.
14. G. W. Noyes, ed., *Religious Experience,* pp. 13–14.

first quarter of the nineteenth century, boys did experience by this time a transitional stage between childhood and adulthood called "youth," which encompassed the early teen years to the mid-twenties.[15] This stage further marked a "coming of age" wherein a boy, at least in terms of sexuality if not career commitment, was expected to move from dependence or semidependence on the family to independence and autonomy—in other words, to manhood. Particular forms of behavior, naturally, were expected from middle and upper-class males. While it may not be quite accurate to say that abundant opportunities for self-improvement were open to all, one cannot deny that a high premium was placed upon the display of initiative and autonomy. The social tensions of the period, however, must certainly have come to weigh heavily upon and even exacerbate the inner tensions individuals experienced passing through this period of youth.

Shortly after graduating from Dartmouth in 1830, Noyes marvelled at the rapid emotional changes that he felt each person must undergo as he passed through the various stages from childhood to manhood. In his own growth he was still wandering somewhere between youth and manhood, indicative not only of his age (19) but also his inability to resolve doubts and to control his fears, to move forthrightly to manhood. Part of the problem stemmed from the environment: paradox and conflict had become "pervasive qualities of existence in New England colleges" during the antebellum period.[16] Noyes, moreover, was one of the youngest members of his class. When he graduated at the age of 19, most of his classmates were at least three to four years older, and several eight to ten years older.[17] It would have been difficult for anyone to assert himself under these circumstances, but it was particularly hard for Noyes because he suffered from *acute* shyness, a

15. John and Virginia Demos, "Adolescence in Historical Perspective," *Journal of Marriage and the Family* 31 (1969): 332, claim that the concept of adolesence did not exist before the last two decades of the nineteenth century. This idea has generally been followed by Joseph Kett, "Growing Up in Rural New England, 1800-1840," in *Anonymous Americans: Explorations in Nineteenth-Century Social History,* ed. Tamara K. Hareven (Englewood Cliffs, N.J., 1971), pp. 1–16; Kett, "Adolescence and Youth in Nineteenth-Century America," *Journal of Interdisciplinary History* 2 (1971): 283–98. Recently it has been suggested that the concept of adolescence can be applied earlier in history. N. Ray Hiner, "Adolescence in Eighteenth-Century America," *History of Childhood Quarterly* 3 (1975): 253–80; Ross W. Beales, Jr., "In Search of the Historical Child: Miniature Adulthood and Youth in Colonial New England," *American Quarterly* 27 (1975): 379–98.

16. Allmendinger, *Paupers and Scholars,* p. 110.

17. *General Catalogue of Dartmouth College and the Associated Schools, 1796–1925* (Hanover, N.H., 1925), pp. 142–45. This age difference was to be found in most New England colleges during the nineteenth century. Allmendinger, "Appendix A: The Ages of New England Students," *Paupers and Scholars,* pp. 129–38.

form of behavior that implies even earlier developmental difficulties
that would have left him vulnerable with regard to certain types of
experiences.

Noyes knew that he was having more than his share of difficulty
passing through this youthful period. "It may be that I have less
stability of character than most men," he confided in his journal, "but
I must confess that my views of men and things change so often and
so essentially even in the course of a single year, that I lose acquaintance with myself."[18] Upon entering Dartmouth his reticence and shyness, especially around girls, was a heavy burden to him. Consequently, he kept to himself and spent most of his free time studying.
But this intellectual perseverance afforded him little gratification. The
only inner contentment he found was in the quiet isolation of hunting
and fishing, activities he felt to be the height of happiness. Suddenly,
or so it seemed to him, his interests and personality completely
changed. Books and arduous study gave way to a desire for acceptance
and popularity among his classmates; to achieve this he "studied
human nature and learned to live with men." Just as quickly, though,
he felt threatened by his boldness, and retreated to the security of his
academic rigors. This mood change lasted for only a brief period
before he was hungering again to reach out and establish relationships
with his classmates. Another swing, however, had him clinging to
"Virtue, honor, and the dictates of conscience" as the only guarantees
of inner peace.[19]

Surely on one level the study of human nature provided the shy,
hesitant youth from Putney with an opportunity to relate to others.
He could happily proclaim in his journal that he now played checkers
with everyone even though they all beat him. For every mood—
frivolous, philosophical, political or religious—Noyes had a friend with
whom he could share his thoughts. At one point he became so utterly
pleased with his newly-acquired acceptance that he found himself able
to console two emotionally distressed classmates. He offered them
some rather typical nineteenth-century advice about the control of
their passions. They were to shun the introspective, romantic entrap-
ments of Byron, avoid contemplations of suicide, and, above all, re-
mind themselves that a shy man never won a woman's heart.[20]

18. "Extracts from College Journal," G. W. Noyes, ed., *Religious Experience,*
p. 24.
19. Ibid., pp. 25–35. On moods see Edith Jacobson, "Normal and Pathological
Moods: Their Nature and Functions," in *Depression: Comparative Studies of
Normal, Neurotic, and Psychotic Conditions* (New York, 1971), pp. 66–106;
Edward M. Weinshel, "Some Psychoanalytic Considerations on Moods," *Int. J.
Psa.,* 51 (1970): 313–20.
20. "Extracts from College Journal," p. 22.

With one friend, who was known for his "extremes in affability and haughtiness," Noyes came close to moving beyond the superficiality that marks the usual run of college friendships. As their relationship seemed to be deepening emotionally, and they were "having a wonderfully jolly sociable time of it," the ties became strained. As the tension increased, Noyes longed for the security of Putney, and whatever frustrations he felt he bore silently. A hurt Noyes, reflecting upon this disrupted relationship, voiced his suspicion and fear of his own tender and hostile feelings. To be emotionally open with others was to be left exposed and vulnerable. The only answer to such rejection was to withdraw inward for self-protection. This whole affair, he remarked, had deeply impressed upon him the necessity of having "resources of enjoyment within himself." As a result, the nature of this relationship changed: the spontaneity was subdued and replaced by lengthy academic discussions carried on in "philosophic coolness."[21]

Noyes complained in his journal, one bleak January day during his junior year, about students who flouted the rules for proper behavior by seeking their own advancement while snubbing everyone else. Noyes was especially sensitive to one classmate who exhibited these offensive qualities, and he took pleasure in branding him one of your *"real pompous boobies."* This person was "unsocial and misanthropic" without having any of those social graces that "palliate and remove the curse of misanthropy." Stingy, but quite willing to spend someone else's money, he often took part "in a jolly scrape," but never had his wallet ready when the bill came.[22]

Indeed, Noyes showed little inclination to tolerate classmates who affected airs of superiority and appeared to be greater and more socially impressive than he. Another classmate, "pedantic and conceited," was detested because his "whole soul seems to be devoted to his own advancement." Noyes believed that whenever this individual talked with others, he did so for the purpose of flaunting his conversational powers. In Noyes's estimation such arrogant behavior was despicable and demeaning to others. He would rather have seen a person drop his arrogance for the conviviality and social acceptance of his friends.[23]

Noyes's journal continued to reflect the heat of his inner conflicts. In a moment of deep anguish during his junior year again, Noyes proclaimed himself a fool because he was unable to control a ruinous habit: "that infernal diffidence, natural or acquired," that made him appear as "a stupid dunce" to himself and everyone else. The limits of

21. Ibid., pp. 22–23.
22. Ibid., p. 19.
23. Ibid., pp. 19–20.

his shyness were endless; truly, he felt he would have an easier time facing "a battery of cannon" than confronting "a room full of ladies" whom he did not know. In the red glow of his shame, reaching the pinnacle of frustration, Noyes brought his thoughts to a close with the shout: "Oh! for a brazen front and nerves of steel! I swear by Jove, I will be impudent!"[24]

One is occasionally perplexed in reading a journal or diary as to why certain intense, and often ambivalent, feelings find expression at the moment they do. Fortunately, Noyes wrote about the incident that aroused his deep-seated feelings of bashfulness and inferiority, and while it did not involve a room full of ladies it did center on a particular woman at a social engagement. Noyes, in fact, blushed whenever he felt himself to be awkward in a social situation with women, and his cheeks were never redder with shame than at a wedding he attended in this period. His mere presence at such an affair must have been unnerving for him, making him ever more keenly aware of and sensitive to how he appeared in the eyes of others. Shortly after the wedding ceremony and during the reception, Noyes felt himself to be socially confident and the center of attention. In the midst of the usual social amenities, he inadvertently misnamed a lady, and from this minor *faux pas* arose the hypersensitivity associated with shame. The "scornful smile" he perceived creeping over the face of a lady nearby immediately signaled to him that he had made a disastrous mistake. His embarrassment was so great that he was hardly able to regain his composure.[25] Standing exposed before the ridiculing glare

24. Ibid., p. 21. Shame ideation says, "how could *I* have done that; what an *idiot I am*—how humiliating; what a *fool,* what an *uncontrolled person*—how motifying; how unlike so-and-so, who does not do such things, how *awful and worthless I am*" (Helen B. Lewis, *Shame and Guilt in Neurosis* [New York, 1971], p. 36). For some it might be enough to explain Noyes's shyness by pointing to "the Atkinson difficulty." Noyes's father had four brothers, all of whom married cousins or some other kin because, as Parker, *Yankee Saint,* p. 6, reported, they had a "general bashfulness toward mankind, and special bashfulness toward the opposite sex." The Atkinson Noyeses were said to be so bashful that "they could not pop the question to anybody but cousins." While it is recognized that genetic inheritance may play a part in personality formation, I think a much stronger case may be made for Noyes's shyness by concentrating upon his separation and loss experiences, identifications, and the environmental tensions.

25. "Extracts from College Journal," p. 21. Heinz Kohut, *The Analysis of the Self: A Systematic Approach to Psychoanalytic Treatment of Narcissistic Personality Disorders* (New York, 1971), pp. 230–31, has several remarks on the *faux pas* worth noting. The pain experienced in many of these situations can best be understood by recognizing that a sudden and unexpected rejection has occurred just when the individual was most vulnerable to it. That is, just at the moment when he had expected to be noticed and receive acclaim in his fantasies. The shame that follows is partially caused by the sudden, narcissistic realization that one was not in control in the very area where he wished to shine.

of those around him, Noyes fervently wished to avert their gaze, to hide from the world, to become a "hermit or a savage."[26]

All these painful feelings linked to shyness were expressed in a contemporary poem; though not aesthetically pleasing, it is an accurate barometer of his anxieties. Noyes wrote, returning to one of his particularly sensitive themes:

> I hate garrulity and self-conceit,
> And vain display of learning or of wit,
> Where'er I meet it. But a greater curse
>   (In man 'tis bad enough, in woman worse)
> Is that affected modesty called cold reserve,
> Which holds in still subjection every nerve,
> Ties down the tongue to merely a "Yes" or "No."
> And chokes the fountains whence kind feelings flow.
> And this vile canker-worn, this deadly pest
> To every joy that's kindled in the breast,
> Is called by some "good breeding," and by some
> Is named "politeness." By my halidom!
> What good it breeds, or where its merits lay,
> 'Twould match the far-famed Oedipus to say.[27]

In the context of this poem and his other concerns as expressed in his journal, we can see that Noyes's sensitivity to arrogance in others reflected not only the cultural strictures against vanity and pride that were a part of the religious and guidance literature of the day, but also something more, something very personal. The anger and resentment he felt towards those whom he perceived as self-confident and self-assured are openly expressed. Their coldness and emotional self-sufficiency acted to diminish his own sense of worthiness. Noyes felt that he did not measure up to those whom he thought to be socially confident, and, as a result, relegated himself to an inferior position. As Noyes himself said about the social reticence, it was a "deep-seated, chronic obstruction to free communication of all kinds," especially when in the company of "superiors."[28] Noyes, of course, took some comfort in knowing that he did not possess those very qualities he deplored. But it should be clearly understood that he also wanted to be assertive and impudent, noticed and admired, to be seen as strong and self-confident, perhaps even arrogant.

26. "Extracts from College Journal," p. 21. Lewis, *Shame and Guilt*, p. 38, points out that these shameful feelings are often connected to the defense of hiding or running away.

27. "Extracts from College Journal," p. 20.

28. Home-Talk by J. H. N.–No. 123, "Fear of Criticism," *Circular* 1 (12 September 1852): 179. The roots of shyness are discussed in Donald M. Kaplan, "On Shyness," *Int. J. Psa.* 53 (1972): 439–52.

The social world presented problems for Noyes. His persistent battles with self-consciousness and shame continually hindered his efforts to abide by society's rules for proper behavior. He had himself stipulated that a man was to be composed and self-contained in social situations—not bashful and awkward. With his heart as faint as it was, how could be ever win a girl? Noyes desperately wished to appear before others as unblemished, which meant that he was constantly preoccupied with, and self-conscious of, his physical appearance, dress, speech, and moral behavior. He was always guarded, trying to perfect behavior, hoping to prevent and ward off any criticism that might undermine his precarious sense of self-esteem. There was no easy solution for this dilemma, and he knew it. As he observed, it would require a virtual Oedipus to solve these conflicts.

Noyes mulled over the meaning of the wedding incident, and in so doing revealed the source of his fears. In his mind there was no quarter asked and none given in any competitive contest. He apparently could not imagine a situation where rivals coexisted on an equal plane. Rather, it was an either/or struggle, with the conqueror "animated by the victory" and gaining even more strength and superiority. The conquered one, dispirited and battered in defeat, would sink further into despair and slowly dwindle away. Immersed in these unhappy thoughts, Noyes remembered a long-time friend who was once as vibrant, sensitive, and intelligent as any boy, but whose transition from boyhood to manhood, "which usually determines the bent of future life . . ." was marked by "a miserable though perceptible change." Noyes concluded his run of thoughts on this whole matter tersely, but in a way that revealed his distrust of emotions and his need for even stricter self-control. "When the mouth is sluggish in utterance, but active and noisy in eating, you may write its owner a fool."[29]

Noyes was still trying to come to terms with his conflicting inner urges as his college career ended. He had sought the limelight again in the spring of his senior year by sporting the latest in clothing fashion: "bell-bottomed pantaloons, square-toed boots, patent leather stock, and pyramid-formed hat." Noyes must have cut quite a figure,

29. "Extracts from College Journal," p. 22. What is being stated here in symbolical terms is Noyes's solution to his earlier separation conflicts and experiences, and in particular the oedipal conflict with which he was once again doing battle in his youthful period. It is also logical to infer that in view of his chronic blushing, shyness and shame, Noyes, in that earlier conflict, had renounced masculinity in response to overwhelming castration threats and therefore had assumed a passive identification as a defense against oedipal strivings. In a sense then, Noyes lacked a psychological background of safety in his youth conflicts. Joseph Sandler, "The Background of Safety," *Int. J. Psa.* 51 (1960): 352–56.

and he even imagined that "a handsome dress actually has some tendency to elevate the mind." This move to be the cynosure lasted but a brief moment before Noyes renounced his narcissistic display and quietly returned to conventional attire.[30]

While the focus has been on Noyes's moods, his intense shyness, and his wishes to be assertive, we should be reminded that he was something more than a jangle of internal conflicts. Noyes had his strengths, even with his emotional problems. He was attempting to reach out to others and to avoid the pitfalls of withdrawal. He was able to survive in the sometimes disruptive social atmosphere at Dartmouth, and he graduated Phi Beta Kappa, with one dean characterizing his mind as "sound and discriminating."[31] Furthermore, like many in his class, Noyes chose the law as a profession, indicative of his wish to compete in the man's world.[32] Thus, with graduation, it was time for Noyes to step out into the world of the marketplace and marriage.

Shortly after leaving Dartmouth, he was welcomed into the law office of his brother-in-law in Chesterfield, New Hampshire. For a while he was the model of perseverance and discipline, with the study of Blackstone consuming most of his time and energy. However, beneath this outward calm lurked those deep rents and fissures that would begin to expand and press toward the surface as he was asked to contend with situations that were perceived by him to be competitive.

Above all, there seemed to be no escape from his shyness and his fear of censure. Noyes's first day in court was "a most shabby performance," even taking into account the normal anxiety one experiences in such circumstances. Noyes was frightened "beyond all reasonable bounds," by the exercise of autonomy and authority, and for a few moments had trouble regaining a semblance of composure. At last, he sputtered his way through the presentation, a performance which

---

30. "Extracts from College Journal," p. 23. Edith Jacobson, *The Self and the Object World* (New York, 1964), p. 198, says that chronic shame reactions and fears of exposure, coupled to a highly sensitive self-consciousness, indicate identity problems wherein the superego usually shows an infantile rigidity and a lack of autonomy. These superego qualities are further indicative of an immature moral system. Also see, Sandor S. Feldman, "Blushing, Fear of Blushing, and Shame," *Journal of the American Psychoanalytic Association* 10 (1962): 368–86 (hereafter cited as *J. Am. Psa. Assn.*); Fred E. Karch, "Blushing," *Psychoanalytic Review* 58 (1971): 40, 43–44 (hereafter cited as *Psa. Rev.*); Jule P. Miller, Jr., "The Psychology of Blushing," *Int. J. Psa.* 48 (1965): 189–91.

31. G. W. Noyes, ed., *Religious Experience*, p. 16.

32. *General Catalogue of Dartmouth*, p. 144, indicates that Noyes graduated Phi Beta Kappa. The catalogue also lists the professions of the graduating class of 1830.

did not escape the acerbic eye of his instructor, Squire Spaulding, who muttered that Noyes "did not plead worth a damn!" Afterwards, in the solitude of his room, Spaulding's "taunting words" festered within Noyes, challenging his already fragile sense of self-esteem. He complained bitterly of having to "bear the curse of other people's contempt," but vowed just as firmly that his self-esteem had suffered "no incurable deterioration." For Noyes it was clear that to be out of control and less than perfect meant to be virtually diminished.[33]

Chesterfield's social world also provided Noyes with more than his share of frustrations—especially close, or potentially close relationships—with women. Noyes wished to master his shyness and feelings of vulnerability, but in mid-November 1830 he lamented the fact that "(thanks to the depravity of human nature) society has been a constant source of misery" to him. Specifically, Noyes had become "bewitched" by two girls who attended a local private academy. As he admitted in his diary, "my fancy was wrought up to such a pitch that I imagined I had at length found that perfection for which I had hitherto sought in vain."[34]

His thoughts about these girls indeed began to intrude upon his study of Blackstone. Surely, thought Noyes, if an outsider had access to his thoughts during the day and his dreams at night, he would have had to conclude that Noyes was happy, but nothing was farther from the truth. Noyes's "excitement" was being diminished by his frustration and "impatience" at being separated from the girls during the day, by his jealousy of his "competitors in gallantry," and his "dolorous reflection" that their school would be closing shortly. These thoughts, laden as they were with sexual excitement, overtones of competition and possible defeat (the jealousy), and fears of loss (the girls were leaving), were too taxing for Noyes. They eventually pulled him down "from the pinnacle of felicity," which seemed to be almost within his reach.[35]

Noyes recovered to climb that peak once more during his stay in Chesterfield. Caroline was her name, which is just about all we know about her from independent sources. However, Noyes's deepest feelings found their way again into verse. In a poem entitled "An Invitation to an Evening Walk," Noyes wrote:

> Mark, Caroline, yon western sky,
> Deep-tinged in crimson light.
> The sun's red glories haste to die,
> And swift comes on the night.

33. G. W. Noyes, *Religious Experience*, p. 29.
34. "Extracts from Diary," G. W. Noyes, ed., *Religious Experience*, p. 28.
35. Ibid., pp. 28–29.

> Now turn again, and mark yon star
> Dim twinkling in the east.
> See, just above the dark belt where
> The sun's domain has ceased.
>
> Then hasten, ere the twilight ends.
> Far down the vale we'll roam,
> Nor pause till o'er us night descends,
> Then Love shall light us home![36]

This bliss was not to last, since Caroline's school would be closing in a matter of weeks. Her imminent departure threatened to undermine Noyes's sense of well-being. Indeed, the mere thought of her leaving provoked great anxiety in Noyes, and "he doubted himself and the consequences of a parting interview." To avoid any further pain he gathered a few scattered belongings and fled home to Putney, never to see Caroline again.

The imagery in Noyes's poem harkens back to his earlier observation that in every contest there must be victor and vanquished. Noyes had no tolerance for thoughts of defeat; he had no wish to challenge his adequacy, perhaps by appealing somehow to Caroline, or expressing his love. Faced with mounting tension and threatened by feelings of depletion and loss—the result of Caroline's forthcoming departure —Noyes sought to control the situation and provide himself with a sense of relief by initiating the break and fleeing to Putney.[37]

These familiar surroundings plus the warmth of an understanding family gave Noyes the chance to repair his image. Exactly how long Noyes stayed in Putney and precisely what kind of nurturance he received from his family, we can not ascertain from existing documents. We do know, however, that in time he returned to Chesterfield and completed his year's study. By the fall of 1831 Noyes was hesitant yet determined to "indulge the lust of the eye and the pride of the life for the present, and risk the consequences." He planned another year of study and practice, but this time in the larger, more prestigious law firm of his uncle in Battleboro.[38] But these anticipations were as evanescent as they were impossible for Noyes to implement. Within a week he had undergone a religious conversion, and within six weeks he had become an ardent student at the Andover Theological Seminary.

Religious revivals and subsequent conversions were common enough events in the second quarter of the nineteenth century. This is espec-

---

36. Ibid., pp. 30–31.
37. Ibid.
38. Ibid., p. 34.

ially true for residents of southern Vermont who had easy access to
the "psychic highway" that wended its way across the rolling hills of
nearby western New York. The many spiritual bonfires, which had
become a conflagration by 1830–31, were ample proof that this region
deserved its sobriquet, "the burned-over district."[39] More than one
historian has remarked how the revivals helped preserve a sense of
national unity in the face of sectarian division, permitted towns to
reestablish a sense of social order, and allowed for personal integration.[40] The revival was hardly new to Putney, since the town had
undergone two within recent times: one in 1819 and another in 1827.
The latest revival, a four-day affair to begin in town on 14 September
1831, would serve the purpose of social reintegration after a disastrous
economic panic four years earlier. Noyes decided at this time to
submit to the emotional call, which might seem surprising, considering
the fact that as recently as 1827 he had shied away from one of
Putney's strongest calls for religious conversion.[41]

Noyes, however, would use the revival now as a means of integrating
the different and conflicting elements of his personality. His graduation from college had signaled that it was time to leave his immediate
family, earn his own living, and be at least semiindependent. In Chesterfield he experienced a great deal of anxiety in his attempts to meet
these demands. Although he negotiated his way through the first
year, his prospective job in Battleboro suggested an even bigger step
into the competitive, adult world—so big, in fact, that he could not
risk taking it. His inability to appear adequate to the challenges, and
his own wishes for mastery, meant that daily life was becoming increasingly problematic and troublesome for him. The twenty-year-old
Noyes wanted to be his own man, but he was losing ground, and he
turned to the revival as an integrative measure.[42]

That Noyes would choose a religious solution to his problems was

39. Whitney R. Cross, *The Burned-Over District: The Social and Intellectual
History of Enthusiastic Religion in Western New York, 1800–1850* (New York,
1965), p. 3. Also see David Ludlum, *Social Ferment in Vermont, 1791–1850*
(New York, 1966).

40. Perry Miller, *The Life of the Mind in America: From the Revolution to
the Civil War* (New York, 1965), pp. 3–95; Donald G. Mathews, "The Second
Great Awakening as an Organizing Process, 1780–1830," *American Quarterly* 21
(1969): 23–43.

41. G. W. Noyes, ed., *Religious Experience*, pp. 16–17.

42. At this time the evidence indicates that Noyes's ego was under increasing
tension and pressure. For conditions leading to ego impoverishment see Otto
Fenichel, "Ego Strength and Ego Weakness," in *The Collected Papers of Otto
Fenichel* (New York, 1954), 2: 70–80; Max Schur, "The Ego in Anxiety," in
Drives, Affects and Behavior, ed. Rudolph M. Loewenstein (New York, 1953),
pp. 67–103.

by no means unusual in his day. Religious conversion and the sense of certainty of salvation provided considerable support for the individual. Horace Bushnell told his listeners that religion never required "the humiliation of the soul," but set free all its powers. No one, he said, would ever be driven into God's arms "to be sheltered there from the loss and ignomy of a defeated life," for salvation assured one of "unequivocal success."[43] In one of his many essays on religious topics, Theodore Parker spelled out how active-passive forces were, through religion, conjoined in the mind. Religious faith not only gave strength to the individual to aspire and achieve, but it also legitimated suffering as an avenue in the search for identity. As Parker succinctly put it: "Religion not only gives the feminine capacity to suffer, but the masculine capability to do."[44] Therefore, religion reconciled two modes of action and in so doing led to an integrated and productive life.

The revival experience required an individual's immediate break from the idleness and sin of his past. The consolations could be great for an afflicted soul; an experience deeply felt could resolve one's inner turmoil. Nevertheless, this was not an easy, automatic step to take; before a person could reaffirm himself, he first had to give free reign to his emotions. And tempting as this spiritual catharsis might appear, such an emotional "letting go" might also contain the power to overwhelm, submerging the self in those very inner forces.

Noyes experienced these mixed feelings himself on the eve of the revival. He was attracted to it but simultaneously "felt a dread of being present at it." He had looked upon religion "as a sort of phrenzy to which all were liable," and feared being "caught in the snare."[45] However, his need for inner peace and a strong desire to please his mother combined to override his fears, and when the revival commenced, Noyes was to be found among the crowd. The religious exercises made little impression upon him for several days, and when they threatened to do so he immediately fortified his resolve not to be carried away by the emotional displays. The scenes of people exposing their deepest emotions did not soothe Noyes's fear of losing control. In fact, he admitted that such demonstrations at the "anxious bench" caused him almost unbearable tension. Noyes was sensitive to how he appeared before others, and even though he was moved by the religious exercises, he held himself in check by the thought that

43. Barbara M. Cross, *Horace Bushnell, Minister to Changing America* (Chicago, 1958), p. 47.
44. *Sermons of Religion by Theodore Parker,* ed. Samuel A. Eliot (Boston, 1908), pp. 174–99, especially p. 186.
45. "Extracts from Diary," pp. 40–41.

as soon as the revival ended he would lose his religious fervor, be left alone and exposed "to ridicule" for his emotional outpourings. With such painful memories as the wedding incident, Noyes was not about to let himself appear foolish.

Unable to participate actively in the revival, Noyes lost ground in his fight to control the inner forces that threatened to paralyze him. He began, on the last day, to slip into a depressive mood, and he braced himself for the inner conflict that was so familiar to eighteenth- and nineteenth-century conversion experiences. Throughout his "painful process of conviction," the consideration that weighed most heavily upon him was that to accept religion fully, he would have to "quit the law and take to divinity."[46] Unlike many others who underwent revival experiences and carried the spiritual message to their vocations, Noyes saw religion and law as diametrically opposed. Religion pointed to the maternal, protective bosom of the family; the law pointed to competitive, isolated relationships. The more he contemplated his alternatives the more intense his feelings became.

The day after the revival ended, Noyes slipped further into gloom, insisting, however, that he was "calm—calm as a soldier in the day of battle." But his "war with God" was not going well, and there seemed to be a good chance that he would join the ranks of the fallen and defeated. The following day a cold brought him down, and in the solitude of his home the cold's severity impressed upon him the vagaries of life. Abruptly, in the throes of this suffering, he was overcome with the realization that his moment of reckoning had arrived; one way or another his future course was about to be determined. "The conquest of my aversion to become a minister was one of the critical points," said Noyes, and after some further agonizing moments on this issue, he decided to accept religion.[47]

Noyes had made his decision: now he felt it was time to master his "fear of man, and though it was like cutting off a right hand God enabled me to resolve and to execute the resolution of communicating to Mother my determination."[48] The symbolic meaning of the dreaded amputation is clear: Noyes had to sacrifice before he could achieve. He wanted to act but he feared the aggressive, assertive, competitive action of the marketplace. He sought his mother, indeed, to declare his resurrection of his father's world of pride and aggression. Noyes would rejoin the world, but on his terms; he would express his passive aim through the spirit of reconciliation and resurrection, through

46. Ibid., pp. 36–37.
47. "Religious History—No. 1," *Perfectionist and Theocratic Watchman* 4 (16 April 1844): 8.
48. G. W. Noyes, ed., *Religious Experience,* p. 37.

identification with Christ as he, Noyes, interpreted the message of the Gospel.

Noyes, having taken Christ as his guide, could now appear before his mother, suffused with her ideals, as pure and innocent rather than worldly and aggressive. His ideals, moreover, assumed a quality of grandeur and perfection.[49] Noyes had created for himself an inner world of harmony and acceptance and opposed it to the world from which he had withdrawn. He chose the nurturance of religion rather than the competition of the marketplace. In this sense Noyes had chosen passivity. We should be perfectly clear on the meaning of this: Noyes had not withdrawn, he had rather outflanked his father's world and acquired for himself *a different and legitimate* mode of activity. As Noyes so accurately put it, he had been a "bashful boy" in college, and not until he had come to religion did he begin "to feel and exercise the strength of manhood."[50]

We must be careful with this metaphor of passivity because during this period Christ could appear to people in such a light. Lydia Maria Child, for example, was keenly aware of the appeal of Christ's passive qualities. The feminine ideal, which tended to depict Christ with a benign, meek expression, and "feminine beauty," came much closer to biblical standards than did the prevalent ideal of masculinity. Very few, said Child, spoke of the masculine qualities of Christ, of his bravery, strength, or intellect. The Devil, instead, was imagined to possess "acute intellect, political cunning, and the fiercest courage."[51]

To some extent Child was right, but her emphasis upon passive

---

49. Regarding Noyes's religious choice, Peter Blos, "The Genealogy of the Ego Ideal," *Psa. St. Chi.* 29 (1974): 82, states, "Whatever the ensuing irrationalities and distortions, which are due to persistent narcissistic self and object realizations, their form and content are always derived from the social system in which the individual lives."

50. John Humphrey Noyes, *Confessions of John H. Noyes, Part I: Confession of Religious Experience: Including a History of Modern Perfectionism* (Oneida Reserve, N.Y., 1849), p. 19. Like Christ, Noyes saw himself sacrificed for the sake of the father. With his renunciation of his incestuous wishes for the mother, there emerges the belief in a great reward awaiting the submissive, obedient son (death and resurrection to the father's side). This placation and denial of castration is analyzed by Henry Edelheit, "Mythopoesis and the Primal Scene," *The Psychoanalytic Study of Society,* ed. Warner Muensterberger and Aaron H. Esman (New York, 1972), 5: 212–33.

51. Lydia Maria Child, *Letters from New-York* (New York, 1844), p. 246. Thought provoking discussions of active-passive are found in Roy Schafer, "On the Theoretical and Technical Conceptualization of Activity and Passivity," *Psychoanalytic Quarterly* 37 (1968): 173–98 (hereafter cited as *Psa. Q.*); Schafer, "Action: Its Place in Psychoanalytic Interpretation and Theory," *The Annual of Psychoanalysis: A Publication of the Chicago Institute for Psychoanalysis* (New York, 1973), 1: 159–94; David Beres, "Ego Autonomy and Ego Pathology," *Psa. St. Chi.* 26 (1971): 12–15.

traits was far too one-sided. Certainly Jesus had a nurturant, protective character, but He also had an active masculine one that struck against the sin that incarcerated men.[52] Theodore Parker had no trouble persuading his audience that Christ introduced into this world "a higher type of manliness" than was ever before deemed possible. His "manly intellect" was united with a "womanly conscience and affection" to produce "one great humanhood of character."[53] Christ, moreover, was full of "well-directed energy," enabling Him to carry on 'his Father's business' regardless "of the busy multitudes absorbed in the pursuits of gain and pleasure."[54] Needless to say, this was a comforting message to those befuddled by the social turmoil of the 1830s and 1840s. And to some like Noyes, it said that the terms "activity" and "passivity" were not specifically sex-linked. Through Christ one was able to embrace the positive, cultural ideal of meekness. In accepting this passive mode of dealing with reality, ultimately one would be given the opportunity to act upon and change reality. Thus, through passivity, activity would be achieved.

Noyes, in the flush of his conversion experience, spent many hours with his mother reading and rereading the New Testament. Each time through he became more fully infused with the spirit of Christ, and the ecstasy seemed limitless. Noyes, immersed in this rapture, prayed with all his inward strength to be like Christ, a perpetually young convert in zeal and simplicity. With his heart fixed on the promise of millennial glory, he dedicated his life to its unfolding and fruition.[55]

Through his identification with Christ Noyes could act and relate to others.[56] But he had to suppress a great deal to achieve this balance. In a sense, the very grandiosity of his conversion experience was

52. Theodore Parker, *Lessons from the World of Matter and the World of Man*, ed. Rufus Leighton (Boston, n.d.), p. 322. Support for Child's observations may be found in Barbara Welter, "The Feminization of American Religion: 1800–1860," in Mary Hartmann and Lois Banner, eds., *Clio's Consciousness Raised: New Perspectives on the History of Women* (New York, 1974), pp. 137–57; Ann Douglas, "Heaven Our Home: Consolation Literature in the Northern United States, 1830–1880," in David E. Stannard, ed., *Death in America* (Philadelphia, 1975), pp. 51–54.

53. Parker, *World of Matter and Man*, p. 310. For more inclusive statements on Christ's dual nature, see pp. 305–26, 327–419.

54. R. S. Storrs, "The Cultivation of Piety in Childhood," *Mother's Assistant and Young Lady's Friend* 4 (May 1850): 100.

55. J. H. Noyes, *Confession of Religious Experience*, p. 2.

56. It should be stressed here that Noyes's narcissistic solution to his crisis did not lead to a general regression to an infantile level. Although his longing for omnipotence and perfection contained regressive features, it did not signal a withdrawal of the entire cathexis from objects. Annie Reich, "Pathologic Forms of Self-Esteem Regulation," *Psa St. Chi* 15 (1960): 215–16.

recompense for what had been sacrificed. Simply to get along with himself would be no easy task for Noyes; what had been suppressed still had its claims and might reappear. Noyes also had to get along with other people. This he would be able to do, even brilliantly, so long as people saw things his way, so long as people did not threaten him by contradicting his sense of virtue and truth. In religious matters, however, people see things differently and they are willing to fight to establish those differences. It would only be a question of time, then, before Noyes was challenged from either, or even both, directions.[57]

57. Kohut, *Analysis of the Self*, p. 150, points out that often in feelings of grandiosity and feelings of being special, unique, and precious, there lies submerged a number of frightening, shameful, and isolating narcissistic fantasies. Also see Edith Jacobson, "The 'Exceptions': An Elaboration of Freud's Character Study," *Psa. St. Chi.* 14 (1959): 135–54; Otto F. Kernberg, "Factors in the Psychoanalytic Treatment of Narcissistic Personalities," *J. Am. Psa. Assn.* 18 (1970): 55–57.

2 On the Road to Damascus:

Andover, Yale, and

a Perfectionist Ideology

Noyes now determined that he should begin his formal training by attending Andover Theological Seminary. Precisely why he chose this school we do not know, but several ideas are suggestive and are consistent with what we know about Noyes's desires to succeed. He carried the twin goals of achievement and success into his newly chosen profession of the ministry, and he was not alone in doing this. Pious young men throughout antebellum society "practiced within religion and reform careers the skills of opportunity-seeking and individual advancement which their society embraced."[1] No religious institution better implemented these values than Andover, "the premier theological seminary in pre-Civil War America," and its graduates were to be numbered among the most influential college presidents, seminary and college professors, and ministers.[2] Given Noyes's high aspirations, Andover was a logical choice.

The two weeks before he was to leave were emotionally charged for Noyes. A few days after his conversion Noyes became so absorbed with thoughts of God's goodness and his merger with the Father that soon, as he wrote in his diary, his mind "seemed to lose its faculty of self-control." For several days he struggled with his inner thoughts to the point where he became physically as well as emotionally enervated. At last he forced those thoughts from religion to any mundane topic—a tactic which slowly lifted his spirits.[3] By 1 November 1831, Noyes was at Andover, although not completely recovered. His health

1. Lois W. Banner, "Religion and Reform in the Early Republic: The Role of Youth," *American Quarterly* 23 (1971): 534.
2. J. Earl Thompson, Jr., "Abolitionism and Theological Education at Andover," *New England Quarterly* 17 (1974): 239.
3. His turn to nonreligious topics was his ego's way of preserving contact with reality. On the ability to "snap out" of it see Andrew Peto, "On Affect

at first forbade "much effort of any kind," but through diet and the "exercise of the Seminary" he recovered sufficiently to attend class, where he began "to feel somewhat encouraged in regard to religious matters."[4]

The stated purpose of Andover's education was to improve the students in heart as well as mind, and to provide for their continued progress "in piety as well as in theological knowledge—for their preparation . . . for the practical duties of the ministry."[5] No one did this better than Moses Stuart with his German Biblical criticism, and Noyes was impressed with him. Two of Stuart's interpretations proved especially attractive to Noyes. One concerned the twenty-fourth chapter of Matthew which gave him *"a glimmering"* (and at this point only a glimmering) that the development of Christianity was progressive. Jerusalem's destruction, instead of being "the birth, ministry or death of Christ, or the day of Pentecost," was the end of Judaism and the beginning of a "mature Christianity." The second of Stuart's interpretations dealt with the seventh chapter of Romans and suggested to Noyes that the sin mentioned there referred to life before conversion. This view, of course, attached itself easily to Noyes's belief that a converted Christian might always remain in the revival spirit, and it confirmed his "purpose and hope of overcoming the world entirely and perpetually."[6] Gradually, however, Noyes grew disenchanted with the curriculum that seemed bent on emphasizing the mind and knowledge over the heart and piety. "I just contrived to live along," he said, "with my understanding convinced but my heart and practical principles at variance with it. I meditated much on divine things, but to little profit."[7]

Obviously, Andover was doing little to support and reaffirm Noyes's desire to be a young convert forever. He sought desperately to recapture this ideal, and in December (1831) he pledged himself to the missionary cause. He believed that the "diffuse, self-sacrificing spirit" that guided Christ's disciples also infused those dedicated to taking the Son's message to Asia. Once Noyes felt himself to be united with this spirit, he reexperienced those exalted feelings of his religious conversion.[8]

Control," *Psa. St. Chi.* 22 (1967) : 36–51. Similar tactics to lift a depression were employed by Richard Henry Dana. Robert F. Lucid, ed., *The Journal of Richard Henry Dana, Jr.* (Cambridge, Mass., 1968), 1: 32.

4. "Extracts from Diary," G. W. Noyes, ed., *Religious Experience,* pp. 42–43.
5. Thompson, "Abolitionism and Theological Education at Andover," pp. 257–58.
6. J. H. Noyes, *Confession of Religious Experience,* pp. 5, 8.
7. Ibid., p. 5.
8. "Extracts from Diary," p. 43.

The conditions at Andover, however, continued to undermine him. Heated debates over the slavery issues, the nature and limits of moral reform, and other social concerns, which seemed to be engulfing all of New England, filled the rooms and halls of the school. The highly respected Moses Stuart was upset by "the spirit of the day" that seemed to be "against solid and patient study."[9] Noyes too was discouraged by the "disputes, excitements, levity, and trifling with Scripture and sacred things." Adrift in this current of dissention, Noyes lost much of his spirituality "and love of prayer and meditation." He felt he had fallen far from his lofty ideals and was depressed to think that he was not measuring up to them.[10] Unable to cope with these mounting pressures, Noyes fled from Andover to Putney where he found the security and emotional comfort necessary to fortify him for a return to the seminary.

In late May 1832, Noyes did return, determined to begin "a new and independent course of life" by setting himself against the bickering and dissent which threatened to disrupt his internal peace. He aligned himself with a small cadre who embraced a religion of the heart and vowed to become missionaries. One of the weekly exercises of this group was to provide spiritual and emotional guidance to each member. At their meetings, every individual at one time or another had to submit to "a frank criticism" of his character by the others. Such open honesty was often embarrassing and painful; nevertheless, Noyes said that he derived a great deal of benefit from it.[11]

Apparently though, this was not enough. The struggle to find moral certainty and spiritual perfection began to take its toll on Noyes. He experienced longer and more severe periods of "sorrow and inward conflict."[12] His mind and body became a battleground between the contending forces of Satan and God. His feelings of anger and impoverishment could be remarkably intense: one night he dreamed incessantly of the cholera, and in the morning his body felt as if it had

9. Thompson, "Abolitionism and Theological Education at Andover," p. 256.

10. J. H. Noyes, *Confession of Religious Experience*, p. 3; "Religious History —No. 2," *Perfectionist and Theocratic Watchman* 4 (20 April 1844): 11.

11. J. H. Noyes, *Confession of Religious Experience*, p. 4. Also see "Mutual Criticism," *Oneida Circular* 12 (20 April 1875): 129–31.

12. J. H. Noyes, *Confession of Religious Experience*, p. 3. Sidney J. Blatt, "Levels of Object Representation in Anaclitic and Introjective Depression," *Psa. St. Chi.* 29 (1974): 117, says that in "the developmentally more advanced introjective depression, there are feelings of being unworthy, unlovable rather than unloved . . . having failed to live up to expectations and standards. There are exceedingly high ideals, and overly harsh superego, a keen sense of morality and commitment, and a constant self-scrutiny and evaluation." In addition, there are "extensive demands for perfection, a proclivity to assume blame and responsibility and feelings of helplessness to achieve approval, acceptance, and recognition."

actually undergone an attack by the dread disease. What better evidence could one have—other than the disease itself—that he was sinful? Such were the thoughts in his mind as he wrote to his brother Horatio. If Horatio ever thought there could be too much anxiety about "the endless consequences of life and death," then he ought to consider the word "eternity," and he would, like Noyes, step back "with horror as from the brink of a bottomless abyss." Noyes felt as if he were in a battle, and chances were that he might be "found among the slain." To prevent this catastrophe, he had to summon up courage, "set all things in order," and then look to Christ for an example "of dying conduct." An unshaken faith in God, Noyes concluded, was the "*only* preventative of that disease" which gripped him and spread "wider and more terrible devastation than the cholera."[13]

Noyes tried different methods in an effort to surmount his depression; he gorged himself at a meal, but this only served to increase his "evils of body and mind."[14] He tried to humble himself before God, but discovered that without a perfect submission to His will, he "was impotent." He finally turned to Christ and tried to measure Christ's love by that which he knew his mother bore towards him.[15] Finding security in this, Noyes declared that his motto would be "*bringing into captivity EVERY THOUGHT to the obedience of Christ.*"[16]

To guide him, Noyes sought in the Gospels and the life of Christ models of thought and action. Discovering a "truth," he would trace it through each of the Gospels, underlining all those passages that related to the particular maxim. When that was done, he would study his notes diligently in order "to obtain a concentrated and comprehensive" understanding of the subject. The harder he studied the

13. "One of the Four, IV," *Oneida Circular* 12 (29 March 1875): 98; "Extracts from Diary," p. 49. Somatic distress and hypochondriacal worry often accompany depressions. Noyes's thoughts about cholera were both culturally and idiosyncratically derived. By 1832 the cholera epidemic had become "a scourge of the sinful" and a sign of God's wrath to most Americans. Charles E. Rosenberg, *The Cholera Years: The United States in 1832, 1849, and 1866* (Chicago, 1962), pp. 40–64. The conflict between Satan and God, which Noyes felt within himself, reflects the aggression that has been turned against the self, Louis Berkowitz, "The Devil Within," *Psa. Rev.* 55 (1968): 28–36; Mortimer Ostow, *The Psychology of Melancholy* (New York, 1970), p. 44.

14. "Extracts from Diary," p. 46. Here Noyes's ego is fighting to halt the regressive pull and maintain contact with reality. One such effort was to eat—to give himself a feeling of fullness and aliveness. Several authors have commented on the oral mechanisms of recovery in depressions. Edward Bibring, "The Mechanism of Depression," in *Affective Disorders: Psychoanalytic Contributions to Their Study*, ed. Phyllis Greenacre (New York, 1953), p. 20; Jacobson, *Depression*, pp. 175–77; Ostow, *Psychology of Melancholy*, p. 48.

15. "Extracts from Diary," p. 53. Noyes's depression lasted, in varying degrees of intensity, from early July to late August 1832.

16. J. H. Noyes, *Confession of Religious Experience*, p. 3.

clearer everything became until it all "seemed to dwell in a focus of glory," and his heart burned with sheer joy. As Noyes acknowledged, these experiences were not chiefly intellectual in nature, for they were geared to secure him a tightly-knit unity and fellowship with the spirit of the Father. Many times, he recalled, when he was about to succumb to the iniquitous atmosphere surrounding Andover, he would repeat this ritual. This occurred almost daily for several months.[17]

This painfully meticulous routine is manifestly suspect. As Noyes emphatically indicated in his underlined resolutions to obey Christ, his quest for control and certainty was rigid and driven, not allowing for any spontaneous, peaceful contemplation. Noyes felt, clearly, that unless he had total and absolute control over his inner wishes and sentiments, he would lose all control and be overwhelmed by them.[18]

The longer Noyes stayed at Andover the more he realized that this kind of self-control was not possible. In the midst of his inner conflicts he wrote in his diary pleading for a new way of sanctification, some method by which sin could be "exterminated once for all." There had been times in the past year when Noyes was certain that he had discovered the cure-all, but just at the point when he thought his "disease was cured, it would break out like a cancer in some other spot."[19]

Noyes suspected that part of his dilemma arose from the external circumstances at Andover; though he also recognized that his "conscience was newly awakened and legality worked wrath" in him.[20] To create the sense of inner security he desperately needed, Noyes sensed that he would have to move, find an environment that could assuage his doubts and anxieties, and support his efforts to become a devoted son of God.

All signs indicated that Noyes should quit Andover for the more liberal atmosphere of Yale Divinity School, but the decision to leave did not come easy for him. Yale certainly offered special inducements to Noyes. At New Haven he would be required to attend the lectures of Nathaniel William Taylor and then would be free the rest of the day to study the Bible as he saw fit. If he stayed at Andover,

---

17. Ibid., p. 5. The adaptive, ego functions of such a ritual are stressed in Volney Patrick Gray, "Psychopathology and Ritual: Freud's Essay 'Obsessive Actions and Religious Practices'," *Psa. Rev.* 62 (1975): 493–506. Also see Leon Salzman, *The Obsessive Personality: Origins, Dynamics and Therapy* (New York, 1968), pp. 39–40, 55–60, 269–70.

18. On the need for impulse control see Seymour L. Lustman, "Impulse Control, Structure, and the Synthetic Function," in *Psychoanalysis—A General Psychology*, pp. 215–16; Salzman, *Obsessive Personality*, pp. 13–17.

19. "Extracts from Diary," p. 51; Parker, *Yankee Saint*, p. 26.

20. "Religious History—No. 2," pp. 11–12.

the second year would be filled with more "technical theology." Taylor's "heretical reputation" seemed to worry Noyes, but this was not really an important factor. Far more significant was the fact that Noyes was "leaving behind valuable connections" in the missionary movement.[21] By going to Yale, he surely would have opportunity to fulfill his pledge, but Andover students held an especially advantageous position in this field. Many directors and founders of the current benevolent associations were centered in Boston, and they drew heavily upon Andover students to act as agents and secretaries.[22] Noyes's transfer to Yale, therefore, was something more than a shift from one religious institution to another, from conservatism to liberalism. The missionary movement provided an avenue for young men "to advance rapidly in pursuits that were innovative and challenging," and Noyes's best opportunity for success lay at Andover.[23] Earlier he had opted to leave behind worldly success as a lawyer to become a minister, a difficult decision for him. Noyes now was thinking of leaving perhaps his best chances of becoming a missionary. He knew what opportunities he was giving up, but he did not know where his emotional and spiritual needs were taking him. This was his dilemma, and it led him to believe that the prospective move was too great for his "comprehension and decision."

Ultimately his decision was made in a way that allowed him to escape the responsibility for it and the dire consequences that might possibly follow from it. In the throes of indecision and doubt, Noyes opened the Bible one day and his eyes immediately fell upon the imperative in Matthew, "Fear not ye! for I know that ye seek Jesus which was crucified. HE IS NOT HERE." The message was clear and Noyes saw no reason "to be ashamed to confess that this little circumstance broke the equilibrium of my doubts, and settled my determination to go" to Yale.[24]

As relieved as Noyes felt, his subsequent journey from Putney to New Haven in the fall of 1832 was not undertaken with an open mind. He had an "instinctive aversion" to teachers and ministers whose views contradicted or challenged his sense of self worth. The "Spirit of truth" as he interpreted it in the Bible, and as he discovered it in meditation and prayer, would be his guide through life, not

21. J. H. Noyes, *Confession of Religious Experience*, p. 6.
22. Banner, "Religion and Reform in the Early Republic," p. 687.
23. Ibid.
24. "Religious History—No. 3," *Perfectionist and Theocratic Watchman* 4 (4 May 1844): 15–16; J. H. Noyes, *Confession of Religious Experience*, p. 6. The quote from Matthew is taken from Noyes's own words and the capitalization in the sentence is his.

the "intellectual treasure" of another man. Thus Noyes resisted "forming any such intimacies with the Professors, and other distinguished men" who might have drawn him "into adhesion to their systems."[25]

Despite this intransigience, Nathaniel William Taylor's modifications of Edwardsean theology were acceptable to Noyes. Taylor rejected the doctrine that man was innately depraved and incapable of saving himself. Though sin was inevitable, it was not "original" and man had the ability within himself to overcome it. In Taylor's phrase, man had the "power to the contrary."[26] Sitting through Taylor's lectures, Noyes "took copious notes of all his prominent ideas, meditated, talked and wrote about them extensively." Indeed, Noyes considered himself to be "as fully a master" of Taylor's doctrines as any of his classmates.[27]

Taylor's method of instruction also appealed to Noyes. He encouraged his students, in their quest for religious truth, "to throw away the authority of names and to think for themselves." He pushed students to question their own beliefs "in light of their own intelligence," to shun blind obedience to the ideas of another, and "to go for the truth themselves to its sources."[28] Given this encouragement, no wonder Noyes could claim that the zeal he brought to his study of the Bible was nurtured by Taylor's doctrines, "which were very favorable to the course I was pursuing."[29] But Taylor's changes in religious doctrine hardly went far enough to meet Noyes's idealized ambitions. As liberal as his ideas might sound, Taylor never broke completely from the Calvinist past. His ideas, though, inspired his students to challenge religious authorities and to discover their own religious truth, which might be far different from his own. Noyes would have agreed with another of Taylor's students who recalled that Taylor's "teaching became the starting point, not the end of my religious thinking."[30]

Noyes did not confine himself solely to Biblical study. Soon he began to channel his energies into other activities, one of which was the religious instruction of New Haven's blacks. Within the seminary, debates waxed hot and strong on the issue of antislavery, and none

25. J. H. Noyes, *Confession of Religious Experience*, p. 19.
26. Sidney E. Ahlstrom, *A Religious History of the American People* (New Haven and London, 1972), p. 420. Also see William G. McLoughlin, ed., *The American Evangelicals, 1800–1900* (New York and Evanston, 1968), pp. 7–10.
27. "Appendix D," J. H. Noyes, *Confession of Religious Experience*, p. 83.
28. Sidney Earl Mead, *Nathaniel William Taylor: A Connecticut Liberal* (Chicago, 1942), p. 162.
29. J. H. Noyes, *Confession of Religious Experience*, p. 19.
30. Mead, *Nathaniel William Taylor*, p. 163.

was more vociferous in a defense of immediate abolition than Noyes. Although this position was an unpopular one in New Haven, Noyes's words were put into action when he took a minor part in establishing the New Haven Anti-Slavery Society, one of the country's first.[31]

Noyes also found a platform from which to express his lofty, perhaps even grandiose, sense of religious devotion. He joined one of the local free churches that were starting to sprout up throughout the Northeast. These churches, with their revivalistic approaches and liberal interpretations of doctrines, embraced "a general radicalism of spirituality," and for a year and a half Noyes was content to remain within this church. In time, however, he would come to realize that they had not gone as far in their evangelicalism as he was willing to go—to sever themselves completely from "the parent denominations."[32]

Noyes had hoped to find in this church the religious organization that could bank the fires of his "burning zeal," but the church was not enough. As Charles Grandison Finney's revivals swept the land, and Noyes attended the services of the free church, he became reinvigorated with the millennial spirit and began to judge the society around him by it. He was depressed to think that Christianity was not converting society the way he once thought it would. And as his confidence in conventional religion waned, his "outward-bound missionary zeal" also declined. His thoughts now turned to "desires, and projects of an *internal reformation* of Christendom. Quality of religion, instead of quantity," became the center of his attention.[33]

In this state of mind, alienated from the established churches, their "missionary madness," and their benevolent societies, Noyes decided that he could no longer "go under the patronage and direction of the American Board [of Commissioners]." Rather, he would carry that evangelical zeal to the heathens by himself, armed with his own interpretations of Scripture, or he would not go at all.[34]

Noyes's continuing estrangement from established institutions had profound effects upon the development of his religious thought. Early in the summer of 1833, his attention became riveted on Christ's intimation that the apostle John would live until the second coming. Perplexed, Noyes wondered how this idea could possibly be recon-

31. "Perfectionism not Pro-Slavery," *Perfectionist* 3 (11 October 1843): 61; J. H. Noyes, *Confession of Religious Experience,* pp. 6–7. On antislavery feeling in New Haven, see Rollin G. Osterweis, *Three Centuries of New Haven, 1638–1938* (New Haven and London, 1975), pp. 296–302.

32. "Religious History—No. 23," *Perfectionist and Theocratic Watchman* 5 (22 March 1845): 2.

33. J. H. Noyes, *Confession of Religious Experience,* p. 7.

34. Ibid., p. 8.

ciled with the customary belief that the second coming was in the future. For the answer, Noyes turned to the ritual he had established at Andover. This time he read through the New Testament ten times, searching out all the passages that dealt with the second coming. He soon perceived that every allusion to the time of this event coincided with his insight that it would take place within John's lifetime. Noyes's mind was now clear on this issue: he no longer "*conjectured* or *believed*, in the inferior sense of that word," he *knew* that the second coming was within one generation "from the time of Christ's personal ministry." That "glimmering" Moses Stuart's ideas had given Noyes at Andover was now a stronger light, but it was still far from a total illumination. The more immediate consequences were that Noyes lost a great deal of confidence "in the theological authorities of the whole Christian church since the apostolic age."[35] As Noyes searched to restore his confidence and reduce his seemingly permanent state of tension, he resorted to another ritual. This time he concentrated on the apostle Paul, whose testimony assured him that Christianity had actually made some believers holy in this life.[36] With this turn to Paul, Noyes's Perfectionism began to take firmer shape, to assume ideological coherence.

Perfectionism, of course, has deep roots in Western culture; it has always been an important element in the national character, as Americans have played out their destiny as God's chosen people.[37] Democracy, asserted one national magazine of the period, was boldly energetic in its quest for a better world and "a higher perfection of social institutions."[38] Henry James, Sr., was even more lavish in his praise of democracy's ideals. He was certain they heralded the moral perfection of man and would usher in a promised age of harmony and "infinite Love."[39]

While the ideal of perfection "floated before the eyes" of the nation continually urging Americans to succeed, it was also suspended before the inner eye of each individual. Every man, Theodore Parker

35. Ibid.
36. John Humphrey Noyes, *Salvation from Sin: The End of Christian Faith* (Wallingford, Conn., 1866), p. 21.
37. The best overview of Perfectionism within Western thought is John Passmore, *The Perfectibility of Man* (London, 1970). For a more detailed analysis of Perfectionism within America see Merrill Elmer Gaddis, "Christian Perfection in America" (Ph.D. diss., University of Chicago, 1954); John Leland Peters, *Christian Perfection and American Methodism* (Nashville, 1956); Timothy L. Smith, *Revivalism and Social Reform: American Protestantism on the Eve of the Civil War* (New York, 1965).
38. "How Stands the Case?" *Democratic Review* 3 (September 1838): 4.
39. Yehoshua Arieli, *Individualism and Nationalism in American Ideology* (Baltimore, 1966), p. 269.

declared, held in his mind "the ideal of what he should be, but is not." It was this gap between one's actual self and this ideal self that kept a man dissatisfied with his present achievements and constantly prodded him to do better.[40] Both for the culture and the individual, therefore, the ideal of perfection was a constant reminder of God's intentions for man.

But the 1830s–1840s were hardly normal times, and for many the disorientation of the period exacerbated and inflamed the tension between the actual and the ideal. Orestes Brownson wrote that the notion that mankind was capable of much greater "moral and physical well-being" than had yet been attained was a popularly held conviction and was daily gaining wider acceptance. The growth of Christian principles, the belief in democratic equality and the rise of the common man, had aroused men's hopes; but as Brownson wisely noted, it was now all the more difficult to measure up to those expectations. Men everywhere believed that they had not reached the ideal social state which they felt they must attain. In every corner people asked: how shall the actual condition of man be made to comport with the Christian ideal?[41]

The answers to this question were not uniform. For some there was no doubt that the past was still the scaffold upon which to build a viable present and future. Emerson, by contrast, would have abandoned the past and reveled in the exhilarating liberation. By the 1830s his distrust of the past and history was well expressed in his complaint, "Why should we grope among the dry bones of the past, or put the living generation into masquerade out of its faded wardrobe?"[42] A break from the past could lead instead to an ideal completeness and perfection within Nature and in the present.

For many others, however, events indicated God's desertion of America. These were real feelings of abandonment and loss. As one writer lamented: "Our age has no power to connect itself with the past or future."[43] Clifford Pyncheon, in Hawthorne's *The House of Seven Gables*, was more somberly confronted with the meaninglessness that stemmed from this loss: "The more Clifford seemed to taste the happiness of a child," Hawthorne wrote, "the sadder was

40. George Willis Cooke, ed., *The Transient and Permanent in Christianity* by Theodore Parker (Boston, 1908), p. 76.

41. O. A. Brownson, "Brook Farm," *Democratic Review* 11 (1842): 481.

42. R. Jackson Wilson, *In Quest of Community: Social Philosophy in the United States, 1860–1920* (New York, 1970), p. 8. Also see R. W. B. Lewis, *The American Adam: Innocence, Tragedy, and Tradition in the Nineteenth Century* (Chicago, 1971), pp. 13–27.

43. "The Voice of the Past," *Ladies' Repository* 8 (January 1848): 24. Also, "Our Country," *Whig Review* 1 (1845): 277.

the difference to be recognized. With a mysterious and terrible Past, which had annihilated his memory, and a blank Future before him, he had only this visionary and impalpable Now, which, if you look closely at it, is nothing."[44]

To overcome this sense of loss, the *New Englander* urged people to unite themselves with God. Through this unity the soul would be ready to endure and achieve. One would be "independent of circumstances," and be able "to master TIME."[45] The *Ladies' Repository* declared that anyone who joined himself to Christ and God united "the past, the present, and the future together by indissoluble links."[46]

And this sense of integration is what religious Perfectionism attempted to accomplish. Perfectionism reflected the concern for self-control, continuity, and direction in life. Charles Grandison Finney sounded much like the famed Sylvester Graham, or any other physiologist, when he asserted that a high level of excitement could not continue long without inducing "inflamation of the brain, and consequent insanity."[47] From the pages of the Perfectionist journal, *The Guide to Holiness*, innumerable essays pelted the reader with the same message. The loss of God, of ideals, would lead to the loss of self-control. This would open the door to brooding indecision, doubts about one's abilities, and self-accusations, all of which would ultimately "cripple the mental energies."[48]

In their attempts to reintegrate man, society, and God, Finney, Asa Mahan, and other Perfectionists exhorted men to submit un-

44. Norman Holmes Pearson, ed., *The Complete Novels and Selected Tales of Nathaniel Hawthorne* (New York, 1937), p. 332. Roy Schafer, "Ideals, Ego Ideal, and Ideal Self," in Robert R. Holt, ed., *Motives and Thought: Psychoanalytic Essays in Memory of David Rapaport,* Psychological Issues, Monograph 18/19 (New York, 1967), pp. 161, 169, states that real events play an important role in the formation, maintenance, and revision of ideal images. If the environment no longer appears stable enough to support the normally developing ideal selves and objects, then it is quite logical to assume that distortions on the personal and collective levels will become manifest.

45. "The True Success of Human Life," *New Englander* 11 (February 1853): 57.

46. "Voice of the Past," p. 277.

47. Charles Grandison Finney, *Views of Sanctification* (Oberlin, 1840), p. 18. Also see Finney, *Lectures on Systematic Theology* (Oberlin, 1887), pp. 229–30; Finney, *Lectures on the Revival of Religion,* 6th ed. (New York, 1835), pp. 425–27.

48. "Letter to a Doubting Friend," *Consecrated Life and Guide to Holiness* 31 (1857): 77–79; "Religious Maxims," Ibid. 2 (1841): 217; Jesse T. Peck, "Cleansed from All Sin," Ibid. 4 (1842): 1–6. From 1839 to 1842 this journal was entitled *Consecrated Life and Guide to Christian Perfection.* After 1842 it was known as *Consecrated Life and Guide to Holiness.* For the sake of clarity, I will use the shortened version of this title, *Guide to Holiness,* throughout this essay.

equivocally to the will of God as Paul and Christ had done.[49] One of man's greatest sins was to have a will separate and opposed to God's, while security and bliss were obtained in an "annihilation of his own will" and a merger with the Lord's.[50] This submission however, did not signify a dissolution of the self; in fact, the opposite was true. It led to an "unruffled and quietness of spirit," which gave men the ability to "endure the smaller and more frequent inconveniences and vexations of life."[51] God's law, Finney said, was the only true and exact standard by which a person could gauge himself. By means of an unwavering faith one could directly communicate with God, grasp the content of His "infallible and invariable" law, and direct his feelings and actions in full accord with it. Men would then know without question "what is their true character in the sight of God."[52]

If an individual's will could conform to these religious demands, his tension between the actual and the ideal would be reduced, and an inner harmony created. The soul would be "in a state to really respect itself," promised Finney; it could "behold its own face without a blush."[53] Hence, through faith, submission, and obedience a person would be saved from a past life of sin; whatever shame and guilt experienced would be diminished; and he could be at peace within himself.

To Finney and other Wesleyan Perfectionists the gap between the actual and the ideal state could be narrowed through salvation and the holiness of perfection, but it could not be closed. A Perfectionist could share in God's attributes even though man's perfection fell far short of the angels' and did not even approach the innocence enjoyed by Adam before the Fall. Man would always be susceptible to doubt,

---

49. *True Submission: Revival Messages of Charles G. Finney* (Grand Rapids, Michigan, n.d.), pp. 50–68; Asa Mahan, *Scripture Doctrine of Christian Perfection,* 11th ed. (Oberlin, 1850), p. 7.

50. "Principles of the Interior or Hidden Life, No. VIII," *Guide to Holiness* 3 (1841): 106–9; "Principles, No. XV," Ibid. 3 (1842): 273–77.

51. "Principles of the Interior or Hidden Life, No. VIII," p. 106.

52. *True Submission,* p. 12. On p. 23, Finney emphasized man's ability to control his thoughts, and by his own actions attain inner harmony. "You can command your thoughts; God has put the control of your mind in your own hands." And, in "Principles of the Interior or Hidden Life, No. IX," *Guide to Holiness* 3 (December 1841): 130, it is stated that "a true quietness of soul involves a cessation from unnecessary wandering and discursive thoughts and imaginations."

53. Finney, *Systematic Theology,* p. 379. For other examples of a reduction of ego-ego ideal tension through perfect holiness see Rev. B. W. Gorham, "Personal Holiness and Ministerial Efficiency," *Guide to Holiness* 31 (1857): 5; "Religious Maxims," Ibid. 27 (1855): 6, where it is asserted that through perfect Christian love, "Shame, which is the indication, as well as result of degradation or guilt, will disappear."

indecision, and anxiety; but through a "muscular" and well exercised faith, he could, in times of stress, control his thoughts and feelings and direct them to God.[54] Perfectionism, then, did not imply stasis, but a continual desire for action and improvement in both the spiritual and secular worlds.

A person may have achieved holiness in perfection, but that did not mean that he was released from his responsibilities as a man and citizen. Even though he might undertake "a higher class of duties," the Perfectionist was still obliged to bring his greater spiritual insight to work for the moral improvement of his fellow man and society.[55] Perfectionists were thus encouraged to maintain ties to their church and other institutions, and criticize them from within. But to present others with a pure morality, to ask them to live uncompromisingly by their own ideals, to demand that they measure up to them, can eventually prove to be highly discomfiting and threatening. "Some persons no sooner hear the word *"perfection,"* reported one believer, "than they immediately take fire."[56] So, like Paul and Christ, perfectionists were warned to be ready to face the attacks and abuse of the nonbelievers. Through self-effacement, self-sacrifice, and suffering for others, they would be able to bring them and their institutions closer to the Christian ideal. One element of Perfectionism, therefore, sanctioned passive nonresistance and encouraged strength through passivity, wherein suffering would be used to achieve greater unity.[57]

Yet, the Wesleyan Perfectionists also recognized that there might be times when such measures would be insufficient. An institution may be so corrupt and the people so mired in unbelief and sin as "to defy all remedial efforts." The duty of God's faithful under these circumstances was to "separate from their churches and societies." Casting off the mantle of meekness, these true believers were to "assume the attitude and the office of vivid and prophetic imagination."

54. "What is Christian Perfection?" *Guide to Holiness* 1 (1839): 1–2; Mahan, *Christian Perfection,* pp. 7–12; Finney, *Systematic Theology,* pp. 403–81, contain good examples of the limits of perfection. On the need for a strong Christianity see "Christian Holiness—How Preserved?" *Guide to Holiness* 12–13 (1847–48): 37; "On the Law of Habit in Connection with Faith," Ibid. 6 (1844): 97.

55. "On the Relation of a Life of Faith to the Discharge of Civil and Political Duties," *Guide to Holiness* 6 (1844): 1–4; "Religious Maxims," Ibid. 2 (1841): 218; On the Doctrine and Duty of Separation from Others," Ibid. 7 (1845): 97–101.

56. N. Bangs, "Christian Perfection," Ibid. 19 (1851): 37.

57. "Principles, No. XXIII," Ibid. 5 (1843): 1–2; "On the Doctrine and Duty of Separation from Others, " p. 101. As Emerson shrewdly noted about suffering during these times: "We fancy it is torture: the patient has his own compensations." Emerson, "The Tragic," *The Dial* 4 (1844): 520.

Perfectionists would endure once more the attacks of others and suffer, but always with the knowledge that like Christ their motives were morally correct and their suffering enhanced the self and promoted God's work. People "called to this terrible work" of active nonresistance would be "equipped within and without, with special armor."[58]

Perfectionism thus covered a wide spectrum of belief and behavior. Responding to the highly unsettling social conditions of the antebellum period, Perfectionism was an impetus to personal and social salvation, and served as an outlet for such individuals as Finney and his cohorts to question existing relationships within institutions and within the given morality. Ideally, however, since it was recognized that no institution could stand between man and God's sovereignty, Perfectionism also opened a way for people such as William Lloyd Garrison to call for immediate abolitionism; for Henry Wright and Bronson Alcott to practice nonresistance; and for the Brook Farmers and Adin Ballou to follow their communitarian ways. Authority would be attacked from *outside* the regular institutions, but still *within* the given morality. At the far end of this spectrum were those random individuals who, paying little heed to the dictum of self-control, embraced Perfectionism because of its implied promises for self-indulgence and other forms of antinomian behavior. Somewhere between these individuals and the others was a man like Noyes who believed in self-control, but whose grandiose ideals would prompt him to confront society with a new and different morality.[59]

These competing views of Perfectionism, given ideological expression and providing emotional integration in existing or newly created institutions, stood as contingent possibilities for action in the social world. These views pushed against each other in the 1830s and 1840s, giving rise to conflicting, contradictory, perhaps irreconcilable orientations, leading to fears of an anarchistic individualism, violent debate, and sometimes to violent action.

Noyes took a significant step towards his new morality when he confronted and assimilated the thoughts of the apostle Paul. Although most Perfectionist publications extolled Paul and paid tribute to his

58. "On the Doctrine and Duty of Separation from Others," p. 101; N. Bangs, "Christian Perfection," *Guide to Holiness* 26 (1854): 130, "A holy person may speak with a fire and zeal against wickedness that may be mistaken for an unholy passion."
59. The impact of evangelicalism and Perfectionism upon these and other individuals and groups during the antebellum period is discussed in Laurence Veysey, ed., *The Perfectionists: Radical Social Thought in the North, 1815–1860* (New York, 1973); Lewis Perry, *Radical Abolitionism: Anarchy and the Government of God in Antislavery Thought* (Ithaca and London, 1973).

life and works as a model for growth in Perfectionism, none equalled Noyes in the number of articles published, and none matched the intensity of his identification.[60] Once Noyes had absorbed Paul, his devotion was life-long and complete. When Noyes defended Paul hereafter, he was defending himself; when he praised him, he was praising himself. The relationship of Noyes to Paul was, to be sure, different from the usual commitment.

To Noyes, Paul's career showed that one was not necessarily "cut off from glorying" by his previous life of wickedness.[61] Before confessing Christ, Paul was "completely carnal," bound hand and foot by his sinfulness—as Noyes himself had been. Indeed, when one first meets Paul, he is not the apostle of Christ; he is Saul the persecutor. Wallowing in unbelief and sin, Paul was a scourge to all believers.[62] And, how well Noyes could identify with Paul's problem of sin. Sin, to Noyes, was a "subjective spiritual evil" that saddled man with a burdensome conscience. Like insanity, sin did not merely affect man's intellectual nature but suffused his whole being. External restraints and changes therefore could no more eradicate sin than a straitjacket could cure insanity.[63]

Doubt and self-accusation grew out of sin and prevented complete salvation. Both, said Noyes, were conducted in "a private contemptible court" where conscience served as the judge, the devil as lawyer, and memory as the witness. But memory, conscience, and the devil were in fact wholly unfit "for the trial of deep questions." The devil, using his full power in this subjective bailiwick, had his way with the judge and witness because of the expanded feelings of sinfulness in these "little conscience courts."[64] It was evident to Noyes that

60. As it has been pointed out in psychoanalytic literature, identification with a religious figure serves multiple functions. In a variety of ways such an identification may support an individual in a crisis and help him to remain active in a world that appears to be chaotic. Albert J. Lubin, "A Boy's View of Jesus," *Psa. St. Chi.* 14 (1959): 156; Gregory Rochlin, *Griefs and Discontents: The Forces of Change* (Boston, 1965), pp. 3–10. For references to Paul within Perfectionist thought see Gaddis, "Christian Perfection in America," pp. 16–22; Mahan, *Christian Perfection,* pp. 38–39; Finney, *Systematic Theology,* pp. 415–16, 423–33.

61. Home-Talk by J. H. N.—No. 76, "Cure for Envy," *Circular* 1 (11 January 1852): 39.

62. J. H. Noyes, *Salvation from Sin,* p. 21; "Cure for Envy," p. 39. Also see Home-Talk by J. H. N.—No. 12 "The Meaning and Use of Suffering," *Free Church Circular* 3 (21 October 1850): 277.

63. "Sin a Spiritual Disease, Requiring a Spiritual Remedy," *Witness* 1 (20 December 1838): 36.

64. "Spiritual Tribulation," *Witness* 1 (22 June, 1840): 157. This metaphor appeared in a letter from Noyes to G. W. Wilder who was suffering from severe religious doubts and self-castigation.

Satan's business was to keep men prisoner to unbelief and entangled in the doubt and indecision that led to self-condemnation. Evidently, the only way to overcome this paralyzing mental confusion was to cease all "private questioning" and submit to God, who would grant salvation and free the mind from uncertainty and "the murky element of doubt."[65]

Noyes himself still wavered between the extremes of passion and sensuality on the one hand, and asceticism on the other.[66] "I covet a state of mind," he said wearily, in which no matter how "varied and multifarious the trains of thought . . . I shall pass from one to the other, with perfect ease and cordiality."[67] In order to assure this, it was essential that the heart and mind be raised to an "*absolute certainty*" in regard to the efficacy of God's goodness to save us from sin. There is such a thing, he stated firmly, "as *perfect certainty* that will make an end to all arguments."[68]

Noyes came to realize, however, that this grace and perfection could not be achieved by the conventional methods of the Methodists, Oberlin Perfectionists, and other Protestant denominations. According to him they made of sanctification a brief, temporary phenomenon, which in effect meant that they denied "or suppressed the most essential element of the new covenant, viz., *security*."[69] The man whose sense of security was based only on "external revelation," said Noyes, could never feel satisfied or complete. He may delude himself into thinking he has found permanent salvation, but in times of "temptation and trouble, he will be liable to sink into darkness and doubts." A man's soul craved absolute certainty, Noyes insisted, and would not tolerate anything less.[70] No man could ever feel that he was perfect, "or to have a good conscience (which is the same thing,)" until

---

65. Alfred Barron and George Noyes Miller, eds., *Home-Talks by John Humphrey Noyes* (Oneida, N.Y., 1875), p. 216. Also see Home-Talk by J. H. N. —No. 112, "Salvation from Doubt," *Circular* 1 (4 August 1852): 155-56, where Noyes declares that "doubt is the element that cripples you in thought and action."

66. Home-Talk, No. 40, "Moderation," *Circular* 2 (2 November 1852): 16.

67. Home-Talk by J. H. N.—No. 64, "Coquetry with the Truth," *Free Church Circular* 4 (29 May 1851): 194.

68. Home-Talk by J. H. N.—No. 98, "The Gospel," *Circular* 1 (23 May 1852): 111. Italics added to the words "perfect certainty."

69. John Humphrey Noyes, *The Berean: A Manual for the Help of Those who Seek the Faith of the Primitive Church* (Putney, Vt., 1847), p. 273. Noyes also stated on p. 169, "Repentance is genuine only when it results in the *forsaking* of sin. That periodical repentance, which implies continuance in the sins repented of, is a most horrible hypocrisy."

70. "Security of the Saints," *Spiritual Magazine* 1 (15 January 1847): 171; Home-Talk by J. H. N.—No. 81, "The Rights of the Mind," *Circular* 1 (8 February 1852): 56.

the righteousness of God was fulfilled in him.[71] What was required, therefore, was a complete merging with the suffering and resurrection of Christ.[72] The usual "vicarious atonement," he asserted, might inspire temporary devotion in some, but fell woefully short of inducing a lasting change in the personality.[73] A man could not rest content to be merely *"with* Christ, he had to be in *him."*[74]

For Noyes, this special kind of identification had been attained by Paul in his instantaneous conversion on the road to Damascus. From a vilifier of Christ he was immediately changed to a militant disciple, and it stood to reason that if a person emulated Paul, he too could be transported to a new spiritual plane where salvation from sin was secured. On this level of morality one would share in the *"perfect security"* and *"absolute certainty"* that Christ had in His relationship to the Father. In this blissful union, an individual would be placed in total dependence upon the Father, but yet, like the Son, he would have a will that was at once separate from the Father's but always in accord with it. And Noyes emphasized strongly the point that Christ did not feel *"his moral agency was destroyed* by his *ABSOLUTE DEPENDENCE upon God."*[75]

Drawing upon his own youthful experiences and religious conversion, Noyes believed that such an acceptance of Christ was analogous to "spiritual puberty." At the age of fourteen, he explained, a new and distinct stage of life began: a time when men and women crossed the line from youth to maturity and were considered born anew. They acquired new "social susceptibilities," and sexual love became an important element in life. Pubescence, therefore, was like a spiritual regeneration because it signaled a "change *within* a person." In many ways, thought Noyes, it was "a latent evolution of life," which contained some elements of the old law and morality but yet was something entirely new.[76]

Once converted and having undergone his change in spiritual pu-

---

71. "True Justification," *Witness* 2 (1 April 1842): 97. Also see, "Spiritual Tribulations," p. 157, where Noyes states that "a *justified* spirit, a *clear* conscience, a *self-approving* heart, is the only soil on which righteousness can grow."

72. The statement which most fully captures the extent of Noyes's identification with Christ is "Perfection of the Man Christ Jesus," *Perfectionist* 1 (20 August 1834): 1–2.

73. "The Cross of Christ," *Witness* 2 (10 December 1841): 65.

74. J. H. Noyes, *Confession of Religious Experience*, p. 15. Also see Home-Talk by J. H. N.—No. 7, "Salvation," *Spiritual Magazine* 2 (1 September 1847): 115–16; "Condensation of Life," Ibid. 1 (15 March 1846): 1–2.

75. "Perfection of the Man Christ Jesus," p. 1. Also, Home-Talk by J. H. N.—No. 2, "Immortality the Result of Obedience," *Spiritual Magazine* 2 (1 June 1847): 17–20.

76. *The Berean*, pp. 246–52.

berty, Paul was put through a rigorous course of discipline and testing, which led to his elevation among the other disciples. In his rise to preeminence, Paul eventually superseded Peter, who in the beginning had been like a father to him. In this accomplishment, as Noyes emphasized, an inversion of roles occurred. Paul became a father to Peter, the pupil became the mentor; but this change was not a source of conflict, as one might have expected. Both disciples worked together to carry the testimony of Christ to the world.[77] In his life, Paul ultimately attained a position analogous to that of Christ, where the spirit of envy toward the Father and all mankind was erased, and the Son was elevated to the side of the Father to share in his glory.[78]

We are here at the very heart of Noyes's wishes for his life and work. To be elevated, but in love, not in conflict; to be great, but not the object of envy; to be admired, but not to stimulate anger; to reach the very pinnacle, but not in the spirit of usurpation and therefore not himself to be usurped. Noyes wanted to reverence that father-son, sexual interrelationship—like Paul—and have it accepted without question that his motives were pure. Noyes would in fact reverence these relationships—but there were those who doubted his motives.

What Noyes found in Paul's life, at least what he would openly tell himself he found, was that to be active and successful a person did not have to be envious and jealous of others, make invidious comparisons, or resort to direct conflict. Enveloped in the pure spirit of love and obedience, the sharp edges of competition would be smoothed and "a love of eminence" could be justified.[79] As Paul wrote, power would be made perfect through weakness.

This sense of power of course influenced one's relationship to social institutions. When Paul confessed himself completely sinful, he was admitting his servility through adherence to the existing norms and values of society, which inherently were "holy, just and good," but had come under the influence of sinful men. Paul's confession of sin, in fact, was a "description of the misery of a soul married to the law."[80] Noyes, like Paul, felt that when a person was married to the law, the only offspring of this union was unbelief and sin. On the

---

77. "Cure for Envy," p. 39.
78. "Appendix G," J. H. Noyes, *Confession of Religious Experience*, p. 92, "Envy, jealousy, rivalry, will forever cease when men become heirs of God." William N. Evans, "The Eye of Jealousy and Envy," *Psa. Rev.* 62 (1975): 481–92, makes connections between envy, jealousy, and omnipotence.
79. "Cure for Envy," p. 39.
80. *Salvation from Sin*, p. 22; *The Berean*, pp. 201–17, 218, 222.

other hand, when one took Christ as his husband, one forsook the law and gave birth to righteousness. Noyes believed that a time would come when it would be impossible to obey the commands of the law and Christ at the same time. If it ever came to this, Noyes knew that he would align himself with Paul. "Death to the law," Noyes said, "must precede marriage with Christ"; and, accordingly, those who believed in Christ as Paul had done were dead to the law and had no responsibility to it.[81]

When Paul's words and deeds became inseparable from his own, Noyes felt able to share in that peculiar affinity to Christ and God that Paul enjoyed. It was a closeness that commingled passive abnegation with feelings of grandeur and omnipotence. Towards God, of course, obedience was to be total and unalterable. Noyes spoke of the need to be "consumed by the love of God." He also spoke of "having eaten of the tree of life," but in this sense: with God as the essence of his spirit, "Adam may return, and eating of the tree of life, became immortal."[82]

Most important for Noyes, finally, was that Paul, through his conversion, broke from an anxiety-ridden past and present, took on a new morality, and was free to act upon his environment in light of that morality. Paul in effect turned defeat, and submission to vice, into victory and activity.[83] Noyes could do the same, and in this elevated state he would be free from any doubt and ambivalence. Like Paul, his writings and actions would abound "with vindications of his own conduct, bold assertions of his righteousness, and appeals from human accusations to the judgement of God."[84] What perils this passive surrender to Christ and God may have held for Noyes were more than compensated by the power he derived. For Noyes could be and was controlling, arrogant, and at times insensitive and ruthless in his ordinary human relationships, as he constantly proposed his own life and thought "as a perfect example for imitation."[85]

From the late winter of 1832 to the early spring of the following year, Noyes studied the Bible and Paul's words intensely. At the

---

81. *Salvation from Sin*, p. 22.
82. "Spiritual Tribulation," *Spiritual Magazine* 2 (15 September 1847): 140. On the nature of inspiration and its active-passive qualities see Ernst Kris, "On Inspiration," *Psychoanalytic Explorations in Art* (New York, 1967), pp. 289–302; Jacob A. Arlow, "The Consecration of the Prophet," *Psa. Q.* 20 (1951): 374–78; Phyllis Greenacre, "A Study on the Nature of Inspiration," *J. Am. Psa. Assn.* 46 (1964): 6–30. 83. *Salvation from Sin*, p. 48.
84. Ibid., p. 30. Italics omitted. A suggestive article on Noyes's self-righteous attitude is Ruth F. Lax, "Some Comments on the Narcissistic Aspects of Self-Righteousness: Defensive and Structural Considerations," *Int. J. Psa.* 56 (1975): 283–92.
85. *Salvation from Sin*, p. 31.

same time, his interest in the exact time of the second coming was rearoused. "With much zeal and under severe pressure of spirit for some days," Noyes read through the New Testament again and again, searching for clues that would pinpoint the exact moment.[86] In the anguish of fervent prayer and deep concentration, Noyes discarded as useless all millennial theories that predicted the second coming in the near future. If it were in the future, he reasoned, then Christ's victory over sin and death had not yet occurred and could not be offered to men in the present. If so, Noyes felt that mankind was like "a misguided navigator," sailing in the direction of "things unknown, mistaking them for things well-known."[87]

Noyes had no tolerance for that kind of uncertainty. In Christ's first coming, He was a *"suffering* victim," but in the second He was to be "a *conquering king."* It was clear, moreover, that "an ordinance commemorating his humiliation"[88] may have been appropriate before the second coming, but highly inappropriate thereafter. Any hope of security in the immediate present and near future, therefore, rested upon the belief that Christ's second coming had already occurred.

Focusing all of his energies upon this belief, Noyes finally determined that the event had taken place in 70 A.D., at the time of Jerusalem's destruction. It was then that "Christ's humiliation ceased."[89] Moreover, in this holocaust the apostolic church, which alone embodied the principles of Christ during his stay on earth, was transfered to the spiritual world where it continued to hold firmly to the principles of purity and perfection. When Noyes linked this insight to the doctrine of salvation, he was bitterly criticized by a bevy of ministers and theologians, but Noyes was braced to meet their attacks. As Noyes said about his millennial theory, "the most decisive and beneficial effect" it had was to give him the strength and courage "to doubt the infallibility of learned doctors, established commentaries, and long-hallowed traditions."[90]

It would take us too far astray to follow the elaborate, exegetical arguments and rebuttals that followed. What Noyes in effect had done with this argument was cut the threads of historical continuity by denying that the present-day church and ecclesiastical authority

86. "Religious History—No. 23," p. 1.
87. Ibid., p. 2.
88. "The Second Coming of Christ," Section VI, *Witness* 2 (18 January 1843): 202–3. Also, Home-Talk by J. H. N.—No. 138, "The Riches of Grace," *Circular* 2 (20 November 1852): 7; "The Second Coming of the Son, of Man in His Kingdom," *Witness,* EXTRA (December 1838), pp. 4, 14.
89. "The Second Coming of Christ," VI, p. 202. Although he disagreed with virtually all of Noyes's theories, Adin Ballou admitted that Noyes's writings on the second coming had changed his mind. Perry, *Radical Abolitionism,* pp. 153–54.
90. "Religious History—No. 23," p. 2.

had any link to the apostles. Their sole connection with the past was with the sinful unregenerate.[91] But at the same time that he was cutting these threads, Noyes was busy stitching a new fabric comprised of two subtle yet distinct patterns. One revealed the imperfect if not evil men and institutions of the present and past. It was this part of his cultural and personal past that Noyes wished to repudiate. The other pattern consisted of a cultural and personal past that had been innocent and pure, and it became imperative for him to link his Perfectionist ideals of the present to this ideal past. He discovered this tie, of course, in the testimony of Paul, which indicated that a person's faith and conviction could link him directly to the invisible church in heaven that "extends itself into this world by attaching itself to individual believers."[92] This was a unique faith, as Noyes pointed out, for it "obliterated the distinctions the world draws between good and bad works," and established "a new method of judgment."[93]

Through his manipulations Noyes could reverse the effects of time. As a son of God, he believed that he had successfully "abolished the time between our hope and its object," as well as "the space between our sight and our heavenly relationships of home and friends."[94]

91. G. W. Noyes, ed., *Religious Experience*, p. 85. Noyes's solution here is but one variation on several nineteenth-century cultural themes: a yearning for the past commingled with an optimism for the future; perfectability of man coupled with doubts about sin; time (history) and timelessness (historylessness). See, for example, Fred Somkin, *Unquiet Eagle: Memory and Desire in the Idea of American Freedom, 1815–1860* (Ithaca, 1967); Marvin Meyers, *The Jacksonian Persuasion: Politics and Belief* (New York, 1960); Major L. Wilson, "Paradox Lost: Order and Progress in Evangelical Thought of Mid-Nineteenth-Century America," *Church History* 44 (1975): 352–66. A pertinent article, from a psychoanalytic standpoint, is Harold N. Boris, "On Hope: Its Nature and Psychotherapy," *International Review of Psychoanalysis* 3 (1976): 139–50.

92. "Our Relations to the Primitive Church," *Perfectionist and Theocratic Watchman* 4 (21 September 1844): 53. Whether Noyes can be labeled a premillennialist or a postmillennialist is discussed by Stow Persons, *Socialism in American Life*, ed. by Donald Drew Egbert and Stow Persons (Princeton, N.J., 1952), 1: 141, and in my dissertation, "The Development of a Utopian Mind: John Humphrey Noyes, 1828–1869," (Stony Brook, 1973), pp. 108–9.

93. Home-Talk by J. H. N.—No. 1, "Faith—Its Conditions—Faith Works and Self-Works," *Spiritual Magazine* 2 (15 May 1847): 2.

94. "Uses of Suffering," *Spiritual Magazine* 1 (15 June 1846): 55. Also, Home-Talk by J. H. N.—No. 161, "The Discipline of Affection," *Circular* 2 (19 January 1853): 75. There is now a vast body of psychoanalytic literature dealing with the concept of time. Hans W. Loewald, "The Experience of Time," *Psa. St. Chi.* 27 (1972): 406, states: "in the experience of eternity, all meaning is condensed in the undifferentiated, global unity of the abiding instant, the *nunc stans*, and may flow out from there again to replenish the world of time with meaning." Other important articles are: Peter Hartocollis, "Time and Affect in Psychopathology," *J. Am. Psa. Assn.* 23 (1975): 383–95; Hans W. Loewald, "The Superego and Ego Ideal: Superego and Time," *Int. J. Psa.* 43 (1962): 264–68; Franz S. Cohn, "Time and the Ego," *Psa. Q.* 26 (1957): 168–89.

When a person's faith was perfect, considerations of time were no longer important because God's all-embracing love expunged the sources of humiliation and shame, of discord and disunity. In his idealized world Noyes could rest assured that "Immortality asks no favors . . . mourns no loss."[95] Essentially, therefore, Noyes's perfectionism was a way of overcoming both external and internal fears of abandonment and loss. He constructed a meaningful past, retrospectively enhanced, and this gave him the basis on which to build a stable present. Both dimensions of his concern would eventually separate him from other men and even from other Perfectionists. But the important point is that Noyes was able to remain active and forward looking. For the time being he had avoided the dreaded defeat, he had avoided collapse. But his worth had yet to be tested.

95. "Correspondence," *Perfectionist* 1 (20 March 1835): 31. On the relationship of time, mourning and immortality see George H. Pollock, "On Time, Death, and Immortality," *Psa. Q.* 40 (1971): 435–45; Pollock, "On Mourning, Immortality and Utopia," *J. Am. Psa. Assn.* 23 (1975): 335–60; Pollock, "On Time and Anniversaries," in Mark Kanzer, ed., *The Unconscious Today: Essays in Honor of Max Schur* (New York, 1971), pp. 249–57; Hans W. Loewald, "Internalization, Separation, Mourning, and the Superego," *Psa. Q.* 31 (1962): 483–504.

3 Perfectionism, Anxiety, "The New York Experience"

As Noyes sipped slowly but steadily from his cup of Perfectionism, he began to fill himself with a new faith. Noyes reasoned that Christ, during His personal ministry, had promised His believers that they would accomplish greater works than He had. "Instead therefore of confining the omnipotence of prayer" to Christ and the past, Noyes now began to believe that the miraculous power of the Son extended to his believers in the present, who were "commissioned to ask and expect power to do greater works than Christ did." Feeling elevated in this belief, Noyes "claimed a share in the promises of *specific* answer to prayer," and argued openly in the seminary that conventional prayer was nothing more than a "solemn mockery." He even had the audacity to tell a group of students that President Jeremiah Day's prayers in the college chapel were fine as moral lessons, but certainly did not qualify as prayers in his sense of the word. Noyes's criticisms soon got back to the faculty, and shortly thereafter he received "an admonitory visit" from a tutor, who happened to be Day's nephew. Duly reprimanded, Noyes admitted his rashness, and the affair was dropped.[1]

Despite his growing disenchantment with accepted religious beliefs, Noyes, along with the rest of his Yale classmates, received his license to preach in August (1833), and for six weeks he "labored as a pastor" in a little church in North Salem, New York. He was out in the world again, and his bashfulness and fears of assertiveness at first seemed to get the better of him, in spite of his resolve. But again he summoned enough courage to plod through a written sermon. As time passed, he grew more self-assured standing before a congregation. With increased confidence his sermons became more

1. J. H. Noyes, *Confession of Religious Experience*, pp. 9–10.

extemporaneous, and as they did so his perfectionist beliefs began to filter into them. "I put my soul into my mouth," Noyes said. But as far as his congregation was concerned, he had also found room for his foot. In the course of one sermon, he compared a drunkard's intemperance with the life of a sinner. In his analogy he observed that a drunk did not have the inner fortitude to honor a pledge of abstention. For the pledge to have any meaning he had to give himself over to a stronger person. This guardian would then "enforce" the pledge. A sinner in the hands of a loving God was in a similar situation. If he vowed to himself to give strict obedience to God, the fallen man would be secured from the power of sin.

At the end of the service, a member of the church board took Noyes to task for this comparison, arguing that the saints never suffered the indignity and sinfulness of a drunkard. This unexpected rebuff struck at Noyes's esteem; it challenged his basic premise that, like Paul, one could have a previous life of wickedness and sin wiped clean by a complete surrender to God. Doubt and indecision crept into his thoughts, and a depressed Noyes lashed out angrily in the privacy of his diary. It was clear to him that he was "in the midst of a domineering set of ministers," who cursed the land of liberty with their spiritual power and arrogance. He cautioned himself to "keep cool and quiet" but to act according to the dictates of his conscience. If that did not work he was ready to take flight. A few days later Noyes recovered from this latest crisis by studying the words of Christ, which opened to him more of Christ's glory than he had previously seen. Confirmed again in his identification with the Son, Noyes expressed this ecstatic unity by meandering through a nearby woods pouring out his soul to God and weeping for joy.[2]

Noyes subsequently returned to New Haven and the free church, with its more congenial atmosphere. He derived a great deal of satisfaction from constant fellowship with his friend and minister of the church, James Boyle, and from readings and discussions of perfectionism with Boyle, Chauncy Dutton, and a group of students at the divinity school.[3] A recurring theme of Boyle's preaching was the be-

2. "Appendix B," *Ibid.*, pp. 74–77. Mortimer Ostow, "Psychological Defense against Depression," in *Depression and Human Existence*, ed. by E. James Anthony and Therese Benedek (Boston, 1975), p. 401, states that weeping itself "signals a wish for reconciliation with someone from whom one has been alienated. Therefore it is not infrequently seen during the clinging defense against depression." Also see p. 406 for more on weeping.

3. J. H. Noyes, *Confession of Religious Experience*, p. 10. Noyes was instrumental in the hiring of Boyle by the free church. For a brief synopsis of Boyle's background in Perfectionism and reform see Cross, *Burned-Over District*, pp. 189–91, 240, 245, 246, 276, 343. Chauncy Dutton was an assistant to Boyle and had learned his revivalist techniques under Horatio Foot.

lief that persecution was the key test of faithfulness, especially for ministers. Reflecting upon his own experiences, Noyes readily agreed, and he began to promulgate this doctrine throughout the seminary, where it was greeted with skepticism and debate. In a long paper on this subject, delivered to a well-attended meeting in the seminary, Noyes's arguments grew bolder. A deeply religious man, he claimed, could not expect to live in a world of corruption and sin without suffering persecution.

In the storm of debate that followed, a calm Nathaniel Taylor remonstrated with Noyes, suggesting that surely Noyes's point was highly exaggerated. Taylor named many of Connecticut's finest ministers as examples of religious men who never had to endure persecution and suffering for their beliefs. To Taylor this advice signaled an end to the debate; he could not know, of course, that Noyes's premises stemmed from his rather unusual character, and that he could not be so easily put off. Noyes persisted, if silently, assuming the criticism to be a sign of persecution and gaining satisfaction from the belief that Christ had suffered similar abuses. Christ had experienced punishment and suffering; why should Noyes expect less; and, following Christ, why should he not be strong in his martyrdom?[4]

During the fall and winter of 1833, Noyes continued to embroil himself in both public and private arguments within the seminary and the free church. Throughout it all Dutton gave his unstinting support, and for a while their friendship was "knit together with a love" that Noyes felt transcended a man's love for a woman. Noyes and Dutton, along with Boyle, frequently discussed the topic of perfect holiness, and their friendly discussions served to reinforce Noyes's belief in a perfection achieved through suffering. By early November, Noyes began to test some of his Perfectionist ideas in the seminary. With a revival atmosphere beginning to settle on the seminary and the rest of New Haven, Noyes's ideas caused little excitement. In fact, on the surface they sounded quite similar to those of other Perfectionists. Briefly, Noyes asked sinners to repent, to submit immediately to God, and to conform to a higher law of perfection, without fully delineating what this higher morality entailed. He proposed to fellow ministers that they all adopt the motto: "Perfection, Prayer, and Preaching."

Noyes of course welcomed the support of his friends. But we know, nevertheless, that he had difficulty implementing his high standards and thus had to guard against his feared inner conflict. Consequently, Noyes was forced to turn to "systematic temperance, fasting, exer-

4. Ibid., p. 11.

cise and prayer" in order to conquer his nervous system, which for quite some time after his religious conversion "had been morbidly excitable." His efforts at self-control extended to his passion for Bible study, and he wrote proudly that he could study twelve to sixteen hours a day without harm. When not studying, he was accustomed to devote not less than three hours a day in his closet in fervent prayer. During these hours of cloistered meditation, he often became infused with the loving spirit of Christ and God, which erased his sins, dried his tears, and filled him with unspeakable bliss. With his heart "burdened with spiritual joy," Noyes subsisted on the love of God for days at a time, while his "body became weak and pined away."[5] A description of him some months earlier by his sister Joanna seems appropriate here: "He is certainly a remarkable person," she declared in a letter home. "I never knew anyone so self-denying, so divested of any worldly feeling."[6]

Strengthened by these ritual behaviors, Noyes at first took an active part in the revival and even bragged that preaching, which once "would shake and disorder" his nerves, was now a "delight and refreshment" to him.[7] Working in this atmosphere of excitement, however, Noyes began to lose his sense of religious security, and no matter how hard he tried there seemed to be no way he could regain it. At twenty, Noyes had experienced a religious conversion, but the social world was failing to sustain him and his lofty ideals. Now, at twenty-two, he felt the need for another intense, religious experience. In the agony of his renewed doubt, Noyes perceived that there came a time when a man knew that his church and his ordinary prayers were trivial matters in the quest for salvation. Purity and salvation from sin were absolutely necessary, but they were not going to be reached in any conventional way. Noyes was stymied, and the "conflict of hope and fear" began: the hope of a new life in God's love opposed to the fear of leaving the old religion and perhaps finding nothing in its place.[8] Noyes was ready to cast all conventions aside, but he feared the consequences, especially isolation and failure. In this new crisis, which Noyes called "a double-minded state," the devil was busy with delusions.[9]

Noyes readily understood that he had to move from the insecurity of the usual relationship to Christ and God and elevate himself to that rapturous plane where a person merged with Christ and gained

---

5. Ibid., pp. 11–13.
6. G. W. Noyes, ed., *Religious Experience,* p. 65.
7. "Religious History—No. 3," p. 14.
8. Ibid.; J. H. Noyes, *Confession of Religious Experience,* p. 13.
9. "Religious History—No. 3," p. 14.

immediate access to the Father.[10] Here, of course, unity and perfection would cancel out conflict and sin. Noyes also saw that the transition from the "double-minded" state to that of perfect holiness and salvation from sin required a radical conversion—a conversion portrayed by Christ as one of "sorrowful agony, like that of childbirth."[11]

To prepare for his own rebirth, Noyes withdrew from the turmoil and confusion of the revival to the seclusion and quiet of prayer, Bible study, and contemplation of salvation from sin. Despite these efforts, the blackness of sin continued to envelope him. He lost his appetite and went days without eating; still, sin overrode all. Noyes groaned "under the full weight of the perfect law of God." Failing to measure up to this ideal, he loathed himself and all his "past works." Noyes was convinced that he was dying.[12]

In this deep state of depression Noyes turned outward for support, but spiritual guidance from Dutton was not enough. Finally, in an evening meeting at the free church, as he sat brooding over his fallen state, Noyes picked up a Bible and began to thumb his way listlessly through it. His eyes suddenly fell upon the passage (Luke 1:35): "The Holy Ghost shall come upon thee, and the power of the Highest shall overshadow thee; therefore also that holy thing which shall be born of thee shall be called the Son of God." The words not only leaped from the page, they glowed, for through them God was promising him the eagerly sought second birth. Encouraged by this revelatory message, Noyes eagerly turned to the Bible for direction; not surprisingly, he found it. This time he was reassured that his previous unity with Christ had been correct and pure, even though his critics had scorned and rejected him. His duty was clear; he was to carry his message of Perfectionism to the outside world, regardless of skepticism and censure of others.

10. "Religious History—No. 5," *Perfectionist and Theocratic Watchman* 4 (1 June 1844): 22–23; "Appendix C," J. H. Noyes, *Confession of Religious Experience,* p. 78.

11. J. H. Noyes, *Confession of Religious Experience,* p. 15. Ostow, "Psychological Defense against Depression," p. 404, indicates that fantasies of rebirth are often used to deny the inner awareness of being drawn further down into depression. Also see Ostow, *Psychology of Melancholy,* pp. 13–17, 44–49.

12. "Religious History—No. 5," p. 23. Bibring, "The Mechanism of Depression," pp. 13–46, has stated that anxiety and depression represent "diametrically opposed basic ego responses." Anxiety indicates the ego's desire to survive. The ego, faced with danger, mobilizes the signal of anxiety and prepares for flight or fight. In a depression the opposite occurs. The ego becomes overpowered and finds itself unable to meet the danger. Depression may occur when a person feels helpless, lonely, isolated, unloved, weak, inferior, or a failure. Furthermore, the tension between high aspirations and the ego's awareness of its real or imagined helplessness to fulfill these aims, also leads to depression.

After the meeting, Noyes returned home assured that he was on the verge of salvation. Awakening fresh the next morning, he again saw that Christ's resurrection was the center of faith, and if a person was in Christ, the miracle of resurrection became his own. Abruptly, Noyes knew that Christ was in him with all His glory, and now it was time to confess it to the whole world.[13]

On the bleak evening of 20 February 1834, Noyes stood before a small gathering at the free church. He believed that he did not yet have all the "feelings" he had hoped for, but he "knew" that he was walking in the path of righteousness and went forward with his proposed sermon: "He that committeth sin is of the devil." This topic in itself caused little stir among his listeners. But, when Noyes insisted upon the literal meaning of the text—that men were either totally pure and perfect in Christ or they were sinners—his attentive audience was bewildered. Such a rigid, implacable distinction between good and evil men, between Christians and sinners, was a frightening supposition. Noyes, however, did not wait around to explain himself. His public confession, the mere fact that he had "stood tall" to test his beliefs, was an electrifying experience for him. That night back in his room he could hardly contain himself. "Three times in quick succession," he recalled emotionally, "a stream of eternal love gushed through my heart" with unspeakable joy. All thoughts of doubt and condemnation were submerged in the stream that cleansed his once-sinful heart.[14]

That pure stream of bliss soon became muddied by a flood of contention from the outside. After all, how was Noyes to explain his idealized world with its rigid dichotomy of good and evil to people who were prepared to accept and live with human fraility and fallibility? To defend it on the grounds of obedience to a higher spiritual law would only put him in the same boat with the Perfectionist groups of western New York, who were already feared because of their antinomian tendencies and sexual irregularities. A theological student, who had heard Noyes's proclamation the night before, cornered him and argued that his categories of good and evil were too rigid. Did Noyes actually mean to say that a sinner cannot be a Christian? Noyes assured him that that was precisely what he meant. Taken aback, the student then asked Noyes if he sinned, and Noyes firmly replied: NO. Absolutely staggered by this reply, the young student shakily took his leave of a triumphant Noyes.[15]

13. J. H. Noyes, *Confession of Religious Experience*, pp. 17–18.
14. G. W. Noyes, ed., *Religious Experience*, pp. 109–10.
15. J. H. Noyes, *Confession of Religious Experience*, p. 18. On the New York Perfectionists see Cross, *Burned-Over District*, pp. 238–51.

Within a few hours the news spread that Noyes believed himself to be perfect, and along with the rumor went the cry that he was crazy. His room was daily filled with the curious and contentious, making Noyes feel like a misfit, but he steadfastly held to his beliefs. On one occasion Noyes's arguments proved to be so upsetting yet persuasive that a theological student fainted. He recovered and fled Noyes's room for the familiar study of his local minister, who quickly reaffirmed his faith in conventional religion.[16]

Noyes was entering the field of spiritual warfare now. He knew that if he did not counter "every fair objection to the doctrine of holiness," he would "sink" into despair and defeat.[17] Within a week or two after his confession of perfection, the question whether man could achieve perfect holiness in this life was the subject of a debate in the Theological Seminary. Noyes had the opportunity to voice his beliefs, and he caused quite a stir among the audience. Nathaniel Taylor got so upset that he accused Noyes of "disrespectful language" and threatened to leave if Noyes was allowed to continue. The furor subsided, but Noyes's days as a licensed preacher were numbered.[18]

Indeed, within a few days Taylor came to Noyes's room to notify Noyes that he was to be tried by the Association that had licensed him. A dispute ensued, Taylor censuring Noyes for voicing his ideas before the Seminary without first asking for Taylor's permission. He also informed Noyes that he had reconverted a Perfectionist once before, and offered to do the same for Noyes. Noyes wanted no part of this, saying that he had "received the Holy Spirit" and could not be turned from his course by any man. Taylor derided Noyes, claiming it was impossible "for any man to feel the Spirit of God" as intensely as Noyes averred. In rebuttal, Noyes insisted that Taylor's own doctrines, if taken to their logical conclusion, led to the very Perfectionism Noyes was espousing. Taylor of course argued to the contrary. In His benevolence God did not ask man to be perfect in his obedience to the law. God was willing to settle for less. Noyes's beliefs, continued Taylor, were nothing more than "the old Wesleyan scheme that had failed," and if Noyes was lucky, he might find a few followers "among women and ignorant people, but not among the intelligent."[19]

---

16. J. H. Noyes, *Confession of Religious Experience*, p. 22. Here is a dramatic example illustrating the basic reality orientation and superego threats that Noyes posed. That is, if Noyes's reality were legitimate, then what of mine? If Noyes's higher law morality were legitimate, then what of mine? Also see "Religious History—No. 8," *Perfectionist and Theocratic Watchman* 4 (13 July 1844): 35–36.

17. J. H. Noyes, *Confession of Religious Experience*, p. 26.

18. Ibid.

19. Ibid.

When Taylor suggested that a young man like Noyes could learn from Taylor's greater experience and wisdom, Noyes insisted that age and experience had nothing to do with this kind of spiritual truth. Noyes then challenged Taylor with his rigid beliefs on the nature of sin, and Taylor's arguments could not budge Noyes from his inflexible position. The two men parted, emotionally and intellectually farther apart than before. In mid-April the Association stripped Noyes of his license, a formal procedure that confirmed what Noyes already knew: his experiences at Andover and Yale had furthered an increasing sense of alienation from existing institutions.[20]

While all of this was transpiring, Noyes was losing support for his ideas on other fronts as well. He tried desperately to convert Dutton, who despaired over his friend's aberrations. Dutton, in time, left Noyes and went to Albany. Boyle, who had been out of town at the time of Noyes's "rebirth," was determined to rid his church of this heresy. He remonstrated with Noyes who could hardly sustain this argument with Boyle, whom he admired and from whom he had expected support and encouragement. "I dreaded his opposition," he lamented. "My feelings were especially tender in relation to him, and his cold words were as daggers to my heart."[21] As if this were not enough, Noyes got little support from home. His usually sympathetic mother was dumbstruck and could only mutter, "What does John mean?"[22] Noyes was in serious trouble; he had feared failure and isolation, he did not want to be bereft of all. In his own words, his "good name in the great world was gone." His friends were deserting him, and he was "beginning indeed to be an outcast."[23]

A twentieth-century person who has to confront highly threatening personal and social tensions might readily seek some sort of psychoanalytic experience, no matter what the school or technique. In the nineteenth century people turned to religion, or to a religious person, for help in mastering anguish and in preparing to return to a more productive life in society. This was particularly true for certain individuals who considered themselves deeply religious and yet continued to face severe doubts about their goodness and capacities. Such people would seek a therapeutic relationship with a religious guide—a relationship akin to that of analyst and analysand, with one major difference being that their roles were often interchangeable. In their

---

20. Ibid., pp. 26–27.
21. Ibid., p. 24.
22. G. W. Noyes, ed., *Religious Experience,* p. 111; "Backward Glancings, IV," *Oneida Circular* 4 (6 May 1872): 146, indicates that an elder sister voiced this surprise.
23. J. H. Noyes, *Confession of Religious Experience,* p. 27.

intellectual and emotional interaction, these nineteenth-century figures were able to provide needed support for each other.

In particular the relationships were like psychoanalytic therapy in the transferences that were established.[24] One might seek to manipulate and win over another, thereby bolstering esteem. One might attempt to devalue the person on whom one had become dependent for help, or one might endow the other with the bad thoughts and feelings that had been the source of the original search for help—and then punish that other person for being wicked and sinful. This would have the effect of turning passive withdrawal into active seeking. But these were mighty contests of will fought by people who felt everything very deeply.

In the midst of Noyes's own despair, then, Boyle introduced him to Charles H. Weld, who had come to New Haven expressly for the purpose of meeting Noyes.[25] Weld was one of the older brothers of the well-known abolitionist, Theodore Dwight Weld. Charles had graduated from Yale in 1822, and four years later from Andover. In 1828 he became a licensed preacher and spent some time traveling throughout Mississippi for the Bible Society. He apparently suffered some sort of emotional breakdown, for in the early 1830s he was to be found recuperating in his father's home in Apulia, New York.[26] During this period he turned to Perfectionism, and although this gave him a firmer grip over his emotions than had traditional evangelicalism, he was still susceptible to doubt and despair. By the time he made his trip to New Haven, Weld had made contact with several Perfectionist groups in western New York, and his name was becoming known in Perfectionist circles.

From the outset Noyes was attracted to Weld and soon they became "very intimate." In many respects Weld seemed to have those very qualities that Noyes felt himself to lack. Weld had profound

---

24. I do not mean to imply here that Noyes and Weld recreated the transference situation in reality, at least not an exact replica of it. Transference in analysis unfolds under controlled conditions while outside it a host of variables intervene. In brief, transference in analysis cannot be considered identical with similar phenomena outside it. Furthermore, Noyes and Weld continued to see each other as real people; they did not solely relate to each other as a projection from each other's past. On these points see Ralph R. Greenson, "The 'Real' Relationship Between the Patient and the Psychoanalyst," *The Unconscious Today*, pp. 213–32; Harold P. Blum, "Transference and Structure," Ibid., pp. 177–93; Rudolph M. Loewenstein, "Developments in the Theory of Transference in the Last Fifty Years," *Int. J. Psa.* 50 (1969): 583–87; Paul A. Dewald, "Transference Regression and Real Experience in the Psychoanalytic Process," *Psa. Q.* 45 (1976): 213–30.

25. J. H. Noyes, *Confession of Religious Experience*, p. 27.

26. Cross, *Burned-Over District*, p. 196.

insight into "spiritual mysteries," was highly intelligent, and appeared to be "fulfilled with the most lovely benevolence." The two men never grew tired sharing ideas, and while Weld accepted Noyes's basic beliefs on salvation, he criticized the manner in which they were presented as being too strong, inflexible, and demanding. Weld insinuated, in the course of their many talks, that he had exercised "a paternal supervision" over such people as his brother Theodore, Charles Grandison Finney, and Boyle, and it did not take long for him to establish himself as Noyes's "privy counsellor." Despite Weld's tendency to assume a *"fatherly* relation" toward him, and despite his own ambivalent feelings about the closeness of their relationship, Noyes acquiesced. His need for support at a time of ever-deepening emotional crisis dictated that he lay aside, for the time being, whatever uneasy feelings he might have concerning Weld.

As their relationship deepened, Noyes learned that ten years earlier at Andover Weld had undergone a severe religious crisis from which he had never fully recovered. Though still vulnerable to despair, Weld believed that this crisis had given him a special insight into salvation that other men simply did not have. As time passed, however, Noyes began to suspect that Weld's greater insight was clouded by his emotional instability. "He was like a sick doctor," thought Noyes, who had now come under the care of another physician, "healthier but not yet wiser." Weld permitted Noyes to apply his spiritual medicines, but took it upon himself to see how "they should be mixed and when they should be administered." When Noyes finally realized that he was not curing Weld, he decided that he must apply stronger measures to aid Weld in conquering his spirit of condemnation.

While Weld and Noyes ministered to each other, Boyle was agonizing over the doctrines of salvation from sin and perfection. Noyes put his demanding, persuasive powers to work with Boyle and succeeded in bringing him to an emotional confession of Christ. To Boyle it felt as if the power of God had rushed upon him like a flood, that he was being born into a new world. "Old things immediately passed away," he averred, "and *all things* became new." Weld stood by, transfixed by this demonstration of instant salvation. There can be little doubt that he was deeply moved by what he saw, but when Noyes again attempted to convert him, Weld was unable to achieve a similar experience. Exasperated by his and Weld's failure, Noyes told him (in much the same way an analyst would tell his patient) that his salvation depended upon his own efforts. Did he really want to still his religious doubts and indecision? If so, then he advised Weld to "look the law of God in the face, and submit to the full pressure of the truth": whoever committed sin was of the devil. Weld nodded his head wearily in affirmation and, according to Noyes, seemed to defer to his leadership.

A short time later, with Boyle attending a revival in another town, Weld was asked to conduct the services of the free church. He did well enough in the morning, but was completely enervated by the experience. Unable to lead the afternoon services, Weld asked Noyes to substitute for him. With the approval of the church deacons, Weld introduced Noyes to the congregation, urging them to accept the truth in Noyes's doctrines. With all his fervor and apparent strength of conviction, Noyes discoursed upon his familiar theme of salvation from sin. At the height of his passion and deep in the intensity of his conviction, Noyes was brought up short by a strange gurgling sound off to his right. Startled and annoyed, Noyes looked around only to see Weld sitting with his eyes closed, "his countenance black with horror, his hands waving up and down, and his lungs laboring with long and rattling breaths." Measured by sheer agony, it was one of the most disturbing conversion scenes Noyes had ever witnessed. Apparently many in the congregation felt the same way, for quite a few fled in utter dismay.

Weld at last gained control of himself, and as he did so his once-anguished countenance reflected great joy. His face seemed to grow brighter and brighter in the radiance of religious ecstasy. He arose slowly to his full height and gazed upon the remainder of the audience "with an eye of angelic brilliancy." He spotted a few people with whom he had recently disputed the doctrine of holiness, and withered them with a malevolent look that could have been matched only by the proverbial destructive eye of God. His eye then met Noyes's, and as Noyes tells it, he returned the look, never lowering his own stare. In that fleeting moment a hidden contest of wills was being waged, and when it was over, Noyes had won. Weld's face relaxed into smile, and his cold eyes softened. Soon, he relapsed into "his former state of horror," only it was not quite as severe this time. A few days later he had sufficiently recovered to return to his brother's house in Hartford, confident that he had met the test, suffered as Christ had, and was now saved.

Near the end of April, Noyes received an invitation from the pastor of the Congregational church in Prospect, Connecticut, to conduct revival services there. Noyes readily accepted, but warned that his "crazy genius" might upset the community and bring disgrace to the church. As it turned out Noyes's presence caused little stir, and after converting two or three people he left. On his way back to New Haven Noyes encountered Weld in the town of Bethany. Feeling stronger and more arrogant, Weld again assumed a dominating influence over Noyes, who once more permitted him to become his spiritual "father and leader."[27]

In between the moments he was convincing Noyes that his recent suffering had made him even more exalted than before, Weld suggested that they attend a conference of ministers in New York City. Since clergy and reformers would be coming from all parts of the country, Weld thought it would be an ideal place to spread their views of Perfectionism. Noyes agreed, but he had additional reasons for wanting to go. Noyes saw himself as totally innocent and pure in his perfection, but this was not the case with certain Perfectionist groups in western New York, whose antics left them open to charges of free love and "spiritual pride." What Noyes intended to do in New York was redeem the good name of Perfectionism from the sexual irregularities that were beginning to disgrace it and his own name.

Noyes's dependent relationship to Weld, however, stirred unwanted desires in him. During their passage to New York, and for as long as Weld remained with him, they bickered over a variety of religious topics. Noyes could not help noticing, though, that Weld continually turned their conversation to subjects that were "too imaginative to be healthy." Discussions on the "*physical* enjoyments of the resurrection state" and on the glories of spiritual marriage indicated to Noyes that holiness was far from the center of Weld's thoughts.[28] Though Noyes considered himself pure, he admitted that for the time being similar thoughts also possessed his mind. Undoubtedly his fantasies were filled with Abigail Merwin, his first convert in the free church, and one of the few people who gave him unqualified support. Throughout his struggles she had stood with him "in the front of the battle, and in the full glare of the public gaze."[29] Although he insisted that his feelings for her never ventured beyond a "calm, brotherly love," he was beginning to have difficulty keeping that love within the bounds of spirituality.[30]

From all accounts of New York with its growing slums and filth, its frenetic pace of life, and its notorious prostitutes, Noyes's description of the city as "a vast accumulation of diabolical influences" may not have been too far off the mark. In any event, it was hardly a suitable milieu for a man searching for, and in need of, inner peace. Further, Noyes quickly discovered to his alarm that the encouragement and support he desperately needed were not to be forthcoming. Reports

27. J. H. Noyes, *Confession of Religious Experience*, pp. 27–30.
28. G. W. Noyes, ed., *Religious Experience*, p. 133.
29. Ibid., p. 114.
30. "Religious History—No. 14," *Perfectionist and Theocratic Watchman* 4 (2 November 1844): 63.

of New Haven Perfectionism had preceded him and were received with "ill suppressed bitterness and anxiety." James Latourette, a central figure among New York Perfectionists, had little sympathy for his ideas as did the noted reformer, John McDowall. Noyes tried to meet Finney but was unsuccessful, although Mrs. Finney, a reformer in her own right, condescended to hear him out. Weld also took him to a number of lesser-known religious leaders, but they gave him short shrift as well. By the week's end Weld had become dispirited and left for Hartford.[31] Plagued by his own self-doubts, his theories derided by others, deserted by Weld, and his funds dwindling rapidly, Noyes suffered through his most prolonged and severe depression—his "New York experience."

Noyes has given us an excellent description of the intense emotions he experienced when the inner world he had created threatened to crumble. Unable to stem the tide of his self-reproaches, Noyes feared that his inward anger would soon engulf and destroy him. Thrown back upon his own meager resources, Noyes found it extremely difficult to maintain a sense of balance and well-being. He felt as if he were being subjectively mobbed and about to lose all control. In many ways his condition resembled a staggering and uncouth man who was being dragged down a street "by an exasperated crowd, under a storm of brick-bats and rotten eggs."[32]

The crisis began, in May 1834, when he felt surrounded by a "strange, murky spiritual atmosphere" within which alien, uncontrolled thoughts possessed him. The Devil, he believed, was nearby waiting to devour him.[33] When at last everything about him seemed to be "full-charged, and . . . crawling with the dark, nauseous spirit of Satan," he grew convinced that he was either going to die or undergo some sort of an immediate transformation. Simultaneously, he felt a

---

31. J. H. Noyes, *Confession of Religious Experience*, pp. 31–32.

32. Ibid., p. 34. On helplessness and hopelessness as the primary affects of depression see the works of Arthur H. Schmale, Jr., "A Genetic View of Affects: With Special Reference to the Genesis of Helplessness and Hopelessness," *Psa. St. Chi.* 19 (1964): 163–88; "Depression as Affect, Character Style, and Symptom Formation," *Psychoanalysis and Contemporary Science*, ed. by Robert R. Holt and Emanuel Peterfreund (New York, 1972), 1: 327–49; Schmale and George L. Engel, "The Role of Conservation-Withdrawal in Depressive Reactions," *Depression and Human Existence*, pp. 183–96.

33. J. H. Noyes, *Confession of Religious Experience*, p. 37. Several important points need to be made here. First, somatic distress and hypochondria are common experiences in depression, especially one this severe. Secondly, the feeling that the devil is within him is an expression of his own hostility, which is threatening to overpower him. This is also commonly experienced in depressions. Thirdly, feelings of death and rebirth are found in depressives, and they too have their roots in aggression that is turned against the self. Ostow, *Psychology of Melancholy*, pp. 44–49; Jacobson, *Depression*, pp. 204–9; Berkowitz, "Devil Within," pp. 28–36.

suffocating pressure on his lungs. This experience was so vivid and real to him that he straightened his room and lay down to die. The pressure was unrelenting, so much so that he thought he had stopped breathing and resigned himself to his fate. Then, the heavy pressure lifted and was supplanted by a vision repeated several times. Noyes saw himself enclosed in a net being dragged to Hell, only to burst the net at the last terrifying moment and return to life. Shortly after the last of these visions, he went through a "protracted process of involuntary thought and feeling" that he equated with a spiritual crucifixion. He had clear impressions of the events of Christ's death and experienced them as his own; he had gone through the crucifixion "not as a spectator, but as a victim." At length, the glorious resurrection lived through, Noyes was released from the agonies of despair to enjoy the rapture of merger and rebirth. He felt the love of Christ as a burning stream flowing through his body, as a "mighty but peaceful river," which emptied into a vast ocean, symbolic of his spiritual unity with God. He was married in perpetuity to the Father, an all-giving husband who would provide for his every need.[34]

Unfortunately these oceanic feelings did not sustain Noyes; his extraordinary inner conflicts welled up again, and he feared he was losing his mind. He imagined at one point that he clearly saw the falsehood of all scientific beliefs and that all of his conceptions of scientific truths had been "turned topsy-turvy." When all semblance of reality had been "prostrated and reduced to chaos," Noyes turned to his Bible for support. Whereas his scrutiny of biblical passages at Andover and Yale had served him well, giving him a sense of control and order, now the ritual failed him. He cast aside the Book with abhorrence, branding it "a monstrous imposition."[35]

In this struggle to maintain contact with reality, Noyes attempted to overcome his deep feelings of abandonment and depletion by redirecting his anger from himself to others. Abigail Merwin, his first and staunchest supporter in the free church, now came under attack. "From her too," he remembered bitterly, "as well as from all other objects of my previous confidence, I was separated by the spirit of

34. "Spiritual Tribulation," p. 140. Ostow, "Psychological Defense against Depression," p. 402, states that among people "struggling against depression, the actual depressive collapse is often represented in dreams as falling or sliding uncontrollably down." On falling also see Kohut, *Analysis of the Self*, p. 154; Leon J. Saul and George C. Curtis, "Dream Form and Strength of Impulse in Dreams of Falling and Other Dreams of Descent," *Int. J. Psa.* 48 (1967): 282.

35. J. H. Noyes, *Confession of Religious Experience*, p. 40. Another manifestation of his depression in New York was his lack of appetite. As his conflicts became more severe, he grew to detest meat and for a while would only eat fish. At the outset of depression there usually occurs a lack of appetite and a refusal to eat. Ostow, *Psychology of Melancholy*, p. 48; Jacobson, *Depression*, pp. 173, 212, 248, 269.

doubt." In a vision he saw her standing alone in her angelic beauty; but a voice, which he could not silence, whispered to him that she was really the Devil masquerading as an angel. In that instant he renounced her as one cursed by Satan.[36]

This maneuver, though, resolved nothing; his hold on reality remained uncertain. Again he turned to Christ in an effort to recapture the feelings of bliss and security, but now Christ's character was also "subjected to the diabolical spirit of analysis." Feeling bereft and abandoned by the Son, Noyes convinced himself that He was disobedient and in league with the Devil. The cloud of doubt then drifted over the image of the Father, and, as His power and purity were lost in the gloomy mist, Noyes renounced God and submerged himself in the "darkness of atheism." With his world empty of any secular or spiritual meaning, Noyes's hostility was turned full force upon himself, and he became the devil incarnate. Succumbing to the intensity of his own anger, Noyes resigned himself to eternal damnation.[37]

Noyes knew that he was on the verge of emotional annihilation and madness, and he fought desperately to come back. To strengthen his weakened grip on reality he avoided sleep, which he felt to be a defenseless position wherein "the powers of darkness had most advantage" of him. Often after a mentally exhausting day he would collapse upon his bed hoping for a "night of repose, if not of sleep." But just as he was about to doze off, the unnamed terrors of sleep would force themselves upon him. He would then spring from his bed to wander the streets and alleys of the city. When he grew tired of this, he would nod off for a few moments on a park bench only to be rudely awakened again by the terror of sleep. For three weeks this constituted his fitful pattern of rest.[38]

During his nightly excursions this unshaven, bedraggled wraith

36. J. H. Noyes, *Confession of Religious Experience*, p. 42. What Noyes wanted was a nurturing, supportive figure, not a sexual one. When his interest in Abigail became consciously a sexual one, she also became a threatening figure to him.

37. Noyes's psychic world was inhabited by totally good and totally bad objects. Through the defense mechanisms of splitting, denial and projection, Noyes was able to see himself and other valued objects (often an extension of himself) as wholly good. Others who posed a threat to him were devalued and seen as wholly bad. What is happening in New York at this point is that the good and bad objects are merging, and as they do the intense hostility is turned on himself. With his world collapsing, Noyes is very close to a psychotic break with reality. See, Otto F. Kernberg, "A Psychoanalytic Classification of Character Pathology," *J. Am. Psa. Assn.* 18 (1970): 811–13; Kernberg, "Treatment of Narcissitic Personalities," pp. 52–66.

38. J. H. Noyes, *Confession of Religious Experience*, pp. 42–43. Noyes's fear of sleep is linked to his fear of death in that both signify to him a loss of reality and ego annihilation. Jacobson, *Self and the Object World*, p. 7; Martin Grotjahn, "Ego Identity and Fear of Death and Dying," *Journal of the Hillside Hosptial* 9 (July 1960): 149; Salzman, *Obsessive Personality*, pp. 69–70.

trudged into the "vilest parts of the city," where he descended into cellars frequented by "abandoned men and women." There in the murky dimness he discussed with derelicts their carnal ways, their sins, and their hopes of salvation. To one poor soul he gave a Bible, to another a Testament, and to some downtrodden strangers he gladly gave what little money he had left. In these scenes of decadence and filth in New York's slums, Noyes found the true representation of his own wickedness and depravity. He purposely sought out the fallen and raised them as he himself wished to be raised, from the depths of despair. Noyes treated these outcasts the way he wished now to be treated—with a nurturing gentleness, encouragement, and respect.[39]

Noyes still struggled as well to find outside support for his Perfectionist ideas. He went to Latourette's home where once more he was treated brusquely, and he returned to his boarding house "in a depth of sorrow." To combat these feelings of emptiness and depletion, he dropped his ascetic diet for the hedonistic pleasures of "ardent spirits" and spicy foods.[40] A short time later he ventured to the home of another clergyman, where his ideas, although not accepted wholeheartedly, were congenially received, and Noyes left in a more hopeful frame of mind. The last visit was important for Noyes; the mere indication that his environment was not entirely hostile and could be supportive helped to lift the depression. A few days later this perception of an amenable environment was reinforced by the arrival of a friend who paid his lodging bill and transporation fee back to New Haven.

A short time after he had arrived in New Haven, Noyes regained the confidence that God meant to favor and protect him. Unabashedly, he related his experience to anyone who would listen, giving little consideration to the impression he was making. Soon he found himself, "an isolated object of ridicule and pity to the whole world."[41] Having been informed of her son's anguish, Polly Noyes showed her sorrow and consternation for his well-being in a letter to John's brother, Horatio. She hoped that John Humphrey would come home to her as soon as possible because he obviously needed her "soothing influence." He must, she confided in Horatio, "expect to listen to the voice of parental love and solicitude."[42] At the end of June, Noyes

39. J. H. Noyes, *Confession of Religious Experience*, p. 43. For a discussion of externalization and how it allows an individual to act upon his anxieties, see Jack Novick and Kerry Kelly, "Projection and Externalization," *Psa. St. Chi.* 25 (1970): 69–95.

40. J. H. Noyes, *Confession of Religious Experience*, p. 44. Once the severity of the depression threatened ego dissolution, it became imperative to take restitutive measures—one of which was copious eating and drinking. To fill himself was to feel full and alive.

41. J. H. Noyes, *Confession of Religious Experience*, pp. 45–47.

42. G. W. Noyes, ed., *Religious Experience*, p. 154.

fulfilled his mother's wishes by trading the hostile and undermining atmosphere of New Haven for the security and support of his family in Putney.[43]

With Noyes resting in Putney, perhaps this is an opportune moment for us to be reminded that Noyes's struggles with shyness, his need for self-control, his retreats to the home and nature, and his growing disenchantment with institutions were not peculiar to him alone. Although his conflicts may have been felt more intensely, other Americans were undergoing similar experiences.

While some saw eventual growth and a stronger America emerging from the disruptive social changes in the antebellum period, Henry Ward Beecher was less sanguine. Casting a wary eye over society, this soon-to-be-famous minister saw an increasing disrespect for authority on all institutional levels and an "effeminate administration of it." Beecher, along with other middle-class Americans, also decried the "manifest decline in family government."[44] Horace Greeley, the liberal reform editor of the New York *Tribune*, feared that this failure of authority to maintain the traditional morality was leading to a "morbid egotism," where each individual might feel free to do as he pleased. In a bitter argument with Stephen Pearl Andrews, which filled the editorial columns of the *Tribune*, editor Greeley complained that Andrews' doctrine of the "sovereignty of the individual" was "in palpable collision with the purity of Society and the Sovereignty of God."[45]

The "horse and rider" metaphor gave striking voice to these anxious feelings of drift and estrangement. Thus, Emerson's oft-quoted plaint: "Web to weave, and corn to grind/ Things are in the saddle/ And ride mankind."[46] Henry Ward Beecher and Theodore Parker used this metaphor with telling effect as they portrayed the emotional disasters awaiting young men in their hurried quest for fame and fortune.[47]

For those acquainted with psychoanalytic literature, the horse and rider metaphor is familiar enough. Freud once remarked that in its relation to the id, the ego resembles a man on horseback, who has to rein in the greater strength of the horse, with the difference that the rider attempts control with his own strength while the ego employs "borrowed forces." In extending this analogy Freud declared that often

43. J. H. Noyes, *Confession of Religious Experience*, p. 47.
44. Henry Ward Beecher, *Seven Lectures to Young Men* (Indianapolis, 1844), p. 34.
45. *Love, Marriage, and Divorce and the Sovereignty of the Individual* (n.p; Source Book Press, 1972), p. 76. This book reprints the famous debates in the *Tribune* (1853) among Greeley, Andrews, and Henry James, Sr.
46. "Ode to W. H. Channing," *Complete Essays*, p. 71.
47. Beecher, *Seven Lectures*, p. 72; Parker, "Traits and Illustrations of Human Character and Conduct," *World of Matter and World of Man*, pp. 93, 105–6.

a rider, if he is not thrown from his mount, must guide it where it wishes to go; thus, in the same manner the ego is accustomed to "transforming the id's will into action as if it were its own."[48]

The ego has its strengths, then, and the nature of these strengths has been considerably amplified by post-Freudian psychoanalysts. This is a useful thought for us because the issue for Greeley was not the fear of rampant id, as emphasized in Freud's use of the metaphor, but the fear of rampant ego. If id-ego conflicts threatened randomly to undermine individuals, the great conflict for the society at large was between ego and reality. The larger social question was whether people could tolerate the strain imposed by rapid change in a burgeoning society, whether the personal, competitive autonomy expressed as self-interest in the economic sphere could be reconciled with society's needs without resort to the shameful alternative of passive retreat.[49] Men especially would have to sustain a sense of personal control in action, reconciling interest to conscience, reserving a portion of their concern for social order, so that society would not indeed dissolve into atomistic parts.

Thus, on one level, a personal experience like bashfulness, one which Noyes was particularly sensitive to, would be held up to opprobrium precisely because shyness implied a failure of nerve and an excessive concern about oneself rather than the welfare of others.[50] Young men would have to master such personal feelings and beware particularly the social effects. They were to demonstrate the qualities of good breeding, which entailed a reassertion of self-command, modesty not bashfulness, and an interest in the well-being of others. On another level, however, there was also little tolerance for the unrestrained egoism so feared by Greeley and others.

Although certainly a number of people in the antebellum period were able to maintain their balance in the midst of normatively perceived disruption, this was difficult for increasing numbers of young

---

48. Sigmund Freud, *The Ego and the Id,* ed. by James Strachey, trans. by Joan Riviere (New York, 1962), p. 15. For other uses of this metaphor in psychoanalytic theory see Heinz Kohut, *Analysis of the Self,* p. 187.

49. Three recent articles are highly informative on the nature of these changes. See, Herbert G. Gutman, "Work, Culture, and Society in Industrializing America, 1815–1919," *American Historical Review,* 78, (1973): 531–88; Daniel Walker Howe, "Victorian Culture in America," *Victorian America* (Philadelphia, 1976), pp. 3–28; Richard D. Brown, "Modernization: A Victorian Climax," Ibid., pp. 29–44.

50. William A. Alcott, *The Young Man's Guide,* 11th ed. (Boston 1837), pp. 76–78, claims to have known young men "*injured* by bashfulness." Also see William A. Alcott, *Gift Book for Young Men, or Familiar Letters of Self-Knowledge, Self-Education, Female Society, Marriage, etc.* (New York, 1852), p. 46; Lydia Maria Child, *The Mother's Book* (Boston, 1831), p. 132.

men.[51] John Todd openly wondered, "who has not mourned that he is doomed to pass through life, accomplishing little or nothing; neither meeting the hopes of his friends nor satisfying his own conscience."[52] Emotionally distraught over this dilemma, Bronson Alcott cried, "There mingles in my reflections, a peculiar feeling of desire to accomplish something worthy the purposes of my existence—The idea that half my life is gone and so little is accomplished worthy a mind and heart destined for such noble activities and acquisitions, overpowers me."[53] Little wonder, then, young men—having difficulty implementing the cultural values of activism, competition, and success—underwent a period of emotional turmoil marked by brooding, introspective relationships, soul-searching walks along the quiet paths of the countryside, and finally turning to religion to help explain not only the existential dimensions of life but also to remain active in life.[54] Indeed, the point needs to be stressed here that among the variety of possible responses to a loss of social and psychic integration with the world, one should expect to see on both the individual and collective levels a heightened narcissism to help bolster a threatened self-esteem.

To stem these emotionally disrupting shocks, many believed that a sense of personal self-control and cultural order had to be re-established. Orestes Brownson put it as simply and directly as anyone. A community without individuality was a tyranny which produced a loss of autonomy, a fate synonymous with death. Individuality without a community's restraints was individualism, and this was tantamount to a Hobbesian state of nature where true autonomy was again extinguished.[55] Horace Mann did not mince his words on this score: "The

51. On this point see Allan Nevins and Milton Halsey Thomas, eds., *The Diary of George Templeton Strong* (New York, 1952), 1: 62; Edward Thomas, "The Conflicts of Mind," *Ladies' Repository* 2 (November 1842): 322–25.
52. John Todd, *The Young Man: Hints Addressed to the Young Men of the United States,* 4th ed. (Northampton, 1850), p. 14.
53. Odell Shepard, ed., *The Journals of Bronson Alcott* (Boston, 1938), p. 21. Also see L. Maria Child, *Letters From New-York,* First Series (New York, 1852), p. 65.
54. See, for example, James Brewer Stewart, *Joshua R. Giddings and the Tactics of Radical Politics* (Cleveland and London, 1970), pp. 24–25; Bertram Wyatt-Brown, "New Leftists and Abolitionists: A Comparison of American Radical Styles," *Wisconsin Magazine of History* 53 (Summer, 1970): 261. Weinshel, "Some Psychoanalytic Considerations on Moods," pp. 315–17, observes that moods may reflect a high degree of ego control and may indicate a predominately intrasystemic tension within the ego. Rose Edgcumbe and Marion Burgner, "Some Problems in the Conceptualization of Early Object Relationships," *Psa. St. Chi.* 27 (1972): 283–313, 315–31, point out that object loss for an adult may be experienced, and dealt with, on the ego level. It is possible then for regression to occur in object relationships within the ego without correspondingly a drive regression or without a regression to primitive bodily needs.
55. O. A. Brownson, "The Community System," *Democratic Review* 12 (Feb-

unrestrained passions of man are not only homicidal, but suicidal"; and a community lacking a conscience would soon perish.[56]

This was all the more true in that these disruptive social experiences were matched by unusual, perhaps dangerous, thoughts and wishes and by hitherto unknown and unwelcome emotional states. An anguished Mann asked: what institutions still remained intact that could secure the allegiance of the people and at the same time "save us from the dangers that spring up in our own bosoms"?[57] People feared "the appetites," which might prove to be destructive of both the individual and society (the fear itself, the feelings above would add to the sense of separation and loss).[58]

The science of physiology, whose widely accepted doctrines established a linkage between man's biological, mental, and spiritual natures, provided some relief by way of explanation. In his famous lecture on the dangers of indulgence, Sylvester Graham solemnly observed that genital organs were "woven" into the same "grand web of organic life" with other organs such as the stomach, lungs, and heart. Through an intricate network of connecting nerves, an overstimulation of the thought may effect the genital organs and vice versa.[59]

---

ruary 1843): 134. Among the variety of possible responses to a loss of social and psychic integration with the world, one should expect to see on both the individual and collective levels a heightened narcissism to help bolster a threatened self-esteem. Therefore, historians must be cautious in their use of such terms as regression, fixation, and neurosis when discussing the young men in antebellum America, who displayed a preoccupation with the self, had mood swings if not depressions, demonstrated aggressive behavior, and callously treated others.

56. Paul C. Nagel, *This Sacred Trust: American Nationality, 1798–1898* (New York, 1971), p. 73. Todd, *The Young Man*, p. 204, voiced similar fears.

57. Michael Fellman, *The Unbounded Frame: Freedom and Community in Nineteenth Century American Utopianism* (Westport, Conn., 1973), p. 65. Robert Seidenberg, "The Trauma of Eventlessness," *Psa. Rev.* 59 (1972): 95–108, writes that the absence of stimuli, a lack of external events, and appropriate internal responses, can be as traumatic as any other assault upon the ego. In addition, an anticipation of more and more eventlessness may be perceived as a serious threat to one's well-being. In the context of the nineteenth century, therefore, the anxiety arising from the social changes likewise produced in many the fear that as they were losing control over external reality, they might also be in danger of losing control over the inner drives.

58. Charles A. Pinderhughes, "Somatic, Psychic, and Social Sequelae of Loss," *J. Am. Psa. Assn.* 19 (1971): 694, has drawn the connection between psychic loss and somatic loss. "Vegetative (cholenergic) processes which regulate the outpouring of body products may express symbolically the loss of objects with the common innervation facilitating the substitution of one symbolic expression for another."

59. Sylvester Graham, *Chastity, in a cause of Lectures to Young Men: intended also, For the Serious Consideration of Parents and Guardians*, 2nd. ed. (New York, n.d.), p. 3. The best study of Graham is Stephen Willner Nissenbaum's fine essay, "Careful Love: Sylvester Graham and the Emergence of Victorian Sexual Theory in America, 1830–1840" (Ph.D. diss., University of Wisconsin, 1968).

There is little doubt that Graham's audience was well aware of the obvious conclusion to be drawn from these facts; that is, all excess, no matter if caused by moral, mental, or physical stimuli, increased "the excitability and unhealthy activity of the nerves of organic life," and more likely than not induced a state of "diseased irritability and sensibility."[60] The heat generated from these inner passions and outer excitments could ruin a man. Hence, William Alcott's advice: "Keep cool, keep cool!"[61]

To Graham, Alcott, and others, keeping cool applied even to marriage, because there, too, sexual indulgence was considered to be harmful.[62] Sexual practices, of course, were not independent of other cultural activities and styles. In one sense, to be sure, sexual urges threatened to undermine the capacity for socially useful activity. But in another sense, sexuality was also an expression of unrestrained willfulness, so that sexual urges presented for this period many of the same problems that competitive, self-seeking individualism did. Both contained elements of heightened narcissism and, if carried to excess, both could dissolve the bonds of community. Ostensibly, therefore, the focus of Graham's lecture was sex, but more fundamentally he was referring to a broader dimension of social relationships and the need for institutional stability in society. For instance, in the same breath that he censured uncontrolled sexuality, he advocated the repression of all hostile feelings such as envy, anger, and jeolousy as a means of neutralizing the competition and aggression that were a part of the authority relationships from the bedroom to the business office. In short, control of sexuality was an element in a more general need to control all the appetites. In this way interpersonal tensions would be reduced and social bonds strengthened.[63]

To therefore insure the health and stability of the social order, writers inveighed against a wide range of solipsistic pursuits and praised those thoughts and actions that enhanced social unity. We can certainly appreciate in these terms the period's exaggerated fears of masturbation, for this act also had its connection to the

---

60. Graham, *Chastity*, p. 4. Also, William A. Alcott, *The Physiology of Marriage* (Boston, 1859), p. 66; George Drysdale, *The Elements of Social Science; or, Physical, Sexual, and Natural Religion* (London, 1867), p. 79.

61. William A. Alcott, *Familiar Letters to Young Men* (Buffalo, 1850), pp. 174-76.

62. For similar fears in England see Peter T. Cominos, "Late-Victorian Sexual Respectability and the Social System," *International Review of Social History* 8 (1963): 18–48, 216–30.

63. On the need to control aggression see Alcott, *Young Man's Guide*, pp. 93–99; "Anger," *Godey's Lady's Book* 4 (March 1834): 156; "Envy," *American Ladies' Magazine* 7 (1834): 514–16.

broader aspects of self-control, narcissistic indulgence, and personal pleasure independent of any social purpose. In sum, then, good health and self-control grew to be moral imperatives in antebellum America, for these meant the salvation of the individual and community. The passivity of sickness was not to be tolerated: sickness "broke down the pride of manhood," and brought back "feelings of infancy" where the "tender mother" was ready to nurture.[64] Even worse, poor health, no matter whether it arose from internal or external causes, eventually became visible to all—a humiliating reminder that one had lost self-control, was no longer his own master, and had given in to indolence. Health implied a sense of individual and communal purpose, a mastery of the environment, and a sense of worthiness.

By the mid-1830s, however, it had become increasingly apparent that if people were to maintain or regain order and direction over their lives, they would need help and guidance. Out of these concerns emerged a spate of advice literature aimed at inculcating the proper morality and social behavior, and a sizeable chunk of these pamphlets and books was directed at the young male, who had to contend with the wiles of the outside world.

In all circumstances it was necessary to control the peaks and valleys of emotion, to keep the self stable, and especially to remain active in the face of obstacles.[65] Self-control, of course, was the key. Readers of the guidance manuals were told time and time again that they must always be "fully conscious" of where they were and what they were doing. They were also encouraged to believe that they had the power within themselves to direct their thoughts and feelings from any unworthy object and "hold them fixed" on a more desirable one.[66] An inner self-control would in this way allow for a mastery of the

---

64. *Godey's Lady's Book* 1 (1840): 148. For warnings and fears of masturbation see Graham, *Chastity,* pp. 16–19; Alcott, *Physiology of Marriage,* p. 86. Also see Charles E. Rosenberg. "Sexuality, Class and Role in the 19th-Century America," *American Quarterly* 25 (May 1973): 134–36; Carroll Smith-Rosenberg, "The Hysterical Woman: Sex Roles and Role Conflict in 19th-Century America," *Social Research* 29 (1972): 669–70. For a highly selective view of masturbation in the nineteenth century see G. J. Barker-Benfield, *The Horrors of the Half-Known Life: Male Attitudes Toward Women and Sexuality in Nineteenth-Century America* (New York, 1976), pp. 135–226.

65. "The Errors of Youth," *New England Magazine* 5 (October 1833): 299. If these fluctuations in self-esteem were not curbed, it was feared that they could lead to insanity. David J. Rothman, *The Discovery of the Asylum: Social Order and Disorder in the New Republic* (Boston, 1971), pp. 109–29; Gerald N. Grob, "Mental Illness, Indigency, and Welfare: The Mental Hospital in Nineteenth-Century America," *Anonymous Americans.* pp. 255–57.

66. Todd, *The Young Man,* p. 255; *How to Behave: A Pocket Manual of Republican Etiquette* (New York, 1856), p. 46.

world, a mastery that occupied the middle ground between passive retreat and egoistic assault.

Despite these demands for "perfect self-control" the guidance literature was hardly calling for the inflexible rigidity that Noyes did. Rather, there was a remarkable flexibility that counter-balanced and ameliorated the more excessive admonitions for control. It was acknowledged that people needed a respite from the onslaughts of a very perplexing social order. A distressed John Todd believed that if a person only knew "the dangers, the sorrows, the haggard cares" that awaited him in the world, he would probably think twice about leaving the rustic simplicity of his town or village.[67] But since many had left, and still more were planning to leave, it was necessary to construct temporary retreats from the emotional storms.

The social club, church group, and reform organization, among others, provided many with a concrete sense of collective unity, psychic integration, and purposive action.[68] As Orestes Brownson stated, in one form or another the "community system" was being looked upon as the remedy for "all our ills, moral and physical, individual and social."[69] By the 1830s, however, two other real but idealized places were especially emphasized: the home and nature.[70]

67. Todd, *The Young Man*, pp. 124–25.

68. Gregory H. Singleton, "Protestant Voluntary Organizations and the Shaping of Victorian America," *Victorian America*, pp. 47–58; Sidney E. Mead, *The Lively Experiment: The Shaping of Christianity in America* (New York, 1963), pp. 103–33; Edward Pessen, *Riches, Class, and Power Before the Civil War* (Lexington, Mass., 1973), pp. 251–80; T. Scott Miyakawa, *Protestants and Pioneers: Individualism and Conformity on the American Frontier* (Chicago, 1964). Historians must be cautious, however, in interpreting symbols and metaphors from the pens and mouths of nineteenth-century figures. Charles Brenner, "Depression, Anxiety, and Affect Theory," *Int. J. Psa.* 55 (1974): 29, points out that "a wish or fantasy . . . expressed in oral terms is not proof, nor always a good indication, that its origin was pre-oedipal. It is often assumed that oral and anal wishes must have originated during the oral and anal phases, i.e. that they must be pre-oedipal in the literal, historical sense. It cannot be too strongly emphasized that this assumption is incorrect. Oedipal wishes are often expressed in oral and anal terms. The instinctual mode in which a wish or fantasy is expressed is not a sure guide to its time of origin in infantile development." Also see Brenner, "On the Nature and Development of Affects: A Unified Theory," *Psa. Q.* 48 (1974): 532–34; W. G. Joffee and Joseph Sandler, "Comments on the Psychoanalytic Psychology of Adaptation, with Special Reference to the Role of Affects and the Representational World," *Int. J. Psa.* 49 (1968): 445-53.

69. Brownson, "Community System," p. 129.

70. The tendency has been to depict the ideal home and nature as a storage place for libidinal and regressive conflicts. For example, see William E. Bridges, "Warm Hearth, Cold World: Social Perspectives on the Household Poets," *American Quarterly* 21 (1969): 764–79; Michael Paul Rogin, *Fathers and Children: Andrew Jackson and the Subjugation of the American Indian* (New York, 1975); Barker-Benfield, *Horrors of the Half-Known Life*, pp. 215–26.

Although Theodore Parker fully understood that the actual home never measured up to the ideal one, he warmly recalled that the home of every man's childhood was a veritable paradise, a private garden of Eden. There a person's father and mother—"the tall parental mountains of humanity, so they seemed"—stood ready to protect "from the cold and bitter blasts of mortal life."[71] What could be more tempting or satisfying to beleaguered youth than to return to this ideal environment, which was devoid of self-seeking conflict and unrestrained passions. For any young man conquered by his appetites, Parker noted, "the smutch of shame" stood out as boldly upon "the white raiment of God's youthful son"[72] as it did upon poor Hester Prynne. But in the ideal home the love of man united youth "unconsciously to God," and a sense of worthiness was restored.[73]

Parker's sentiments were widely accepted, but it would be a mistake to interpret this as a cultural expression of the desire for a passive life, or the yearning for a regressive merger with childhood figures.[74] Some of course were bound to see it that way, but in the main, while youth might be permitted to seek emotional comfort in the family, it was understood that this was not to be an ongoing, lasting situation. As soon as the young man had been replenished at home, he was encouraged to move out and once more attempt "great things" on his own. If a man intended to achieve anything noteworthy in this world, he had to continue to possess "the love of improvement" and lead an active, productive life.[75]

In many respects nature fulfilled the same psychic functions as did the ideal family. No one drove this point home more forcefully than Emerson in his essay "Nature." According to him, in the tranquillity of the landscape health was restored and life was no longer "irksome."

71. "Phases of Domestic Life," in *World of Matter and Man*, p. 188. Also see Parker, "Home Considered in Relation to Its Moral Influence," Ibid., pp. 209–10.
72. Parker, *World of Matter and Man*, p. 104.
73. Parker, *Sins and Safeguards of Society*, ed. by Samuel B. Stewart (Boston, n.d.), p. 213.
74. An important article on this point is Joseph Barnett, "Dependency Conflicts in the Young Adult," *Psa. Rev.* 58 (1971): 111–24. Conflicts, he says, often take the route of a return to the ideology of the family. This should not be read as a return to the "womb, or uncontrolled regression or fixation, but a temporary return to the "safety of the known." From this position, psychic integration and an ability to cope with the complexities of life can result. Also see Joseph Sandler, "Psychological Conflict and the Structural Model: Some Clinical and Theoretical Implications," *Int. J. Psa.* 55 (1974): 53–61.
75. Alcott, *Gift Book for Young Men*, p. 15. "Be Not Too Fastidious," *National Magazine* 1 (July-December 1852): 25–26, urged young men to recall that "in order to do anything in this world worth doing, we must not stand shivering on the bank, and thinking of the cold and danger, but jump in, and scramble through as well as we can."

Man had no reason to fear "age or misfortune or death," because he was "transported out of the district of change." Just as importantly, a man's self-esteem was not injured in nature; he did not have to suffer the ignominy of rebuff and defeat. There, Emerson wrote, he felt no sense of shame, because "nothing can befall me in life—no disgrace, no calamity (leaving me my eyes), which nature cannot repair." In this emotionally unified world, there was no feeling of loss or separation. "I become a transparent eyeball," Emerson declared, "I see all; the currents of the Universal Being circulate through me; I am part or parcel of God."[76]

Everywhere in nature it seemed that men were able to discover signs and symbols that confirmed life and self. Once again, some might see in this the justification for passivity and withdrawal, an escape from the exigencies of life. But by and large people were not so encouraged and they did not so act. Change and growth occurred in nature too, and men were supposed to act accordingly.[77]

The unifying embrace of Mother Nature, the warm hearth of the ideal home, and the nostalgic yearning for a less complex, golden age thus were partially "strategies in the service of identity."[78] They were, that is, psychic measures employed to cope with a disturbing or even disorienting reality. The nurturant, protective figures and symbols represented a psychic bridge linking past, present, and future in a land becoming even more complex in its urban, industrial growth.

---

76. "Nature," *Complete Essays*, p. 6. Also see W. F. Lowrie, "Deity and Nature," *Ladies' Repository* 1 (December 1841): 360; Theodore Parker, "The Divine Presence in Nature and in the Soul," *The Dial* 1 (July 1840): 59–61.
77. Paul H. Tolpin, "On the Regulation of Anxiety: Its Relation to 'The Timelessness of the Unconscious and Its Capacity for Hallucination'," in *The Annual of Psychoanalysis: The Publication of the Chicago Institute for Psychoanalysis* (New York, 1975), 2: 161, says that such fantasies as the ideal garden (or nature) constitute a recathexis of pleasure, and if it is strong enough, *"allows the ego to regroup its forces and to face frustration with new determination, having been reminded that gratification is a true possibility."* On p. 175, Tolpin also states that such positive memories of the garden or nature offer the psyche "an invaluable protective device which can oppose the innate tendency to react to real or symbolic dangers with disorganizing fear, and allows the mind some degree of autonomy from the immediate impact of unpleasant or anxiety-evoking realities of life." Finally, these fantasies help to "reduce the danger of experiencing too intense degrees of self-dissatisfaction, and of longing, depression, anxiety, and rage."
78. Weinstein and Platt, *Psychoanalytic Sociology*, p. 109. Also see, Pinchas Noy, "A Revision of the Psychoanalytic Theory of the Primary Process," *Int. J. Psa.* 53 (1972): 243–48; Noy, "Symbolism and Mental Representation," *The Annual of Psychoanalysis*, 1: 125–57; Gilbert J. Rose, "Narcissistic Fusion States and Creativity," *The Unconscious Today*, p. 496; Nathaniel Ross, "Affect as Cognition: With Observations on the Meanings of Mystical States," *International Review of Psychoanalysis* 2 (1975): 79–92.

These wishes and thoughts, then, were not dangerous in themselves: the question was whether any individual or group saw these as practicing temporary respites or permanent solutions.

After recuperating from his New York experience, Noyes would be ready to play out the active-passive dilemma in a variety of the cultural contexts just presented. A general loosening of authority, unrestrained egoism, family governance, health and sex would all come under his scrutiny as he sought support for his Perfectionist ideas.

4 Obsessional Behavior:

Perfection, Assertions of Leadership,

and Disrupted Relationships

June to July 1834 was a period of retrenchment for Noyes. He yearned to carry his Perfectionist beliefs to the rest of Putney, but after second thoughts he decided it was best to limit his religious discussions to his family. And well he should have. Rumors of his insanity had preceded him to Putney, and Noyes's father had given up hope for his oldest son. The rest of the family, as Noyes wrote Horatio in New Haven, were in "great suspense and tribulation." Neighbors were hesitant to speak his name around the family for fear of embarrassing them, and, consequently, Noyes had to spend many an hour assuaging the doubts of his family and easing the community's suspicions. He attended the local congregational church and scrupulously avoided initiating any dispute or argument. As he related to Horatio, "I am at present living under an embargo."[1] During his hours of meditation, Noyes reflected upon his New York experience and the lessons he had learned from it. His brush with madness impressed upon his mind more than ever before the need for absolute control in all aspects of life. What a person "positively *knew*," he asserted, should be the rule for all thought and subsequent action. It was both foolish and harmful to trust in speculative thought or muddle over conflicting ideas. "The true method of mental economy," he determined, was to select those thoughts he "absolutely *knew*" to be valid and deny all others. This was, Noyes concluded, "the only way to get and keep a sound mind."[2]

1. "Backward Glances, VI," *Oneida Circular* 9 (12 August 1872): 259 (letter dated 2 July 1834). Noyes became involved in one minor dispute in the church over his Perfectionist ideas. G. W. Noyes, ed., *Religious Experience*, pp. 159–60.
2. J. H. Noyes, *Confession of Religious Experience*, p. 41. In the original quote Noyes italicized the word "know." The obsessive's need for absolute control of all feelings and thoughts (not just hostile and sexual but tender and

We know, however, that Noyes was not well prepared to cope with his world. He lacked the inner resources that might sustain him when confronted by an unstable environment. Pressed by inner urges and by fears of outer conflict, he resolved to sustain himself by exercising *absolute control* over all forces. This resolution was too rigid for comfort: Noyes was compelled to view all situations and encounters in extremes, and he was capable of extreme responses. He lived in an "all or none" world, which nevertheless he insisted could be brought under control by rational and logical means.[3] As a result, all emotional responses including the sexual, the tender, and the aggressive had to be mastered and contained.[4]

To be an ordinary person meant to Noyes that one was weak and helpless, a passive victim controlled by others and by events. Noyes, of course, had surmounted this by his Perfectionism, claiming that he not only *sought* perfection but had *attained* it. Noyes attempted in this way to dress himself in an armor that would strengthen and protect him, though it is evident that underneath he still felt weak and was easily threatened. His Perfectionism, then, was not indicative of true self-esteem. Equally important, as long as he continued to see himself exalted, many of his real assets were denied, and he constantly provoked the very conflict he sought to avoid by making impossible demands upon himself and others.[5]

---

unworthy feelings as well) is a device for preventing "any thought or feeling that might produce shame, loss of pride or status, or a feeling of weakness or deficiency—whether such feelings are hostile, sexual, or otherwise." Salzman, *Obsessive Personality*, p. 13. Noyes was flexible enough so that his Perfectionism could reflect changes within himself and the social world. Noyes's flexibility and adapatability were derived from further revelations that simultaneously enhanced his power as a leader and a controller of events.

3. David A. Freedman, "The Genesis of Obsessional Phenomena," *Psa. Rev.* 58 (1971): 376, 382, notes that obsessive behavior may arise not only from instinctual pressures, but also from "specific environmental pressure." He goes on to say that aggression in obsessive states may be partially induced by the "failure of the parent or surrogate . . . to fulfill its role in the implied contract, 'If I am good, then you will gratify my needs.'" If we may add a sociological dimension to these statements, then it may be suggested that vast social changes that lead to perceived violations of the morality may also produce obsessive concerns. Salzman, *Obsessive Personality*, pp. 89–90, notes that obsessive defense mechanisms are associated with a "general atmosphere of doubt and uncertainty about one's ability to modify or influence the environment to satisfy one's needs." Moreover, the "consistent theme in all obsessionals is the presence of anxieties about being in danger because of an incapacity to fulfill the requirements of others and to feel certain of one's acceptance."

4. On the need for this control in the obsessive see Salzman, *Obsessive Personality*, p. 32; David Shapiro, *Neurotic Styles* (New York and London, 1965), pp. 25–53.

5. On the need for and the use of these mechanisms see Salzman, *Obsessive Personality*, pp. 17–36, 51–52, 163–65. Also note the discussion of the nirvana-like state in Freedman, "Genesis of Obsessional Phenomena," pp. 376–77.

Noyes's unwillingness to settle for anything less than perfection thus had a profound, and often severe, effect upon his relationships with others. Security and self-assuredness would be his only when he could erect a rigid and unyielding control over himself and others, exercise infallible judgments, and be absolutely certain of his status as the "chosen one." The reaction to any disclosure of inadequacy in his contact with others would induce feelings of failure, bring on fits of discouragement and despair, and activate intense anger as he sought to rectify the situation and restore his preeminent position.

While still in Putney, Noyes received a letter from Dutton with the crushing news that Abigail, along with her brother and several others, had deserted the free church. On top of this, Boyle had been dismissed. Faced with Abigail's apostasy, yet hopeful of starting a religious newspaper, Noyes left Putney in late July 1834.[6] After a leisurely journey he arrived in New Haven in August. Although too timid and hurt to contact Abigail, Noyes was eager to begin the paper. Like many others in antebellum America, Noyes had come to look upon the press as the ideal vehicle to modify and mold society.[7] Noyes's impression was bolstered by his faith in the efficacy and power of his ideas. Words were action and commitment to him; the magic of the press would carry the magic of his Perfectionist ideas.[8] Indirectly, therefore, Noyes hoped to exert his influence and control his environment. Unfortunately, his two friends had come under the influence of one Amos Smith, who was undermining their perfectionist beliefs. Noyes was aghast. It looked as if he was about to be silenced before he had a

6. Dutton, Boyle, and Noyes, before they had embraced Perfectionism, had discussed the possibilities of starting a religious paper. After Noyes had returned to New Haven in June (after his New York experience), they had again briefly discussed the need for a paper. J. H. Noyes, *Confession of Religious Experience,* p. 50.

7. For example, S. G. Goodrich, "Responsibility of Authors and Readers," *The Mother's Assistant* 1 (January 1841): 7–9; "The Press," *Democratic Review* 30 (1852): 359–60; Allan R. Pred, *Urban Growth and the Circulation of Information: The United States System of Cities, 1790–1840* (Cambridge, Mass., 1973).

8. On the omnipotence of ideas and the obsessive see Salzman, *Obsessive Personality,* pp. 26–28. Also see Arnold H. Modell, *Object Love and Reality: An Introduction to a Psychoanalytic Theory of Object Relations* (New York, 1968), pp. 10–27. On p. 23, Modell makes the point that magical thought can act to mitigate the danger of overwhelming fears of loss and abandonment through the creation of an illusion of a lack of separateness between the self and the object. In this sense Noyes's omnipotent thought is a way of establishing and recreating a stable world for himself. It is also essential to reemphasize the fact that Noyes attempted to reach his goal of self-aggrandizement through active achievement and did not indulge in a regressive confusion with reality and fantasy.

chance to be heard. Thus threatened, Noyes launched into a bitter attack against Smith.

Angrily, he accused Smith of assuming "a paternal or pedagogical care" over Boyle and Dutton, and that for the worst reasons imaginable, he "loved to rule boys." For several days, Noyes later recalled, he and Smith "wrestled as for life," and the contest was a fierce one. Smith did not come unarmed. With "an unspeakeably obstinate will" of his own, Smith parried Noyes's religious arguments and thrust boldly with his own. The "mysterious and sometimes hideous roll of his eyes," along with "strange working of his wide-spread fingers," lent Smith an air of part insanity and part inspiration; he had successfully converted minds weaker than Noyes's.[9] Ultimately, the contest was declared a draw, although Noyes was successful in weaning Boyle and Dutton from Smith's side. Now nothing stood in the way of the paper but its naming. Reminiscent of William Lloyd Garrison's vow in the first issue of the *Liberator* that he would not "retreat a single inch—AND I WILL BE HEARD," Noyes pleaded that they "hoist their colors" for the country to see. He proposed the name "The Perfectionist," and although they argued that it was too pretentious, Boyle and Dutton agreed to it.[10]

On 20 August 1834, the first number of the paper was issued, and for six months Noyes's mind was busy exploring the ramifications of his Perfectionist truths. The first issue set the tone for the paper and established Noyes's influence on its content. A preponderant number of articles dealt with perfection in obedience, the security of obedience, and the perfection of holiness through suffering.[11] His ideas, of course, did not go unchallenged. Often before he printed an article, Noyes and Boyle would engage in lengthy debates over Noyes's account of the Second Coming and his stringent demands for perfection. Nevertheless, by dint of his tenacity of argument Noyes would win his point, and the articles were published with his ideas intact.[12]

Back in Putney, Noyes's family continued to worry about him. His father anguished over the fact that his son did not hold a respectable

---

9. "Religious History—No. 17," *Perfectionist and Theocratic Watchman* 4 (14 December 1844): 74.

10. J. H. Noyes, *Confession of Religious Experience*, p. 53. Garrison quoted in George M. Fredrickson, ed., *William Lloyd Garrison,* Great Lives Observed Series (Englewood Cliffs, N.J., 1968), p. 23.

11. These articles, heavily freighted in religious language and often tedious to read, were reprinted in John Humphrey Noyes, *"The Way of Holiness." A Series of Papers Formerly Published in the Perfectionist, at New Haven* (Putney, Vt., 1838).

12. J. H. Noyes, *Confession of Religious Experience*, pp. 53–54.

position. Both parents urged him to return home, or for that matter to go anywhere other than New Haven, to begin to earn a living and return to a more sensible religious position. In a series of letters Noyes acknowledged their concern but insisted that his work on the paper had for the first time given him a feeling of self-worth. He felt on top of the world again, and he had no desire to come down. He politely informed his father that in doing God's work, money was a secondary concern. He thanked him for whatever financial support he had given in the past, and stated that this did not represent a dependent tie; it was a gratuity, which enabled Noyes to continue his work for the Father in heaven.[13] He tried to convince his sister Elizabeth that he was neither a *boy* nor crazy, but a sane *man* filled with the spirit of Paul and Christ and thus God's devoted servant.[14] To his mother he snapped brusquely that he did not wish to trade the activity and independence he had attained in New Haven for the passivity and dependence that would be waiting in Putney. He reminded her that now he was "writing for the press and preaching," while at home— as she well knew—he "could do comparatively nothing." Where, he asked edgily, was he more dependent—in New Haven or at home? The answer was obvious, and he pleaded in angry tones: "Give me up, Mother! For the Lord's sake give me up!" If she could not accept his way of life and religious beliefs, then he had pity for her and wanted nothing more to do with her.[15]

In many respects these disagreements with his family were not as enervating and severe as the hostility he had to endure from the rest of society. Throughout the spring and summer of 1834 the established clergy denounced Perfectionists of all kinds. More than that, as the school of New Haven Perfectionism began to take loose shape around Noyes's beliefs in the Second Coming, security, and freedom from law, the New York Perfectionists represented by Latourette, John B. Foot, Charles and Simon Lovett, and the Annesley sisters of Albany turned against him. Latourette withdrew his subscriptions to the *Perfectionist* and dubbed it "the Delusionist." Another blow was struck against Noyes at a general convention of Perfectionists held at Canastota, New York, on 1 January 1835. The various factions of the New York group pushed through a resolution strongly denouncing Noyes and the New Haven wing. Submerged in this flood of spiritual

---

13. "Backward Glancings, X," *Oneida Circular* 9 (9 December 1872): 395 (letter from Noyes to his father dated 8 October 1834).
14. "Noyes to His Sister Elizabeth," G. W. Noyes, ed., *Religious Experience,* pp. 172–73. My underlining the words "boy" and "man," which Noyes used in his letter, is to emphasize the fact again that for Noyes religion was his means of remaining active and a way of negotiating the step from youth to manhood
15. Ibid., p. 175.

contention, Noyes felt as if he were about to be "wrecked" and "cast forth to desolation."[16]

To add insult to injury, the New Yorkers sent Simon Lovett to convert Noyes to their persuasion. Someone should have warned poor Lovett of the risk; Noyes was in no mood to tolerate anyone's spiritual tyranny. As Noyes was later to say, "When I first meet a self-righteous minister, otherwise a false prophet, I am usually girded for battle. Saul hauls his javelins, but David cannot be hurt."[17] Lovett represented to Noyes a means of overcoming his discouragement and despair. If he could convince Lovett that his views were correct, it would help restore his image as an exalted leader. In their ensuing battle, David successfully deflected each of Saul's javelins. Noyes was victorious; Lovett for the time being had been converted.[18]

In February 1835, these two set out to visit several Perfectionist groups throughout New England in order to convince them of the righteousness of Noyes's philosophy. In Massachusetts they first stopped at Southampton where Noyes became acutely aware of "a seducing tendency to freedom of manners between the sexes." When a young woman greeted Lovett with a kiss, it was Noyes who felt uneasy and blushed. At Brimfield he encountered another group of nubile women whose interest in the two itinerant Perfectionists appeared to be something more than spiritual. Two plus two began to equal a very threatening four to Noyes. He felt himself to be the object of attentions that ostensibly were innocent, but he knew them to be quite dangerous. One evening while conducting a meeting in a private house, Noyes attempted to give spiritual comfort to a distraught girl. Deeply involved in the emotionality of the moment and the girl's plight, Noyes inadvertently put his arm around her waist. When they separated, she kissed him in token of her gratitude. Noyes was nonplussed. That night in the anxiety of deep prayer he got a "clear view of the situation" and received "orders" to withdraw. However, what should have been an orderly retreat ended in a hasty rout. Early the next morning, without telling his intentions to anyone, Noyes "took a bee-line on foot through snow and cold—below zero— to Putney, sixty miles distant," which he reached in a remarkably brief time.[19]

16. J. H. Noyes, *Confession of Religious Experience,* pp. 54–55. See "Appendix D," Ibid., pp. 79–88, for a concise explanation of his differences with the New York Perfectionists. Also see "New York Perfectionists," *Witness* 2 (10 December 1842): 181–82.

17. "Noyes to Boyle, March 15, 1835," in G. W. Noyes, ed., *Religious Experience,* pp. 215–16.

18. "Religious History—No. 18," *Perfectionist and Theocratic Watchman* 4 (28 December 1844), p. 78.

19. G. W. Noyes, ed., *Religious Experience,* pp. 198–99.

Luckily for Noyes he left when he did. Joined a few days later by Dutton and left to his own devices, Lovett allowed his interests to deviate from the spiritual to the sexual. Late one night in March two girls, Mary Lincoln and Maria Brown, made their way into Lovett's bedroom. They intended to demonstrate that they could conquer the devil's passions within themselves and emerge victorious. That night spirituality lost, but Lovett did not. When the scandal broke, Mary Lincoln was particularly devastated by the wrath of the community. In her anguish she imagined that God was about to destroy Brimfield with fire and thus warned the villagers of the impending disaster. She urged them to join her in fleeing to the mountains. All but one thought she was insane, but a young woman, Flavilla Howard, decided that there was some truth in the presentiments. Late at night Mary and her convert set out for a nearby mountain. Sloushing through the rain and mud, they threw off their clothing as they ran. When these two bizarre Dianas on the hunt reached the top of their climb, they prayed that God might spare Brimfield His avenging bolts of lightening and fire. Afterwards, they were convinced that their efforts had saved the town.[20]

Safely ensconced in Putney, Noyes began daily to preach there and in some of the surrounding villages. Nevertheless, the rumors of sexual irregularities that followed Perfectionism wherever it went could not be stilled. Despite his protestations of innocence, his proximity to the Brimfield bundling, plus the fact that he was a Perfectionist, worked against Noyes. In the public imagination, which was often quite vivid, he was also charged with lascivious conduct and branded an antinomian.

Near the end of April 1835, Lovett and Charles Weld arrived in Putney to assist Noyes in the religious meetings he had been conducting there with modest success. The presence of these three together in his own home was too much for the elder Noyes; he chastised his son for his choice of friends and pleaded with him to restore his own reputation and the good name of the family. In rebuttal Noyes insisted that a son of God could not be concerned about his worldly reputation when he was busy doing the Lord's work. An exasperated father Noyes grew angry, and for the sake of peace Noyes and his two friends moved out. Then days later they left Putney, with Noyes and Weld going off together to deliver their spiritual dogma to other towns.[21]

This would be a trip that Noyes would long remember, for it set into

20. Ibid., pp. 197–98.
21. J. H. Noyes, *Confession of Religious Experience,* pp. 56–57.

motion a bitter conflict with Weld. Ever since his crisis in New York, Noyes had become more fully determined never to be placed in a subordinate, dependent position again. In the course of their meditative jaunt through Massachusetts, Weld tried to establish a spiritual control over his younger Perfectionist companion. He told Noyes that the Spirit had been communicating with him, and among his instructions, he was directed to take a detour through the northern towns of Vermont. Noyes was prone to see things differently, and he immediately felt "some involuntary disgust" at Weld's suggestion. Noyes acquiesced eventually and they continued their journey. A few days later Noyes decided that it was time to leave Weld in order to attend to some business in New Haven. This display of independence did not sit well with Weld, and for the next several days he remonstrated with Noyes. Refusing to be weakened by Weld's entreaties, Noyes abruptly told him that enough was enough and that he would soon be leaving. Weld relented and asked if he might walk with Noyes for a mile or two before they separated. At the end of the walk, and just as Weld was about to depart, Noyes suddenly changed his mind and suggested that Weld accompany him to New Haven, which he more than willingly did.[22]

By the time they arrived in New Haven the "war of wills" between them had reached a feverish intensity. Years later Noyes was to admit that he could not single out the perverse aspects of Weld's character since his "outward conduct was inoffensive." For Noyes the conflict was primarily a subjective one carried on within "the spiritual language of the heart and brain." Asked how he knew the inner tension came from Weld, Noyes answered that "it always involved in some way or other, the old question of his preeminence; and secondly, because when I communicated with him externally, I always found him in a process of internal strife parallel to mine."[23]

Weld's ensnaring ways were difficult to counter and eventually brought Noyes to "a kind of internal debate, similar to that which often occurs in cases of morbid conscientiousness." Depressed, Noyes wished either to submit to it or break free.[24] At length, after repeatedly fighting Weld off, though with little hope of lasting relief, a beleaguered Noyes informed Weld that the central issue between them was "whether he or I had the strongest mind, and that one or the other must fall."[25] After a day or two of "infinite spiritual hair-splitting,

22. Ibid., p. 58.
23. Ibid., pp. 58–59. Also see "Religious History—No. 20," *Perfectionist and Theocratic Watchman* 4 (25 January 1845): 86–87.
24. J. H. Noyes, *Confession of Religious Experience,* p. 58.
25. G. W. Noyes, ed., *Religious Experience,* p. 224.

with alternate advantage and defeat," Noyes at last gained enough control over himself to subdue Weld's invidious spirit. Once the break had been effected in his mind, Noyes informed Weld, who solemnly acknowledged the inevitable truth. Instead of rejoicing at his liberation from Weld, Noyes felt a deep sense of loss and hurriedly stole to the fields south of town. There he mournfully paced to and fro, agonizing as one who had "barely escaped a whirlpool."[26] Later, Noyes was convinced that this suffering arose from an emphathetic understanding of Weld's feelings, and it did not surprise him, upon his return to New Haven, to find Weld sunk in "a paroxysm of horror" quite similar to that which he had experienced in the free church a year earlier.[27]

In the early days of their friendship, it will be recalled, Noyes had idealized Weld as he sought spiritual certainties and personal integration. Even after Weld had deserted him in New York, Noyes confessed that he still "loved him with much credulous confidence and affection."[28] Upon his final separation from Weld, however, Noyes's idealization gave way to outright contempt and deprecation.[29] Noyes saw himself as completely virtuous and innocent, while his former religious mentor was the devil incarnate. He reviled him as a scoundrel who "insinuated sensual ideas about the kingdom of God" in his Perfectionist ramblings, and for that reason was a "bad man—a very dangerous man." Where Weld was once highly regarded for his greater spiritual insight, he was now demeaned for his "imbecility of will," and his "ineffectiveness of thought." In a parting shot, Noyes gloated in telling Weld that by "delusion you have driven me to certainty; by bondage . . . into liberty; by damnation . . . into heaven."[30]

To add to his difficulties Noyes had to contend with a disputatious James Boyle. For quite some time an undercurrent of tension existed between the two, and when Noyes left the paper in January 1835, Boyle took it upon himself to exercise greater editorial independence in the *Perfectionist*. As Noyes grew bolder and more vociferous in his brand of Perfectionism, Boyle became less and less enchanted with

26. Ibid. Here again the struggle has taken on an either/or quality for Noyes, with a victor and defeated. Although Noyes felt he had subdued Weld, he did so at some psychic cost. In terms of separation anxiety we can see that in his use of the term "whirlpool" Noyes was fighting against a strong regressive pull. On this last point see Kohut, *Analysis of the Self*, p. 154.

27. J. H. Noyes, *Confession of Religious Experience*, p. 59.

28. Ibid., p. 57.

29. On this point see Kernberg, "Factors in the Psychoanalytic Treatment of Narcissistic Personalities," pp. 52, 58; Salzman, *Obsessive Personality*, pp. 221–22, 233.

30. J. H. Noyes, "Appendix J," *Confession of Religious Experience*, p. 96.

him. It was soon obvious to Noyes that Boyle had no understanding and little sympathy for the "warfare" in which he was engaged, and was upset by "the apparent mysticism and fanaticism which attended it."[31]

In time Noyes's "external spinnings" so disconcerted Boyle that he asked Noyes not to submit any more articles to the paper. Their relationship waned rapidly when, in the fall of 1835, Boyle started publishing his opinions doubting the existence of a once-and-for-all perfect holiness and questioning the fact that Paul was a living example of such perfection. Although Noyes admitted that he was never named in any of the articles, to assail Paul was to attack and belittle Noyes. Noyes lashed back angrily at his former coeditor, the man who "whipped me in the paper as hard as he could." He accused Boyle of being jealous of him because he was becoming a leader. "And to cut me off forever from that position," he noted with umbrage, Boyle "became a leader himself."[32] When Boyle openly disagreed with Noyes's assessment of Weld's character, a final break in their once close relationship was inevitable. When it came, Noyes was openly relieved to be rid of his dependence upon Boyle.

In the midst of his struggle with Boyle, and shortly after he had left a distraught Weld in New Haven, Noyes joined Lovett for a spiritual crusade in some nearby towns. However, weakened by his encounters with Weld and Boyle and highly upset over the flood of abuse that continued to engulf the name of all Perfectionists, Noyes succumbed. In Prospect, he experienced for several weeks a turn of mind similar to the one in New York, though on a far lesser scale.[33]

One afternoon in the latter part of June 1835, Joanna, Noyes's sister, received a surprise visit from her brother, who had just returned to New Haven from Prospect. Having been "loosed from all the moorings of ordinary prudence, and sent adrift once more with no pilot or helper but God," Noyes presented a harrowing figure to his sister. After "a long crying fit about him," Joanna wrote their mother, and from this letter we catch a quick glimpse of Noyes's harried mental state.

The first time she saw him he was terribly upset, "would not reason at all, but denounced everything and everybody." Physically, he was "haggard and careworn," and Joanna was positive that he was un-

---

31. G. W. Noyes, ed., *Religious Experience,* p. 199.

32. "Organization—No. 1," *Witness* 2 (20 January 1841): 4; "Religious History—No. 21," *Perfectionist and Theocratic Watchman* 4 (8 February 1845): 90; "Boyle versus Paul," *Witness* 1 (22 February 1840): 135–36; "Boyle and Socialism," *Perfectionist and Theocratic Watchman* 4 (14 December 1844): 75.

33. "Religious History—No. 21," pp. 82–83.

balanced. A few days later Noyes seemingly regained his composure. While in this frame of mind he exhibited some "gentleness and kindness," and told her that for the last six months he had been fighting the battle against the Antichrist. Although he believed he had suffered through some of his greatest turmoil since he was last in Putney, he now felt that victory was near and that he would be at peace once more.

Joanna, however, doubted the claim. His strange behavior, she continued in the letter, had alienated him from the other Perfectionists in New Haven, and he mourned the fact that he had "no home and no friends in the wide world." In this abject condition he had been contemplating how to change his fortunes. Joanna urged him to go to New York and become a countinghouse clerk, and for a while Noyes considered this idea. The more she saw of him, though, the more grieved she became. Taking everything into consideration he seemed to be rational, but still there were times when "something wild" would come over him, especially when he began to espouse his views. Basically, she found his beliefs on holiness to make sense, but on other religious subjects and in his manner of talking to people, he appeared "deranged." As a last resort, Joanna suggested to her mother that if Noyes's mind could be diverted to more practical pursuits, his religious aberrations and strange behavior would eventually improve.[34]

In search of rest and tranquillity, Noyes made his way to Milford, a town about ten miles west of New Haven. There he lived with an acquaintance, who, although not a Perfectionist, had been friendly to him earlier. As it happened, this man had been an editor of a paper in New Haven, which had some delinquent accounts needing collection. For the sake of diversion and a desire to earn money for his keep, Noyes volunteered his services. He spent a few days journeying from town to town collecting what he could, and preaching whenever he could find an audience. Once he completed this task, Noyes had another waiting. His friend was in the middle of writing a history of Milford and wished to include a map of the town in his book. Noyes wasted little time; he grabbed a compass and for two or three weeks surveyed the town. While defining the lines and contour of Milford, Noyes had ample time to reflect upon and plot out his own direction.

A lengthy letter to his mother most fully reveals the outcome of Noyes's reflections during this interval of peace. As reprinted in the book edited by G. W. Noyes, the letter runs approximately seven pages

---

34. "Noyes's Sister Joanna to Her Mother," G. W. Noyes, ed., *Religious Experience,* pp. 226–27.

and is truly a rich document in confirming so many of our impressions to this point.

At the outset Noyes revealed the intensely narcissistic roots of this current lull in his stormy life. He gained his temporary and fragile peace by denying his dependence upon others, by assertions of his omnipotence, and by his identification with a perfect world free of all conflict. Noyes certainly gained his peace, but he was in "splendid isolation." His "work of bloodshed" was a thing of the past; he was now free to do God's work as if he had never known "father, or mother, or brother, or sister." Previously he had felt compelled to find support for his ideas of perfection, but now he felt strong enough to abide by them even if others derided him. Right now he saw nothing but goodness in the universe. "All that is called evil," he wrote, "is good to one whose head is above the clouds."[35]

Aware that this might be misinterpreted, Noyes assured his mother that his self-satisfaction was only a manifestation of God's spirit, which alone made him what he was. So completely merged was he with His spirit that it was impossible for him to have "goodness, or greatness, or glory separately from him." From this merger a meek son inherited the strength and greatness of the Father, or in Noyes's words, "As with him I glory." In such a state he could not conceal God's righteousness and could not feign "a voluntary humility."[36]

For the next several paragraphs Noyes tried to assure his family that he was not insane. He justified the apparent irrationality of his behavior by insisting that "severe suffering of the body and mind" was essential for true spiritual growth. He rejoiced in the knowledge that his suffering had separated him from other Perfectionists, his own family, and other earthly mortals. Freed from these "spiritual and natural relations," Noyes was able to devote his services to God and in so doing become more God-like.

Noyes also discussed some "practical conclusions" that he had formed over the past year or so. He had learned that a love of God, of self, and of mankind were all the same; that is, in his wished-for perfection there was to be no gap between the actual and ideal self. He also had come to know, as he informed his mother, that perfection of the self depended upon "perfect self-knowledge and perfect self-control," and until he had acquired these traits, he would not be able to preach the truth to anyone else. Though he felt himself superior to

35. "Noyes to His Mother," Ibid., p. 233; J. H. Noyes, *Confession of Religious Experience,* p. 60.
36. "Noyes to Mother," p. 233.

most everyone, he also realized that in terms of perfection he was still "but a sophomore."[37]

Self-confident and intact in his blissful state, Noyes discovered that "the love of independence" was one of his most pressing desires, and that he could never be satisfied until he earned a living as other men did. Even though money was the root of all evil and the "reigning idolatry" of New England, he did not fear it. He realized that the aggressive-competitive qualities associated with it were "forever extinguished" in himself, permitting him to act in good conscience in pursuit of a living. His head "full of Yankee notions about money making and economy," Noyes claimed that he had suddenly become a great admirer of Benjamin Franklin.

Noyes tried to persuade his mother that this change was not ephemeral. No one knew more fully than he "the chaotic ocean of change" over which he had been tossed. Yet, he had never lost confidence in himself because God had been his pilot, and he now was securely "at anchor in the haven of God's peace." Noyes had no reason to suspect that any future "shipwrecks" lay ahead. He confidently assured his mother that he feared "neither ocean, nor storm, nor quicksands, nor whirlpools." An innocent person need have no fear, he reminded her.[38]

Noyes then focused his attention on his mother's failing health. We do not know the full story of "her strange affliction," but years later Noyes's sister Harriet discussed their mother's illness and indicated that Noyes's behavior as a Perfectionist often induced it. No doubt her high expectations for her first-born son, her desire to see him a respectable minister, had been shattered. Whenever word came of Noyes's misadventures, she experienced such overwhelming anxiety that she was often kept awake for days at a time. In this state she once more was beseiged by an "unnatural activity of the brain, and . . . a morbid action of the conscience." Despondent, and at times overcome by waves of guilt, she would berate herself unmercifully. Ultimately she would recover, only to be submerged again in "the waves of her disease everytime she saw him swing loose in the righteousness" of his Perfectionism.[39]

---

37. Ibid., pp. 232–35.
38. Ibid., pp. 236–37. For the moment Noyes's ambivalent feelings regarding autonomy and passivity are resolved in the merger with God. He can now partake of the Father's power (phallic grandiosity), and feel that he can compete on equal terms. It is also significant that in this magical merger and feelings of narcissistic bliss, Noyes no longer feared those regressive pulls represented by the quicksand, whirlpools, and fears of drowning in the water. On this point see Kohut, *Analysis of the Self*, p. 154.
39. "Memorial of Mrs. P. Noyes," *Circular* 3 n.s. (2 July 1866): 122.

As Noyes addressed himself to the problem of his mother's health, the tone of the letter changed dramatically from that of a pleasant, even subdued, grandiosity to that of a more insistent, intransigent demand for control. It is surely significant that no sooner had he declared his wish to be independent then he attempted to establish a fatherly position in relationship to his mother, younger sisters, and brother. He assured his mother that if he had her infirmities he certainly would find some way of restoring his health. He informed her that her mind was undermining her body. Although she probably felt as if she could not control her mind, Noyes knew differently. From his own experiences, unrestrained thoughts and impulses had on more than one occasion wreaked havoc on his body. With God's help, however, he was able to regain control of his mind and thus of his health. "The pilot of a steamboat," he said, "can stop his vessel in a moment even when it is under full pressure." Under proper control the mind was "as obsequious to the will of its pilot as a steamboat." Steeped in the most severe conflict, Noyes felt he was now able to control his suffering, become "perfectly thoughtless," and attain a feeling of inner peace. Finally, Noyes asserted that he would have preferred to be the "slave of a southern negro driver" rather than suffer the torture of, and be a slave to, his own mind.[40]

Noyes returned again to his theme of perfection. He had recently noted that he was a "glorious kingdom" unto himself, a kingdom that lay partially in ruin and darkness but was still capable of being restored and of glorifying God. When Noyes himself had fully ascertained the nature and resources of this kingdom, and was able to control the entire conflict within it, and when he was utterly certain he was doing his Father's work, he would then be able to assist his benighted relatives in their own quest. Noyes thus concluded the letter with expressions of his desire and need to remain active and purposive. He urged his sisters to become more spiritual and reminded his mother that should she want help in breaking from her spiritual and mental bondage, he, in time, would be the one to help her.[41]

These thoughts were a consistent expression of Noyes's elevated state. But reality pressured him vengefully and rudely, acting always to throw him off balance, to render him despondent. One Sunday in October Noyes was asked to address a small gathering in the Milford schoolhouse. Perfectionist doctrines with their overtones of anti-

---

40. "Noyes to His Mother," pp. 237–38. For a similar expression linking slavery to a loss of control and autonomy see Shepard, ed., *Journals of Bronson Alcott*, p. 243; Ronald G. Walters, "The Erotic South: Civilization and Sexuality in American Abolitionism," *American Quarterly* 25 (1973): 177–201.
41. "Noyes to His Mother," p. 239.

nomianism were not well received in this community, and many townspeople were apprehensive even before Noyes had a chance to speak. At this meeting Noyes had to face what many abolitionists were encountering in other parts of the country—violence.[42] Just as the meeting was about to be adjourned, some of the town's more irate citizens hurled rocks through the windows. The glass shattered, and so ended Noyes's interval of peace. Confronted with the possibility of physical harm, Noyes's immediate response was flight. He went to New York and shortly thereafter to Newark where he stayed with Abram C. Smith, a recent convert to Perfectionism. From there he made his way to Philadelphia in order to confront T. R. Gates, who had recently become friendly with Boyle. Their meeting was short and stormy, Gates stridently declaring his superior spirituality and proximity to God. Completely unnerved by this, Noyes hurriedly made his way back to Newark. A few days later, both monetarily and spiritually destitute, Noyes set out for New Haven. During the first day of his journey, Noyes's anxiety became so great that he lapsed, predictably, into a depressive mood. For relief Noyes turned to Nature, as he previously had done in New Salem. Meandering off the main road, he travelled a short distance until he came to a quiet, beautiful spot overlooking Long Island Sound. There he lay down and resolved not to move until his inner state matched the quietude of his surroundings. After a while he fell asleep, and when he awoke his spirit "was in blessed harmony with the warm sunshine and the tranquil ocean."[43]

Upon arriving in New Haven, Noyes went directly to Joanna's home. It was early December now, and the cold New England air must have cut through his tattered clothing. His appearance and manner once more distressed Joanna so greatly that she wrote home asking for advice. Their parents sent money at once, and Polly Noyes urged that her son be sent home right away. Joanna could not guarantee this, for Noyes insisted that he was entirely in the hands of God and that he must follow the Lord's will and plans. Thus, she believed it was senseless to try to push him one way or the other because he would not act until he felt God wanted him to. By mid-December Noyes had apparently received the Word, since he now decided that he should

42. On this point see Leonard L. Richards, *"Gentlemen of Property and Standing": Anti-Abolition Mobs in Jacksonian America* (New York, 1970); David Grimsted, "Rioting in Its Jacksonian Setting," *American Historical Review* 87 (1972): 361–97; Lorman Ratner, *Powder Keg: Northern Opposition to the Anti-Slavery Movement, 1831–1840* (New York, 1968); Theodore M. Hammett, "Two Mobs of Jacksonian Boston: Ideology and Interest," *Journal of American History* 62 (1976): 845–68.

43. J. H. Noyes, *Confession of Religious Experience,* pp. 61–62.

return to Putney. Preceding him was a letter written by Joanna to their mother, which contained words of caution and advice. She urged Polly not to dictate to him or try to persuade him that he was wrong in any of his beliefs. The only way to handle Noyes, Joanna thought, was to leave him alone and let him think as he pleased. He was so afraid of "being influenced by man's wisdom and of being under bondage," that he could not tolerate any advice or contradiction, especially from members of his family. "So," Joanna warned, "beware!"[44]

At this point, we are as well aware of Noyes's range of moods, his predilections, preoccupations, as we can be. To be sure, over the next years Noyes had many adventures, some of them remarkable, but most of them repeating the pattern we have already established: elevation, contradiction, despair, recovery, elevation. He could function, even admirably, when under control. After this we will focus on themes that relate specifically to his communitarian enterprise: for example, leadership and sexuality. He wanted to be a leader, but only on his own terms. And he came to realize that if he was going to create some ideal community he had better start soon.

By the fall of 1836, then, Noyes had once more taken to the offensive. He lashed out at those who besmirched the good name of Perfectionism. While engaged in this battle, he wrote his stinging, denunciatory letter to Weld letting him know that he was a "child of the devil" and an enemy to all righteousness.[45] Within a year Noyes's verbal and written forays were directed at his old nemesis, James Latourette, the very same man who had snubbed him twice during his New York experience. In an exchange of acrimonious letters Noyes reminded Latourette of the callous treatment he had received from him, and told him that he was now ready to prove the leader of New York Perfectionism a sinful fraud. After this correspondence Noyes had a short interview with Latourette, charged him with the crime of "spiritual tyranny," and declared that in relation to such a mental slaveholder, he, Noyes, was an abolitionist.[46]

In the winter of 1837 Noyes spent several months with Abram C. Smith in his Kingston, New York, home. Much of their time was spent in "arguments and semi-contentions" about Noyes's "claim of leadership." As Noyes "plainly and repeatedly" told Smith: "I would never go on board any ship again unless I could have the helm, meaning that I would never connect myself with any individual or association

44. "Joanna to Her Mother," G. W. Noyes, ed., *Religious Experience,* p. 246.
45. J. H. Noyes, *Confession of Religious Experience,* pp. 95–96.
46. G. W. Noyes, ed., *Religious Experience,* pp. 302–4; also see Noyes's diatribe against Latourette in "Secret History of Perfectionism," *Witness* 1 (2? September 1837): 19–20.

in religion unless I was acknowledged leader." Smith balked at this, and at first was reluctant to accept Noyes as his spiritual leader. Through persistence, however, Noyes eventually converted Smith and understandably was pleased with his conquest.[47]

Noyes could never rest easy when he had been challenged. The years of the decade 1837–47 especially were punctured by a serio-comic battle with Charles Torrey, who cast doubts upon Noyes's sexual morality.[48] A somber struggle emerged over the control of Perfectionists in the village of Belchertown, Massachusetts. There Noyes had to meet the challenge of a number of would-be Perfectionist leaders, who openly attacked him and who in return were hotly abused by him. As one of his adversaries said about Noyes, there was evidently an overpowering desire in him "to be a leader and the originator of every new truth that is good." He was a worthy antagonist, full of "self-justification" and seemed to relish "the downfall of others." This same opponent held high hopes that one day Noyes's arrogance would be broken and that his fall from spiritual pride would be a long one.[49] In those years Noyes would suffer some defeats, but he would always bounce back. "Thank God," said a relieved Noyes, "I am equipped for war on the field of morality."[50]

47. G. W. Noyes, ed., *J. H. N.—The Putney Community,* pp. 25–26.
48. On the ups and downs of Torrey's career see Gilbert Hobbes Barnes, "Charles Torrey," *The Dictionary of American Biography,* ed. Dumas Malone (New York, 1936), 18: 595–96. Theodore Dwight Weld characterized Torrey, who was also a well-known abolitionist, as "an exceedingly vain, trifling man, with no wisdom or stability." (Quoted in Barnes, "Torrey," p. 595.) On Noyes's correspondence with Torrey, see the reprint of their letters in *Witness* 1 (25 September 1839): 73; *Witness* 2 (20 January 1841): 6; *Witness* 2 (22 February 1841): 12-14.
49. G. W. Noyes, ed., *J. H. N.—The Putney Community,* p. 128, but also see the fuller account in pp. 126–50.
50. Ibid., p. 58.

5 *The Quest for Security:*

Love, Sex, and Marriage

Noyes's attempts at complete self-mastery and manipulation of others were continually influenced, as we have seen, by his precarious self-esteem, his fears of being contradicted by authority, and his need for control. These factors, in the ensuing years, also contributed in creating a sexual arrangement that would cover familiar experiences without threat, that is, to be actively passive, without competition, as an ingredient in love, sex, and marriage.

Even though Noyes did his best to avoid sexual encounters, he still yearned for Abigail Merwin. In the summer of 1835, while he felt bereft of all outside support and caused great alarm in Joanna, Noyes continued to linger in a hostile New Haven. Undoubtedly the reason for this was the presence of Abigail. Intensely shy, for almost a year Noyes was afraid to ask her why she had left his side as a Perfectionist. She was never far from his thoughts, and he continued to pursue her—but always at a distance. Whenever he passed her house at night, the light from her window reactivated his feelings of loss and yearning. One day, while walking the town's streets, he rounded a corner and met her face to face. Noyes blanched. What seemed to him an interminable moment of awkwardness and embarrassment passed before he could utter a formal greeting and hurry on his way.[1]

During his trials at Prospect, however, Noyes had undergone an experience that emboldened him in his relationship to Abigail. In the midst of his sufferings, he again envisioned her clothed in white robes; this time, unlike his vision in New York, she remained an angel, and God promised her to him in an everlasting spiritual union.[2] Armed

1. G. W. Noyes, ed., *Religious Experience*, p. 355.
2. "Noyes to Abigail Merwin," Ibid., p. 353. Also see "Religious History—No. 19," pp. 82–83.

85

with this, Noyes called upon her hoping for a reconciliation. Receiving him politely, Abigail claimed that she was still a Perfectionist and that she continued to have confidence in him. Encouraged by her response, Noyes paid another visit and spent several hours with her in lengthy conversation. Unfortunately for him, at this time reports of his altercation with Weld and his untoward behavior in Prospect were being bruited about. Abigail's father, fearing for his daughter's reputation, forbade Noyes to see her again. Not long thereafter Noyes heard the crushing news that Abigail had become engaged to another man.

Hurt and brooding over this loss for several months, Noyes finally wrote to her in late December 1835. He assured Abigail that he had no wish to interfere with her "earthly engagement," for now he was beyond such concerns. As a spiritual representative of the Father, he could not return to those whom he "had left asleep," so he had no desire "to disturb their dreams until they shall hear that voice of the Son of God, which will effectually break their slumbers and sever every earthly tie." If God wished her to marry before the advent of His kingdom, then Noyes would acquiese in this judgment. However, Noyes felt compelled to give Abigail a brief account of his feelings for her.

He confessed "without shame" that from their association in the free church he had come to love her more deeply than anyone previously. Naturally, marriage had crossed his mind, but "remaining self-suspicion" precluded any such step on his part. Noyes next rehashed the sufferings he had borne in New York, when he had cast Abigail aside and offered himself to God "as a virgin." He described as well his experiences in Prospect and his most recent vision of her. In the ecstasy of this communication from God, Noyes strongly felt that Abigail would always be his, but he dared not "declare it openly." At the same time, though, the place and nature of marriage relationships in the coming dispensation were also disclosed to him. Since then, he had been with Abigail in Spirit, never doubting that she would return to him, and they would dwell together "in the bosom of God."

When he heard of her engagement, Noyes felt he was put to the full test. Like Paul before him, Noyes called upon God three times hoping that he might be rid of her, and three times he was refused. This signified to Noyes that Abigail was "the gift of God, pure and free, above all jealousy and above all fear."[3] Indeed, Noyes's solution for his attachment to Abigail bears a strong resemblance to that which

3. "Noyes to Abigail Merwin," pp. 351–54.

Hawthorne provided Hester and Dimmesdale in *The Scarlet Letter*. Denying the ambivalence of love and hatred in the passions, Hawthorne constructed an edenic world where "a man and woman, who are still essentially the old Adam and Eve, deceive themselves for a moment into believing that they can escape the consequences of sin."[4] Stating it more bluntly, Sarah Grimké felt that men and women would never be able to enjoy the true spiritual relationship God had intended until "our intercourse is purified by the forgetfulness of sex."[5]

Noyes grew a bit sheepish and uneasy over the baring of his love, whether it be sexual or spiritual. By "frankly declaring" his love for her, Noyes wished to assure Abigail, in the last paragraph of the letter, that he was in no way confessing "bondage" or lasting commitment to her. A single word from God, and Noyes stood ready to renounce her. In concluding, he once more rejoiced in the thought of her coming marriage, but still claimed that he had "the right and will" to love Abigail as "the workmanship of God, as my sister, as my neighbor, as my self." He would ask no more of her until God had demonstrated to her that they were joined indissolubly "in an immortal marriage."[6]

At length, in January 1837, Noyes received the news of Abigail's marriage, one more blow to his self-esteem. In a letter to his close friend, David Harrison, Noyes indicated that even though many people refused to recognize him "as the right hand of God," his own faith in this self-image was growing daily. Noyes was positive that the second resurrection and the second day of judgment were close at hand. Until that time and the creation of God's kingdom on earth, all men would live in a period of chaos. But Noyes felt that God had sent him to "cast up a highway across this chaos," and he was now busy "gathering out the stones and grading the track as fast as possible."

Noyes was thankful that Harrison had known the strength of his character and was sure that he would regain his former greatness. As Noyes expressed it: "I would that you know the exceeding greatness of the power which through me is searching the bowels of the whole world."[7]

Noyes's bombshell was contained in the last paragraph of the letter. "I will write all that is in my heart on one delicate subject," he scribbled passionately but deliberately in his now-famous Battle-

---

4. Leslie A. Fiedler, *Love and Death in the American Novel*, rev. ed. (New York, 1966), p. 233.
5. Quoted in Walters, "The Erotic South," p. 188.
6. "Noyes to Abigail Merwin," p. 354.
7. "Noyes to David Harrison," Ibid., pp. 307–9.

Axe Letter, and Harrison was to use his own discretion as to whether this passage should be revealed to anyone else. Much of the paragraph repeated his plea for a spiritual unity in heaven that he had expressed earlier to Abigail. God, for His own good reason (which Noyes did not elaborate upon), had established a wall between men and women "during the apostasy," and for equally good reasons this barrier would be destroyed during the resurrection!" Once perfection had been attained and sex had been elevated to spirituality, a new morality would follow. Conventional marriage would be obsolete when God's will reigned on earth as it did in heaven. "The marriage supper of the lamb," he continued, was a feast where *"every dish is free to every guest."* Under these conditions such base passions as exclusiveness, jealousy, and quarreling were disallowed for the same reason that "guests at a Thanksgiving dinner" were not permitted to "claim each his separate dish, and quarrel with the rest of his rights."[8]

Noyes fantasized that in a spiritually innocent community the incest barrier would be lifted. In his own words, he saw no more reason why "sexual intercourse should be restrained by law, than why eating and drinking should be—and there is as little occasion for shame in the one case as in other." The guests of the marriage supper may have their special dish, but that favorite was to be held "with the jealousy of exclusiveness." In effect, once all true believers became one in Christ, their new morality cut "directly across the marriage covenant of this world, and God knows the end."[9]

Noyes's advocacy of sharing spiritual mates may appear on the surface to have been an invitation to indulge in the unrestrained pleasures of free love and the "sociosexual anarchy" of Josiah Warren's Modern Times community.[10] But when we place Noyes's statements in the context of his need for control, his wishes to be a Perfectionist leader, and his disdain for the sexual excesses of the New York Perfectionists, it seems highly unlikely that Noyes was now offering a rationale for simple lechery. Uncontrolled sexual pleasure, in fact, was just about the last thing in Noyes's mind. Faced with a series of defeats, of which Abigail's marriage was one, Noyes's writing of the Battle-Axe Letter may be seen as a cathartic attempt

8. G. W. Noyes, ed., *J. H. N.—Putney Community*, p. 3; Parker, *Yankee Saint*, p. 44. Harrison kept the letter, which Noyes wrote on 15 January 1837, for several months but then disclosed it. Eventually, it appeared in T. R. Gates's paper, *The Battle-Axe and Weapons of War*.

9. Parker, *Yankee Saint*, p. 44. "Battle-Axe Letter," *Witness* 1 (23 January 1839): 49, has a full quote of the letter.

10. For a brief discussion of Warren's radical thought see Arieli, *Individualism and Nationalism in American Ideology*, pp. 279–80, 285–92.

to "cast from himself the fear and shame of guilt" for being rejected.[11] Indeed, the warm ecstasies of love held terror for him. "Falling in love," he once said, was a "kind of fatality—something that people *fall* into as a man walking in the dark might fall into a pit or into the jaws of a wild beast—that there is no help for it, no resisting it, no restraining it."[12] While perhaps not as frantic as Noyes, Lorenzo Fowler expressed similar feelings, although he never considered tampering with conventional morality. Fowler was saddened by the fact that marriage was "too often made a matter of *feeling* and not enough of *reflection* and *judgment.*" Too many young people considered no other motive when they married than "being in love," and thus were "led by the blind impulses of their nature" that in the long run could have disastrous consequences for their health and marriage.[13]

If romantic love continued unchecked, Noyes believed that it would result in disease and death. So, he recommended that love be treated not as an end but as a spiritual means subject to rigorous controls within the new morality. Sharing of spiritual wives was in part, therefore, a defensive maneuver. While sharing, Noyes would be able to avoid becoming emotionally and sexually involved with one particular person.[14]

---

11. "Battle-Axe Letter," *Witness* 1 (23 January 1839): 51.
12. *Oneida Circular* 9 (27 April 1874): 140. Weinstein and Platt, *Psychoanalytic Sociology,* p. 31, have said that within a complex, industrial society the "isolated nuclear family and the need for mobility place . . . a special emphasis on romantic love as the basis for mate selection and marital integration." Thus, with romantic love linked to modernity with its diversity and ambiguity, it is little wonder that Noyes, who sought to overcome all ambivalence and ambiguity in his relationships, and who sought to replace the emotional isolation of the nuclear family and industrial society with that of an affective-expressive community, opposed romantic love.

Noyes's cultural fears and admonitions regarding romantic love also had their psychoanalytic roots. Several authors have discussed falling in love in terms of separation and loss anxiety and threats to self-esteem. See, for example, Otto F. Kernberg, "Barriers to Falling and Remaining in Love," *J. Am Psa. Assn.* 22 (1974): 486–511; Charles T. Sullivan, "On Being Loved: A Contribution to the Psychology of Object Relation," *Psa. Rev.* 52 (1965): 5–16; Robert C. Bak, "Being in Love and Object Loss," *Int. J. Psa.* 54 (1973): 1–8.

13. From L. N. Fowler, *Marriage: Its History and Ceremonies,* in Walters, ed., *Primers for Prudery,* p. 93.
14. Robert Seidenberg, "Fidelity and Jealousy: Socio-Cultural Considerations," *Psa. Rev.* 54 (1967): 583–608, has stated that the sharing of a mate with others is most likely one of the main sources for feelings of infidelity and pathological jealousy. For Noyes, sharing would be a way of denying these feelings and protecting his self-sufficiency. Also see, Arnold H. Modell, "A Narcissistic Defense Against Affects and the Illusion of Self-Sufficiency," *Int. J. Psa.* 56 (1975): 275–82.

On another level, no concupiscience was to intrude between the relationship of men and women in this spiritually perfect order. Theoretically, this meant that any man could legitimately have "spiritual" intercourse with any woman, including his mother and sister. Even though Noyes and his Communities never condoned or practiced incest, the implications were there, as his attackers were quick to point out. While we can not ignore the oedipal content in the Battle–Axe Letter, we would be making a mistake to reduce any part of Noyes's perfectionist ideology to the sexuality of an unresolved oedipal wish. Other aspects of this wish, however, need to be stressed here. "The oedipal wish," as one psychoanalyst recently stated, "is stimulated by our search for lost omnipotence." That is, the wish to enter the mother may also include the quest for "the unlimited, the absolute, the perfection of an ego whose wound (the result of being torn away from our narcissistic perfection) would at last be healed."[15] Such a wish, of course, has social roots that go well beyond Noyes's personal problems and reaches out to others having difficulty adjusting to the social changes of the 1830s and 1840s.

By the summer of 1837, Noyes felt it was time to promulgate his Perfectionist beliefs to as wide an audience as possible. His efforts to convert his family had produced good results (as we shall see in chapter 6), and in the spring of that year he had received encouragement for his Perfectionism from William Lloyd Garrison and Charles Grandison Finney. He was stimulated, as a result, to reestablish a newspaper. His choice of location was Ithaca, which, as the center of New York state, was ideally situated for starting the "Kingdom of God." But another fundamental reason lay behind Noyes's choice of this small town. Here Abigail and her husband had settled after their marriage, and now Noyes was going to pursue and confront the woman "who had deserted her post" as his helper.

In August 1837, Noyes began publication of the *Witness* under less than auspicious circumstances. The Battle-Axe Letter found its way into print at virtually the same time his paper came out, and it was not long before a morally outraged public heaped abuse upon Noyes. Although he felt assured that God's inspiration lay behind its disclosure, he also thought, somewhat uneasily, that God had taken "fearful advantage" of him and pushed him into taking "an awful step" against his will. Caught in the snare of his own confidential whisper, and "hung up as a gazing stock of the world," Noyes had second thoughts about his writing of the letter, and his sanguine out-

15. J. Chassequet-Smirgel, "Some Thoughts on the Ego Ideal, A Contribution to the Study of the 'Illness of Identity'," *Psa. Q.* 45 (1976): 370.

look quickly gave way to gloom.[16] Just as bad, the *Witness* fell into dire financial straits as readers withdrew their subscriptions in light of the Battle-Axe furor.

One ray of hope for Noyes at this time was the news that Abigail and her husband had separated. Noyes immediately instructed Harrison to let Abigail know of his continued love for her, and that it was up to God to determine what she would do. If God did not give her to him, Noyes felt certain that the Lord would present someone to him soon, because the Kingdom of God was swiftly approaching its predicted collision with the secular world. "Like two mighty ships," he explained, "they are coming to a crash, which will shatter and sink one of them. The timbers that bear the blow must expect a crushing shock."[17]

Apparently God never intended Abigail for Noyes, because his overtures again went unheeded. The expected collision was also delayed, although support was on its way in the form of one of his most devoted converts to Perfectionism, Harriet A. Holton.

Three years older than Noyes, Harriet came from an illustrous New England family. Her maternal grandfather was Mark Richards, a nephew of the theologian, Samuel Hopkins. Richards had been Lieutenant Governor of Vermont and a member of Congress. One of Harriet's uncles was an eminent lawyer, well known throughout New England. An only child and orphaned at an early age, Harriet was raised in the home of her grandfather Richards.[18]

Harriet, like Noyes, agonized over a childhood that was "cramped by bashfulness." Homely and possessing a "plodding and thorough" mind, Harriet seemed to outgrow her shyness in youth as she attended card parties, dances, and boat rides on the Connecticut River. Yet, she admitted privately that she never felt at ease in social situations. "I was too self-conscious, felt small, and always thought I did not look well," she recalled unhappily, even though she "had no lack of dress to make a display," had she the courage to do so.[19]

Brought up under the stern eye of her grandfather, Harriet often struggled with him, especially over affairs of the heart. At the age of eighteen she became engaged to a young lawyer in her uncle's office. During this time the country was being torn by the Adams-Jackson election, and soon the grandfather and fiancé were embroiled in a bitter political debate of their own. Grandfather Richards grew so incensed that he threw the young man out of the home and threatened

16. G. W. Noyes, ed., *J. H. N.—The Putney Community*, pp. 2, 10.
17. "Noyes to Harrison," Ibid., p. 12.
18. "A Community Mother," *Circular* 3 n.s. (17 September 1866): 212.
19. Ibid.; "A Community Mother," *Circular* 3 n.s. (29 October 1866): 259.

to disinherit Harriet if she married him. Defiantly, Harriet told him that he could do as he pleased with his money and property, but that she would continue to see her fiancé, which she did for several years. Meanwhile, Harriet had begun to believe that her Unitarian beliefs were no longer fulfilling. In 1831, at the age of twenty-three, she turned to revivalism and chose to devote her life to God. Breaking off her engagement, she joined the Congregational church, and for the next three years busied herself with a variety of church-related functions. In 1834 she agreed to marry a widower who lived in Mississippi. Anticipating her move South, Harriet took in a ten-year-old girl with the hope of raising her "as a daughter and assistant." The joys of surrogate motherhood soon soured for Harriet. Frequently upset by the child, she "sometimes punished her in a passion." Feeling guilty, Harriet "condemned herself for something every day, and longed for a new grace."

One day in 1834, Maria Clark, Harriet's friend from a nearby town and a follower of Noyes, told her of Noyes's faith in Christ and belief of salvation from sin. Later when Maria returned home, she sent Harriet some of Noyes's writings, which Harriet avidly devoured. Not long thereafter she publically announced that she was a Perfectionist.[20]

From then on, Harriet never wavered in her devotion to Noyes and his Perfectionism. She read everything he had written, and as she studied Noyes's writings she began to contribute money periodically to his cause. During the winter of 1837, she sent him money to help resuscitate the *Witness*, and in the early spring of the following year Noyes wrote thanking her for her kindness and support during a difficult period. In the last paragraph of the letter we get a vivid picture of the wide fluctuation in moods that Noyes was experiencing during the winter and spring of 1837–38. Alternately submerged in feelings of despair and joy, Noyes believed that love and joy would ultimately prevail, because he sensed that salvation was nearer than he had first anticipated. Until then, he had to face his struggles with the world and cope with his tensions. His ever-present feeling, he ominously concluded, was that he would "either be killed or crowned soon."[21]

Events now moved rapidly for Noyes. By the spring of 1838 he had come to realize that Abigail would never be his. He wrote her a farewell poem, which again reminded her that her flesh may belong

20. "A Community Mother," *Circular* 3 n.s. (5 November 1866): pp. 267–68.
21. "Reminiscences—III," *Oneida Circular* 9 (4 November 1872): 355. Letter dated 3 April 1838.

to someone else, but that spiritually she would always be his.[22] To compensate for this loss, Noyes had Harriet to fill the void with her unflagging spiritual devotion and financial aid. Buttressed by her support and a growing belief in his divine commission by such people as Abram Smith and David Harrison, Noyes regained a sense of control and stability. In this frame of mind he wrote Harriet a letter of proposal in early June. As one might have expected, this was no ordinary marriage proposal. Before turning to it, however, we should be reminded that it was written in a period when passions in all aspects of life were expected to be controlled.

The courtship of Theodore Dwight Weld and Angelina Grimké, for example, has been described as "a veritable orgy of restraint."[23] In one of his letters to her, Weld took pride in assuring Angelina that he had "acquired perfect self-control, so far as any expression or appearance of deep feeling is visible to others." Angelina was hardly offended by this need for emotional control; in fact, it neatly dovetailed into her own needs and outlook. "I have been tempted to think marriage was sinful," she replied to Weld, "because of what appeared to me almost invariably to prompt and lead to it. . . . Instead of the higher, nobler sentiments being first aroused, and leading on the lower passions captive to their will, the latter seemed to be lords over the former. Well I am convinced that men in general, the vast majority, believe most seriously that women were made to gratify their animal appetites, expressly to minister to their pleasure."[24]

In the opening paragraph of his own letter, Noyes informed his bride-to-be that he had been waiting patiently for over a year for an indication of God's will, and now he was permitted to offer her a partnership. Noyes hesitated to call it marriage until he had fully defined it. As he had done earlier in the Battle-Axe Letter, Noyes sought to desexualize marriage. He reiterated his claim that all true believers in Christ related to each other in "a more radical and . . . more important" way than people did in conventional marriages. In a spiritual marriage the partners would love each other with a warmth, strength, and piety that normal lovers could never experience. Neither would act so selfishly as to possess the other. Instead, they would give each other freely to the "fellowship of God's universal family."

A few "matter-of-fact considerations," which weighed heavily in

---

22. "Noyes's Farewell Lay to Abigail," G. W. Noyes, ed., *J. H. N.—Putney Community*, pp. 14–15.
23. Walters, "The Erotic South," pp. 189–90.
24. Ibid. As Walters goes on to indicate, the Welds, with their passions controlled, had a happy marriage.

Noyes's decision to offer Harriet a proposal of marriage, were listed next. He told her that he respected and loved her for the spiritual, moral, and intellectual qualities she possessed as well as for her attributes of "faith, kindness, simplicity, and modesty." Noyes explained to her, moreover, that at this particular time he concurred with Paul that a secular marriage, although a temporary institution, was for some a necessity and "honorable in all." The marriage, in addition to this, would release the two of them, or at least himself, "from much reproach and many evil surmisings which are occasioned by celibacy in present circumstances."

Finally, Noyes assured Harriet that he no longer cared for Abigail, though he cautioned Harriet that she should have no illusions as to his position and duty in this world. If she judged him by outward appearances, she undoubtedly would discover the "irregularity and seeming instability" of character, which might lead her to have serious reservations about marrying him. In defense of his behavior, Noyes argued that behind "the vagabond, incoherent service," to which he had thus far been called and which had "almost been intolerable" to him, was the grace and protection of God. He would eagerly welcome God's order for his "release as an exile after a seven years' pilgrimage would welcome the sight of his home." Noyes could see no reason why he could not now enter "that certain dwelling place" and assume the responsibilities and duties of married life.[25]

Harriet was overjoyed and responded quickly, telling Noyes that she would take any place he wished to assign her. She was honored to march with Noyes in his quest for religious perfection and would gladly assume the most menial position. In accepting the terms of Noyes's proposal, Harriet was also confident that God would exclude jealousy and every other thing that acted to defile the usual marriage. Their marriage relationship, she hoped, would be placed on a spiritual plane equal to that which Noyes's mother and younger sisters enjoyed. In other words, Harriet wanted John's "society and instruction as long as the Lord pleases and when he pleases."

Such obedience was heartily received by Noyes, and he praised Harriet for her frankness, which made "courtship what it should be, an easy and pleasant, instead of a crooked and foolish business." A week or so later in another exchange of letters with Noyes, Harriet expressed the feeling that God had sent him to her so that she might be able to contribute to his happiness "and usefulness in this act of his drama" in the same manner that Abigail had done in the begin-

25. "From J. H. N. to H. A. N.," *Circular* 3 n.s. (10 September 1866): 202–4.

ning. In the future, if her fate happened to be that of the Empress Josephine's, well, she trusted the Lord to give her the strength to understand and acknowledge it. Furthermore, if she proved to be unfaithful to Noyes by betraying him "with a kiss," she fully expected the wrath of God to punish her for being a traitor to his "gentleness, goodness, and truth." Finally, Harriet briefly noted that she had wanted to discuss with Noyes her inclination towards celibacy, but she had second thoughts and decided that they would talk about this when they met later.[26]

The allusion to Napoleon and Josephine brought a hasty reply from an angry, impatient Noyes. Talk of infidelity, of a future possibly clouded with doubt and tragedy, was intolerable to him. An innocent love destroyed by treachery and desertion was the way of all relationships in the world, but he forcefully told Harriet that such an outcome would have no place in his life. In regard to Harriet's concern about celibacy, Noyes was not sure to what extent she had "imbibed the spirit of Shakerism," but he suggested that fears of sexuality would be dissolved in a spiritual union with the son of God.[27]

Three days later—less than three weeks after his proposal—Noyes married Harriet, a woman whom he had written to more often than he had seen. The ceremony was conducted by Larkin G. Mead, Noyes's brother-in-law, in Chesterfield, New Hampshire. It is now clear that a variety of factors entered into Noyes's decision to marry. Seeing himself as an object of ridicule and abuse in an unfriendly world, forced once more to face the loss of Abigail, and in a constant struggle to convert his mother, Noyes desperately needed a protective, supportive figure like Harriet, with her unstinting emotional, spiritual, and financial support, to help restore his self-esteem.[28] In addition, Noyes carried his ideals of perfection and need for absolute control into the marriage relationship. Before he committed himself he had to be reassured that the sexual and aggressive feelings would have no place in their marriage. As Noyes bluntly put it, there was "no particular love of the sentimental kind between us," but she had "respected" him, and believed in him "as a man of God."[29] With her

26. Ibid.

27. Parker, *Yankee Saint,* p. 63; "From J. H. N. to H. A. N.," p. 204.

28. Noyes admitted many years later that, "By this marriage, besides herself, and a good social position, which she held as belonging to the first families of Vermont, I obtained enough money to build me a house and a printing-office, and to buy a press and type." Parker, *Yankee Saint,* p. 64. Ostow, *Psychology of Melancholy,* pp. 88–89, has pertinent information on the relationship of depression to marriage.

29. "Financial Romance," *Circular* 2 n.s. (8 January 1866): 337.

sexual inhibitions and few demands, Harriet was an ideal, safe person for Noyes.

Upon settling in Putney after his marriage, Noyes continued to establish his leadership over his small but faithful group of followers and attempted to extend his influence among other Perfectionists. He went to meetings held by rival Perfectionist conventions in order to propagate his beliefs. Throughout his proselytizing ventures Noyes still felt that the paper was the best medium for reaching vast numbers and gaining more disciples. The *Witness* in time was replaced by the *Perfectionist*, and it in turn was succeeded by the *Spiritual Magazine*.[30] These periodicals, in addition to containing lengthy articles on Noyes's theology, carried accounts of Perfectionism on all fronts. Although Noyes's ideas were too extreme and threatening to attract a large number of adherents, he did find support among small groups of Perfectionists in central Massachusetts, central New York, northern Vermont, and northern New Jersey.

Of course it was not always easy to keep his disciples in tow. Early in 1840 he traveled to Abram Smith's home in order to break up a liaison between Smith and Mary Cragin, one of Noyes's converts.[31] The Smith-Cragin affair convinced Noyes that if he were going to create a new moral order, he needed a more tightly-knit organization. One way to accomplish this unity would be to have more group discussions centering on the meaning and benefits of his Perfectionism. In the first months of 1840 the Putney group held meetings on Sundays in Noyes's house, which had just been finished. By the end of the year the number of meetings had increased to three a week, and when a chapel was built in 1841, they met daily.[32]

At the end of January 1841, Noyes took another step towards consolidation by transforming his Bible School into the Society of Inquiry. Among the reasons Noyes gave his small band of followers was that in their unorganized state they were open prey to attacks from all sides. But through organization they would be in the secure position "to step forth as the independent organized representatives of the doctrine of perfect holiness," and free to renounce "the formalities of the old churches, and the anarchy of pseudo-Perfectionists."[33] Among the articles of the corporation's charter it was explicitly stated

---

30. In 1844 the name of the *Perfectionist* was changed to *Perfectionist and Theocratic Watchman*.

31. A full discussion of this affair may be found in G. W. Noyes, ed., *J. H. N. —Putney Community*, pp. 37–45.

32. Ibid., p. 46. On the need for organization also see "Organization—No. 2," *Witness* 2 (22 February 1841): 9–10.

33. "The Putney Corporation," *Circular* 3 n.s. (27 August 1866): 191.

that the chief business of their meetings would be to aid each other in the faith of salvation from sin.[34]

In February, while the Society of Inquiry was being created, Noyes's father, eight months before his death, divided his estate among his children. Nearly twenty thousand dollars went to the four who were members of the Putney group, and for the first time Noyes was freed from immediate financial worries. At last, Noyes could invite others who lacked capital to join his growing community, and by the end of March 1843, thirty-five people were being supported by Community funds.[35]

This burgeoning Community brought in what income it could by running two farms in addition to a store in Putney. Many of the Community members lived in one or another of the three houses owned by the Noyeses, with the women taking care of the household chores and the men tending the fields and store.[36] Economics, however, was relegated to a secondary or even tertiary role by Noyes. Far more important to him was the need of his supporters to accept his beliefs beyond reflection, and thereby create an atmosphere of emotional security for both them and himself. Noyes insisted that men and women should spend three hours a day reading the Bible, along with contemplating and discussing his beliefs. When George Cragin, who was placed in charge of the farming, suggested that these daily, religious rituals reduced the working hours and profits, Noyes silenced him by saying that if a person's growth in religious perfection required that he contemplate half the day away, he should do so. "I would much rather that our land should run to waste," Noyes advised, "than that you should fail of a spiritual harvest."[37] We must "not allow worldly affairs to swamp us," continued Noyes. "If they come in upon you and oppress you" and cloud the truth, then drop all you are doing and turn to God.[38] Some time later Noyes reinforced the idea that the object of the Putney Community was "to publish the gospel and help one another in spiritual things."[39]

Spirituality may have been the first consideration, but Noyes also had to contend with his sexual feelings during the Putney years.

34. G. W. Noyes, ed., *J. H. N.—Putney Community*, p. 48.
35. Ibid., p. 50.
36. Ibid., p. 55. The growth of communism was a slow one. Property was held in the name of the original owner throughout the Putney period and for several years after the Community reorganized at Oneida. Some of the members continued to live in their own houses in Putney and to maintain their previous occupations.
37. Ibid. Also, "Episodes in the Life of John Humphrey Noyes," *Community Quadrangle* (December 1927): 6.
38. "The Putney Corporation," *Circular* 3 n.s. (3 September 1866): 198.
39. G. W. Noyes, ed., *J. H. N.—Putney Community*, p. 55.

Within a six-year period after their marriage in 1838, Harriet had given birth to five children in succession; all but one was stillborn. While an agonizing ordeal and bitter disappointment to her, Noyes too brooded over the deaths and the direction his marriage was taking.[40] With the birth of his son Theodore and the loss of his other children during those six years, Noyes sustained a series of wounds that helped threaten to crumble his Perfectionism. No doubt the deaths shook his faith in the ability of the perfect to overcome sin and death as Christ had, and thus undermined his belief in his role as an inspirational leader.[41] On another level these deaths were a staggering blow to his creative (procreative) fantasies, and consequently aroused feelings of shame for being a failure.[42] In response to these emotional setbacks, which again threatened uncontrolled anxiety and depression, Noyes pondered over the meaning of sexual and marital relationships. From these weighty considerations flowed his ideas on male continence and complex marriage. These theories were, in other words, an outgrowth of his own crises and depression, and not primarily, as most writers contend, a true empathetic suffering with the plight of his wife and other women.[43]

As a result of his own marital experiences, Noyes now understood how sexual intercourse could be considered "a momentary affair, terminating in exhaustion and disgust." Subsequently, this emotional and sexual depletion bred "self-reproach and shame," because it created a feeling that one was a failure, that one was not a man. As Noyes expressed it, when exhaustion, self-abasement, and shame united, they made the "eye evil not only toward the instruments of excess, but toward the person who tempts it." In this manner did Noyes account for the "cooling off" that took place between a man

---

40. Ibid., p. 113; Parker, *Yankee Saint*, pp. 66–68.
41. Although these deaths produced great disappointment among his followers, none lost faith in Noyes as a messianic leader. Their need to believe in him, that is, led them to deny that Noyes's prophecy of victory over death had failed. Leon Festinger, Henry W. Riecken, and Stanley Schachter, *When Prophecy Fails* (Minneapolis, 1956), pp. 3–32.
42. The preoedipal and oedipal roots of creative fantasies are explored in Daniel S. Jaffe, "The Masculine Envy of Woman's Procreative Function," *J. Am. Psa. Assn.* 16 (1968): 521–48; Wilbur Jarvis, "Some Effects of Pregnancy and Childbirth on Men," *Ibid.* 10 (1962): 689–700; Edith Jacobson, "Development of the Wish for a Child in Boys," *Psa. St. Chi.* 5 (1950): 139–52; John Munder Ross, "The Development of Paternal Identity: A Critical Review of the Literature on Nurturance and Generativity in Boys and Men," *J. Am. Psa. Assn.* 23 (1975): 783–817.
43. See, Parker, *Yankee Saint*, p. 178; Carden, *Oneida*, p. 49. Psychological factors underlying empathy are discussed in Ralph R. Greenson, "Empathy and its Vicissitudes," *Int. J. Psa.* 41 (1960): 418–24; Kohut, *Analysis of the Self*, pp. 300–307.

and woman: an emotional withdrawal that more often than not resulted in "indifference and disgust."[44]

But this was all wrong, said Noyes, and here he found agreement with Dr. Elizabeth Blackwell. Although she too was a severe critic of sexual indulgence and general licentiousness, she argued that "physical passion is not in itself evil; on the contrary, it is an essential part of our nature." Like every other aspect of human nature, it had the potential of becoming "an enobling or a degrading agent in our lives."[45] Noyes agreed: "To be ashamed of the sexual organs, is to be ashamed of God's workmanship . . . of the most perfect instruments of love and unity." To lower one's eyes in ignominy at the sight of the sexual organs was "to be ashamed of the image of the glory of God—the physical symbol of life dwelling in life, which is the mystery of the gospel."[46] Why, pondered Noyes, did a person have to think of his sexual nature in terms of "sensuality . . . vice, and woe," when with a little effort it could be just as easy and much truer to the spirit of God and nature to associate with it "images of the Garden of Eden . . . and thoughts of purity and chaste affection."[47]

The issue confronting Noyes, as well as a host of others ranging from Sylvester Graham and William Alcott to Robert Dale Owen and Blackwell, was how to impose a voluntary control over the sexual drives that led to excess, poor health, and agony of childbirth for women, and the birth of unwanted children. Noyes realized that this would be a difficult task since sexual desire was "a stream ever running" and to dam it would cause it "to break out irregularly and destructively." The only way to make these desires "safe and useful" was to give them "a free and natural channel."[48] Celibacy did not flow into Noyes's definition of a free natural channel, and he would

44. (Oneida Association), *First Annual Report of the Oneida Association: Exhibiting its History, Principles, and Transactions to January 1, 1849* (Oneida Reserve, N.Y., 1849), p. 33. Noyes also contended that the "shrinking of shame is produced by a feeling that the sexual nature is vile and shameful." Once this was admitted a person could begin to control his sexual drives and thus control the painful feelings of shame and inferiority. *First Annual Report*, p. 36.

45. Blackwell, *Counsel to Parents*, p. 73, quoted in Walters, ed., *Primers for Prudery*, p. 44.

46. (Oneida Association), *Bible Communism: A Compilation from the Annual Reports and Other Publications of the Oneida Association and Its Branches; Presenting, in Connection with Their History, a Summary View of Their Religious and Social Theories* (Brooklyn, N.Y., 1853), p. 28.

47. *First Annual Report*, p. 37. For sexual feelings to be tolerated they had to be denied and submerged with the dual nature of God, who combined the masculine and feminine qualities. Only then could a person be active sexually. As noted previously, this was the crux of Noyes's resolution to his earlier conflict.

48. Ibid., p. 25.

have been in complete agreement with Samuel Wells's evaluation that celibates were "in violation of Nature's laws."[49] Noyes considered it an unnatural separation of the sexes that was usually accompanied by a withdrawal in reaction to shame. Once a person withdrew into himself, moreover, his sexual desires would have no other outlet than in harmful, degrading masturbation, and Noyes's opinion of this solitary vice was no less harsh than those of Graham and Alcott.[50]

While celibacy was discounted as a practical alternative, so too were a variety of methods that to Noyes actually seemed to encourage sexual indulgence and subsequent feelings of shame and guilt. In this category Noyes denounced the practice of abortion, the douching techniques discussed by Charles Knowlton in his *Fruits of Philosophy,* and the practice of *coitus interruptus* advocated by Robert Dale Owen in his widely read *Moral Physiology.*[51] "The useless expenditure of seed certainly is not natural," said Noyes. God did not create men to sow their seed "by the way-side, where they do not expect it to grow, or in the same field where seed has already been sown and is growing; and yet such is the practice of men in ordinary sexual intercourse."[52]

Discarding these methods as impractical and immoral alternatives for the control of sexual desires, Noyes continued to seek a way in which the sexes could remain together, yet avoid the deleterious effects of indulgence and excess. To be ideally happy in life, thought Noyes, a person had to have the power "to withdraw instantaneously from any specific method of happiness, any particular kind of enjoyment." Through obedience to a strong inner will, Noyes believed that a man would be able to draw a "positive pleasure" from his passions,

---

49. From Samuel R. Wells, *Wedlock; Or, the Right Relations of the Sexes,* quoted in Walters, ed., *Primers for Prudery,* p. 42.

50. "Prostitution, masturbation, and obscenity in general," Noyes declared, "are injurious explosions, incident to unnatural separations of the male and female elements." In addition, ordinary sexual intercourse, that is, "performance of the propagative act, without intention of procreation," was to be classed with masturbation." *First Annual Report,* pp. 25, 33; *Bible Communism,* p. 51.

51. J. H. Noyes, *Male Continence; or Self-Control in Sexual Intercourse; a Letter of Inquiry Answered by J. H. Noyes* (Oneida, N.Y., n.d.), pp. 2–3. The letter is dated 26 July 1866. Noyes was ambivalent about Owen's book. He thought it was one of the best yet worst books he had ever read. For Noyes, *coitus interruptus* "forges and gilds the chains of guilt." "To Correspondents," *Witness* 1 (23 September 1837): 22; "Letters to the Editress of the *Advocate of Moral Reform,*" Ibid. 1 (23 January 1839): 53. In the *First Annual Report,* p. 31, Owen's book was condemned in even stronger language. It was called "unnatural, filthy, and . . . wasteful of life." See Robert Dale Owen, *Moral Physiology; or a Brief and Plain Treatise on the Population Question* (London, n.d.).

52. J. H. Noyes, *Male Continence* (Oneida, N.Y., 1872), p. 13.

while still controlling the evil imaginations that accompanied them.[53] By 1844, spurred on by the death of his last child with Harriet and forced to endure attacks on his sexual morality by outsiders, Noyes thought he had discovered a morally justifiable system of sexual control for the male.[54]

Three steps constituted ordinary sexual intercourse, Noyes observed. Initially, "the *simple presence* of the male organ in the female," was followed by "a series of reciprocal *motions*" that brought on "a nervous reflex action or ejaculatory crisis which expels the seed."[55] Noyes insisted that the process up to this point of emission was capable of being controlled by "the moral faculty." In other words, all acts of sexual intercourse were capable of being controlled or stopped at will, except for the fateful climax, which was automatic and uncontrollable.[56]

He then wondered what the effect would be if the person stopped at the first stage. Would it be harmful? Noyes said "no"; how could a control of "furious excitement" be injurious? He appealed to the memory of every man who had had a satisfying sexual experience to acknowledge the fact that on the whole "the sweetest and noblest period of intercourse with woman" was the first moment of penetration and "spiritual effusion" before the "muscular exercise" began.[57] Noyes carried this conjecture one step further. What if a man decided he wanted to enjoy the act of penetration and reciprocal motions but not the final crisis—would there be any danger of serious injury? Noyes was confident that there would not be, since every instance of self-denial contained an interruption of some "natural act." The man who virtuously contented himself with a glance at a beautiful woman, and the lover who stopped at a kiss were fully

---

53. Home-Talk by J. H. N., No. 156, "The Secret of Happiness," *Circular* 2 (5 January 1853), pp. 59, 60. Although one could stress the sado-masochistic elements in *coitus reservatus* for Noyes, the fact should also be emphasized that this system of regulation and control provided him a means of staying in contact with the world of objects, and thus permitted him to remain active. On this point see the discussion of secondary gains in Jay Katz, "On Primary and Secondary Gain," *Psa. St. Chi.* 18 (1963): 9–50; Kernberg, "Barriers to Falling and Remaining in Love," pp. 508–10, for an analysis of love and object relationships.
54. G. W. Noyes, ed., *J. H. N.—Putney Community*, pp. 126–28.
55. *Male Continence* (1866), p. 3; *Male Continence* (1872), pp. 7–8.
56. Noyes analogized that male continence was like rowing near a waterfall. The closer one got to the falls, the more alluring it became, and the harder it was to return. If a man was willing to learn, Noyes declared, "experience will teach him the wisdom of confining his excursions to the region of easy rowing, unless he has an object in view that is worth the cost of going over the falls." *Male Continence* (1872), p. 8.
57. *Male Continence* (1866), p. 3.

aware of such interruptions. It was an easy "descending" series of steps "through all the approaches of sexual love, for the first touch of respectful friendship to the final complete amalgamation." Was there to be no interruption of this loss of control, asked Noyes? While the "Brutes, animal or human, tolerate none," a righteous man was enjoined by the Father "to self-control in ALL THINGS."[58]

To underscore this point, Noyes stressed that intercourse should be divided into two separate elements: the amative and propagative. By its very nature the propagative act was the "cost" factor, while amativeness kept "the capital stock" of life circulating between a man and a woman. By introducing "a third partner" between the two, propagation ruined their peace and happiness; and the "emission of the seed" drained the life of man. When this practice was habitual and excessive, Noyes felt, as did John Cowan, that it produced debility and disease.[59] Embroidering upon his economic analogy, Noyes suggested that if expenses exceeded income, then surely bankruptcy would ensue. After the Fall, sin and shame had joined to curtail amativeness and in so doing diminished the profitable department. Propagation, in turn, increased as did the cost factor. If a country's expenses exceeded its profits, a financial panic would follow, and it would most likely end in a depression. For Noyes this also held true for sexual matters. "Death; i.e., vital bankruptcy," he anxiously spelled out, "is the law of the race in its fallen condition, and it results more from this derangement of the sexual economy."[60]

The inescapable conclusion that Noyes drew from this analogy was that a balance had to be struck between the amative and propagative functions, with the weight shifted preferably to the amative side. By doing this, lovers, who employed their "sexual organs . . . as the servants of their spiritual natures," and who abstained from conception except when they intended, would enjoy "the highest bliss of sexual fellowship" without "satiety or exhaustion."[61]

In Noyes's theory of male continence we find the separation of pleasure and propagation common to the growing Victorian morality of the period, but there was something more to it, and this something more related directly to the degree and quality of self-control he needed in all aspects of his life. As noted earlier, despite the support of his Putney group, by the mid-1840s Noyes had continued to face a series of attacks to his preeminence, among which were the deaths of his children. As these feelings of loss and abandonment continued

58. *Male Continence* (1872), pp. 9–10.
59. *First Annual Report*, p. 30; *Bible Communism*, p. 45. John Cowan, *Science of a New Life*, quoted in Walters, ed., *Primers for Prudery*, p. 89.
60. *First Annual Report*, p. 30.
61. Ibid., p. 33.

to build and feed upon each other, Noyes had to work hard to forestall another serious depression. On a social level he took steps to strengthen the Community and his grip on it, while on a personal level, control over his tender and sexual feelings became urgent.

"Male continence," Noyes stated succinctly, "in its essence is self-control, and that is a virtue of universal importance," which pertained not only to sexual relationships but to relationships on all levels of interaction.[62] In any fellowship—such as that of the Father and Son, the Son and the Church, and man and woman—one was superior, the other inferior. Running smack into a wall of popular belief that considered the woman to be spiritually more pure and innocent than the male, Noyes believed (as will become clear in the next chapter) just the opposite. In the fellowship of a man and woman, Noyes insisted that the man was superior and therefore responsible for "his own limitation . . . and that of the female."[63] This responsibility carried over into the realm of love and sex where Noyes believed that "woman is comparatively passive, and man is active; and the active party should be responsible for the passive."[64]

To satisfy his demands for perfection, dominance, and control, Noyes believed that he could transcend the usual practice of coitus by maintaining an erection and postponing ejaculation at his will. As Noyes asked: "what is a man, knowing his own power and limits, should not even *approach* the crisis, and yet be able to enjoy the presence and the motion *ad libitum?*" To those who answered that it was impossible, Noyes proudly replied that he *knew* from experience that it was possible and easy, and correct in the sight of God.[65] Moreover, as Noyes wrote in the summer of 1844, through this system of sexual self-control his "enjoyment was increased" and his wife's "experience was very satisfactory, as it had never been before."[66]

Indeed, control of the sexual erection in male continence and

---

62. *Male Continence* (1872), pp. 18–20.

63. "The Law of Fellowship," *Circular* 5 (28 February 1856): 21. Interestingly enough, Noyes believed that shame in men consisted of a sensual excess that produced exhaustion and a consciousness of "uncontrolled and ruinous passion." This in turn led to an aversion of "the instruments of mischief." The active elements in this masculine shame were contrasted to the passive ones in women's shame, which consisted of untimely and excessive child bearing. *First Annual Report*, p. 35.

64. Home-Talk by J. H. N., "Woman's Rights," *Circular* 5 (28 February 1856), p. 21.

65. *Male Continence* (1866), p. 3.

66. John Humphrey Noyes, *Dixon and His Copyists: A Criticism of the Accounts of the Oneida Community in "New America," "Spiritual Wives," and Kindred Publications* (Wallingford, Conn., 1872), p. 34. On the obsessive's need to control ejaculation see Salzman, *Obsessive Personality*, pp. 77–78; on the need for perfection of sexual performance see Blos, "Genealogy of the Ego Ideal," p. 61.

spiritual resurrection were inextricably linked in Noyes's mind. In the winter of 1834, while he was undergoing the anguish that would lead to his declaration of perfection, Noyes remarked that the "subject of sexual morality was early forced upon my attention, by its close connection with the peculiar views of the law, of the leadings of the Spirit, and of the resurrection."[67] In discussing the relationship of revivalism to socialism many years later, Noyes made the observation that "man's deepest experiences are those of religion and love; and these are just the experiences in respect to which he is most apt to be ashamed, and most inclined to be silent."[68] That is, just as Noyes's own religious conversion and subsequent resurrection led to a fresh feeling of manhood and a new morality, the same held true in male continence. Both signified to him strength and autonomy; the failure in either indicated weakness and unmanly behavior.

Although Noyes's concern for control might be viewed as obsessional and a distortion of true autonomy in contemporary terms, the ramifications of this practice went well beyond Noyes's own personal conflicts. To people within and outside his Communities, Noyes was offering in the sexual realm a system of control that related directly to the broader social anxieties and concern for health and self-control. A reader of the *Circular* in New York eagerly related that male continence did not "injure the health" half as much as incontinence did, and, furthermore, it led to happier relations with his wife. Another reader in Vermont claimed that his practice of it cured him of many painful afflictions, while from Illinois came the testimony that male continence would put an end to "unwelcome offspring," elevate women to an equality with men, and in general restore the health of the nation.[69]

By late 1845, Noyes had grown weary over his participation in the Belchertown imbroglio, where his sexual morality and the Battle-Axe Letter had come under question and attack. The whole affair had strengthened his conviction that he must "slowly and silently" build a small community in Putney where the true gospel of sexual and

67. "Statement by J. H. Noyes," *Spiritual Moralist* 1 (13 June 1842): 1.
68. *Male Continence* (1866), p. 3.
69. "Male Continence—Letters of Endorsement," *Circular* 3 n.s. (1 October 1866): 228–29. K. R. Eissler makes the point that "one of the ego functions of orgasm is to ascertain . . . truth." Further, "The truth that is affirmed by orgasm is not represented by words and not necessarily by explicit fantasies . . . orgasm is endowed with the power to confirm, create and affirm conviction." Heinz Lichtenstein adds to this last statement by saying that orgasm can affirm "conviction of one's own reality and the reality of another." Eissler quoted in Lichtenstein, "The Effect of Reality Perception on Psychic Structure: A Psychoanalytic Contribution to the Problem of the 'Generation Gap'," *The Annual of Psychoanalysis*, 2: 360.

marital relationships could be carried out. By the spring of 1846 the time was propitious, he felt, to "take the final step out of marriage."[70] His enthusiasm and optimism for such a step were predicated on several factors. He had succeeded in tightening his hold over the Community by breaking up a love relationship that threatened to disrupt the entire Putney group.[71] Moreover, by the spring of 1845 his small band of Perfectionists had advanced to a communal sharing of property.[72] Male continence had become the general rule of sexual conduct, and indeed it seemed as if Noyes's ideas on Bible Communism were about to be fulfilled. To one follower, Noyes wrote words to this effect, and voiced his growing confidence that God was preparing to give them the kingdom. Noyes suggested to his friend that when he was tired of the confusion and social tension in society, he should look to the Putney Community where he would "catch a glimpse of a better world."[73] The one ingredient that was missing in Noyes's ideal world was the sharing of spiritual mates; that is, complex marriage.

What Noyes needed now was the ideal person to join him in this sexual experiment. Abigail Merwin had been his predestined mate, but as we have seen she spurned him more than once. Harriet Holton never fulfilled that function, and in their marriage contract Noyes had reserved the right to introduce a spiritual sharing of mates at his discretion. In the latter part of 1845, he heard that Abigail's husband had died, and once more Noyes's hopes were rekindled that she would become his partner. Unfortunately, she quickly snuffed out the sparks. All the while this was transpiring, Noyes had been devoting a great deal of time counseling Mary Cragin. Although not a particularly attractive woman, it was no secret that "every man who came near her fell beneath her sway."[74] Like Ado Annie in Rogers and Hammerstein's *Oklahoma!*, Mary had difficulty saying no, and more than once Noyes had to intercede to untangle her

---

70. G. W. Noyes, ed., *J. H. N.—Putney Community*, pp. 192–93. As early as 1842 Noyes had stated: "We believe that the philosophy of the sexual relation is a science, which, next to theology, demands the attention of every moral being." Moreover, "God has the right though man has not, to abolish the present regulations of sexual intercourse." "Our Principles," *Spiritual Moralist* 1 (13 June 1842): 1.
71. G. W. Noyes, ed., *J. H. N.—Putney Community*, pp. 51–53.
72. Ibid., pp. 68–73.
73. Ibid., p. 193. Harriet, Noyes's sister, seconded her brother's observation. "The improvement that has been made among us the past winter is so palpable and universal that I cannot forbear acknowledging it. There has been a marked increase of union. The grim cowards of Accusation and Despondency, that so terribly harrass the lonely pilgrim, fly from out closed ranks, and in their place came Innocence, Courage and Strength."
74. William Hepworth Dixon, *Spiritual Wives* (Philadelphia, 1867), 2: 289.

extramarital affairs.[75] At times her anguish over her fallen state became so great that she contemplated suicide, but with constant encouragement and support from Noyes and his wife, Mary pulled through.

In the course of his spiritual concern for Mary, Noyes was allured by her charms and at first did his best to stifle his aroused sexual feelings. When he was rebuffed by Abigail, however, he turned to this Mary Magdalen to replace Abigail as his Eve in the Garden.[76] And, from this time on, an element of what Noyes called "Bible secretiveness" obscures our view of the intimate developments that led to complex marriage. What is left are a few entries from a journal kept by Mary Cragin, a small number of edited letters, and one short piece of writing by Noyes. From these tantalizing yet ultimately frustrating bits and pieces, we shall attempt to reconstruct the early stages of this system of relationships.

At the request of Noyes, Mary Cragin began a journal in January 1846 in order to record "the increase of brotherly love" that had recently taken place among them. In that same month she relates how her husband, George, had gone on a trip, and while away had written to Noyes's wife, "expressing his love for her as a sister in Christ." When Noyes questioned Harriet about the letter, she admitted her feelings of love for George, which Noyes accepted, and to clear the atmosphere he called for a meeting with the Cragins. At the meeting, which took place about the middle of the month, Noyes had words of caution about loose passions, but he also saw a positive side to the recent events. He asked his wife to speak and she said that "she was pleased by Mr. Cragin's letter, and that her heart was drawn out toward him by it." George confessed reciprocal feelings for Harriet, and now the attention was turned to the feelings Noyes and Mary held for each other.

Noyes did not hesitate to say that he loved Mary, who could not believe what she was hearing. As she wrote in her journal: "I said that I have loved Mr. Noyes so much that I feared he would find it out; for I was not certain, my awe of him was such, that he wanted me to love him so much." After these confessions of love, and after they had considered themselves "engaged to each other," they quickly put a lid on the sexual implications of their avowals. Together they agreed to "live in all conformity to the laws of this world until the time arrives for the consummation of our union."

75. Background information on Mary is to be found in Erik Achorn, "Mary Cragin, Perfectionist Saint," *New England Quarterly* 28 (1955): 490-518. Also, Parker, *Yankee Saint*, pp. 74–88, 121–24.
76. Parker, *Yankee Saint*, p. 79.

A few days after this meeting Noyes talked to his sister Harriet, who had married John Skinner, and found her to be much more amenable to "a community of hearts" than he had anticipated. Sister Charlotte's husband, John Miller, also expressed approval. Throughout all of this, Noyes realized that he was on touchy if not dangerous ground. He consequently gave a lecture to the Community on the proper limits of tenderness between the sexes, specifically prohibiting kissing and any other expressive act that might lead to uncontrolled passions and licentiousness.

In March, at a gathering of this select group of the Putney Perfectionists, Noyes commented upon their growing unity and stated that a nucleus must be formed in order to bring the other Community members into this kind of fellowship. He also asked, if he found it necessary to introduce complex marriage on a larger scale, had they enough faith in his ability "to prevent evil surmisings and jealousies?" They all affirmed Noyes's leadership in this area and expressed their confidence in him and his "undoubted right to do as he pleased."[77]

It did not take long for Noyes to exercise this right. One balmy spring evening in May he and Mary went for a leisurely stroll. When they came to a secluded spot along the roadside, they sat down and relaxed into idle chatter. Soon the warm night air was matched by the heat of their caresses. As Noyes delicately put it: "All the circumstances invited advance in freedom," and in surrendering to his desires, he took "some personal liberties." The temptation to go further was almost too much for Noyes, but he abruptly checked himself. On their way back to the Community, these two lovers again "lingered," but Noyes exercised restraint once more and told Mary that he must report their intimacies.[78] Upon reaching the Cragin home, Noyes summoned their respective spouses. A searching and discomfiting talk then took place. Disappointed, angry, and fearing himself cuckolded again, George Cragin lashed out at Noyes and branded him another Abram Smith. After some persuasive justification of his actions, Noyes convinced Cragin of the purity and innocence of his acts. Harriet Noyes, obedient as ever, gave her approval, and as a result the four of them "gave each other full liberty."[79] Complex marriage was thus born.

Noyes now carefully and slowly introduced the plan to the rest of the Community. To disciples of Paul and Christ, he reminded his followers, certain things were promised in the third heaven that were

---

77. "Mary E. Cragin's Journal," G. W. Noyes, ed., *J. H. N.—Putney Community*, pp. 197–201.
78. "My First Act of Sexual Freedom," Ibid., p. 201.
79. Ibid.

not lawful according to the dictates of common morality. There existed, he said, a "wisdom which ought to be communicated only to the perfect."[80] When Christ died the same principle that made the cross "the end of circumcision, also nailed to it the worldly ordinance of marriage."[81]

Noyes argued that the idea rooting monogamy in the nature of human relationships was false and could not withstand a close investigation. Experience, the best guide of all, "testifies that the human heart is capable of loving more than one at the same time." Not man's loving heart but his selfish and jealous one established "the one-love theory."[82] Complex marriage, however, would open "the prison doors to the victims both of marriage and celibacy." For the married who were oppressed by their incontinence and lust, or shackled by quarrels and "uncongenial natures," or "separated from their natural mates," complex marriage offered freedom. The same held true, Noyes suggested, for the unmarried who were abject in their loneliness, "diseased by unnatural abstinence," or plunged into prostitution by desires that were incapable of finding a lawful outlet.[83] Thus, while most people divided the question of marriage and sexual behavior into the diametrically opposed camps of conventional morality and free love, Noyes believed a secure middle ground between the two was attainable. In complex marriage people were far more chaste and pure than the free lovers were; but, on the other hand, they were in a certain sense more "lawless" than the adherents of the standard morality.[84]

The practice of complex marriage, over the course of the next several months, did not always run smoothly among the Community's leading members. Although Mary had shown great love and devotion to Noyes, she also harbored amorous feelings for John Miller. Early in 1846 Noyes had to intercede because the budding Cragin-Miller *affaire de coeur*, if carried too far, threatened to disrupt communal harmony.[85] Nevertheless, their affection for each other did not abate

80. "Letter to Garrison," *Witness* 1 (23 January 1839): 51.
81. "Marriage Nailed to the Cross," *Witness* 2 (24 December 1841): 76–77; J. H. Noyes, *The Berean,* pp. 431–35. In psychoanalytic terms, to understand why Noyes coupled marriage and circumcision see: Martin H. Stein, "The Marriage Bond," *Psa. Q.* 25 (1956): 253; Jarvis, "Some Effects of Pregnancy and Childbirth on Man," p. 689; Milton Malev, "The Jewish Orthodox Circumcision Ceremony," *J. Am. Psa. Assn.* 14 (1966): 510–17.
82. "Bible Communism," G. W. Noyes, ed., *J. H. N.—Putney Community,* p. 118.
83. Ibid.
84. Home-Talk—No. 111, "Third Party Politics," *Circular* 1 (1 August 1852): 151–52.
85. "Mary E. Cragin to John R. Miller at Boston," G. W. Noyes, ed., *J. H. N. —Putney Community,* p. 203.

over the next few months. In August 1846, Noyes wrote to his sister Harriet informing her that their brother-in-law, Miller, was proving obdurate to Noyes's will on many matters, while all the time "availing himself of the privileges" of complex marriage. Just the other evening, Noyes revealed, Miller embraced Mary, and consequently Noyes urged Harriet to repel any advances that Miller might make to her. This man was not to be trusted, Noyes said, until he had adopted all the Community's rules and submitted wholly to Noyes. In the meanwhile, Miller had to be "instructed in regard to secretiveness and the law in relation to propagation before he can safely be trusted with liberty."[86]

Later in August, Miller wrote Noyes that in due time he believed God would reveal the whole truth to him on the matter of complex marriage. Until then, he had the utmost confidence in Noyes's leadership and was certain it was God-inspired.[87] By November, God had revealed His intentions, and Miller was reinstated. Along with his wife Charlotte, the Skinners, the Cragins, and Harriet Noyes, they signed a "Statement of Principles" that affirmed the basis of their "social union." All individual ownership of "either persons or things" was surrendered, and an "absolute community of interests" was to replace the laws and customs that regulated "property and family relations in the world." God was accorded His role as supreme ruler over all, and Noyes was recognized as "the father and overseer whom the Holy Ghost has set over the family thus constituted."[88]

By the summer of 1847 the Community had come to accept the idea of complex marriage and its practice among many of its leading members. As a result, in a meeting held on 1 June, Noyes stood before his followers and asked: "Is not now the time for us to commence the testimony that the Kingdom of God has come?" Surely enough evidence indicated that it had. Together in Putney they had been able to cut their way through "the isolation of selfishness" that characterized regular society, and they had attained a spiritual condition that allowed them "to trample under foot the domestic and pecuniary fashions of the world." Separate households and private property had ended with them; their association was established on principles "opposed at every point to the institutions of the world."

86. "Noyes to Harriet Skinner," Ibid., p. 202.
87. "John R. Miller to Noyes," Ibid.; Parker, *Yankee Saint*, p. 124.
88. "Statement of Principles," G. W. Noyes, ed., *J. H. N.—Putney Community*, pp. 205–6. As early as March 1846, it was evident that a sense of cohesiveness was taking place within the Putney Community. In regard to the doctrines of holiness, perfection, and the second coming, it was now stated that: "We feel that our testimony on these special topics is in a certain sense finished." "Our Title and Motto," *Spiritual Magazine* 1 (15 March 1846): 8–9.

In light of all this, Noyes's followers unanimously agreed with him that the kingdom of God had come to earth with the Putney Community as its shining example.[89]

Within a few months after the introduction of complex marriage, Mary became pregnant, and there is good reason to suspect that Noyes was the father of her twins born in September 1847.[90] In view of Noyes's boasts of the ease with which he practiced male continence with Harriet and his success in not impregnating her, it does not seem likely that Mary's pregnancy was an accident. One might infer that sexual involvement no longer caused Noyes great anxiety because the Community and Mary provided him the necessary "background of safety" to support his feelings of self-worth. Yet, one should not rush to the conclusion that Noyes's relationship with Mary was a sign that he had at last been able to give free reign to his tender feelings and had become fully committed to another person. This is doubtful; in fact, it can be argued more convincingly that in complex marriage Noyes found a system of control complementary to male continence, in that both satisfied his personal needs and simultaneously performed as cohesive mechanisms for his Communities.[91] In other words, at moments of closest intimacy Noyes was able to keep emotional distance. Legally, Noyes was not bound to Mary, and thus the emotional demands one usually finds in a marriage were not binding upon him. Freed from feelings of commitment and entrapment, Noyes, we can speculate, probably found the sexual act more satisfying with Mary than with Harriet.[92] This in turn may

89. "Has the Kingdom of God Come?" *Spiritual Magazine* 2 (15 July 1847): 65–68; G. W. Noyes, ed., *J. H. N.—Putney Community*, pp. 235–38. Also see Arthur E. Bestor, Jr., "Patent-Office Models of the Good Society: Some Relationships Between Social Reform and Westward Expansion," *American Historical Review* 58 (1953): 505–26. One must question this unanimity. Stress and tension did exist within the Community, and most likely some of the problems stemmed from the institutionalization of complex marriage. Mary Cragin, for one, continued to have emotional difficulties. See Chapter 7, p. 138.

90. The question of Noyes's paternity was hinted at in Achorn, "Mary Cragin, Perfectionist Saint." It was openly suggested in Sandeen, "John Humphrey Noyes as the New Adam," p. 90.

91. Boundary-maintenance mechanisms are discussed in Rosabeth Moss Kanter, "Commitment and Social Organization: A Study of Commitment Mechanisms in Utopian Communities," *American Sociological Review* 33 (1968): 499–517.

92. As Salzman, *Obsessive Personality*, p. 79, points out: "when the issue of control is not crucial, such as in fleeting relationships or if intimacy is entirely lacking, the sex act may be far more successful. This explains the contradictory situation in which the sex act can be far more satisfactory with others than with one's own wife."

have accounted for the temporary relaxation that produced the children.[93]

There is one bit of evidence to indicate that Noyes was not possessive of Mary and that he might have shared her with at least one other. In mid-February 1847, when she was some two months pregnant, Mary and John Miller, in the company of their spouses and the Noyeses, reaffirmed their attraction for each other. Mary told Miller that she was "desirous of entering into partnership with him," but first there had to be certain qualifications. Before any move on their part she felt they had to have the approval of Noyes, and they had to keep an "open and direct communication with him" in order that he might teach them "how to love each other in that way which would be the most improving to our characters and tend to make us the happiest."[94] Unfortunately, no documents remain to indicate what Noyes's response was to this request. However, it is significant that Mary felt confident enough to broach the subject, and her journal entry does have an air of assurance that she was in no way challenging or being unfaithful to Noyes. In fact, one gets the impression that two children, John and Mary, were asking Father Noyes for permission to enter into a relationship. Noyes was in control. Secure in his perfection, he was in no danger of feeling attacked or rebuffed.

93. We must not overlook the chance that the births of Victor and Victoria were accidental. It was possible that the births were not a result of Noyes's failure to restrain ejaculation. Masters and Johnson have indicated that "Frequently a preorgasmic secretory emission . . . usually . . . no more than two or three drops . . . escapes involuntarily from the urethral meatus . . . Frequently, actively motile spermatozoa have been demonstrated in microscopic examinations of this preejaculatory fluid emission. . . . The fluid appears most frequently during voluntarily lengthened plateau-phase experiences. . . . Such situations tend to increase both frequency of occurrence and secretory volume of the preejaculatory material." Masters and Johnson, *Human Sexual Response* (Baltimore, 1969), pp. 210–11, quoted in Carden, *Oneida, Utopian Community to Modern Corporation*, fn. to pp. 51–52. Carden was discussing this in reference to birth control at Oneida and not in a discussion of Noyes and Mary Cragin.

94. "Mary E. Cragin's Journal," p. 209.

6 Institutional Order and Disorder:

Paternal Authority and the Family

Noyes's concern over interpersonal relationships drifted easily from sex and marriage into worries about the health of the American family. As his anxieties during the 1830s and 1840s increased, often proving unbearable, Noyes's response to the tensions besetting the nineteenth-century, middle-class family was colored partly by his own intrafamilial conflicts and his resolution of them. On a psychic level this meant that to a degree Noyes translated the present in terms of the past. In time he worked out a unique solution to his conflicts within his own personal family, and carried this over to his larger "families" at Putney and Oneida.

As we have already seen, Noyes's need for self-control and total acceptance led him into bitter altercations with his mother and an attempt on his part to supplant her (and his father) as the sole authority within the family. In the late fall of 1836 Noyes was in Putney conducting his numerous battles to purify Perfectionism, and, most importantly, to establish it on a "permanent foundation." The past two years had not been peaceful for him, and as a battle-scarred veteran of too many religious confrontations to recall, Noyes yearned for quiet and security. To achieve this Noyes realized that he would have to forego "stirring up excitement over a large field" as he had been doing. Furthermore, he would no longer waste his efforts organizing and disciplining "broken and corrupted regiments" as he had tried to do at Prospect and at countless other New England towns. Instead, he knew that for his own emotional security he had to devote himself "to the patient instruction of a few, simple-minded, unpretending believers, chiefly belonging to my father's family."[1]

1. J. H. Noyes, *Confession of Religious Experience*, p. 69.

112

That is, if Noyes was going to create a Family Government with himself as head—an undifferentiated, or rather a *de*differentiated society based on hierarchy, dependence, and emotional healing—then actual family government, the family as an institution alongside others, could go. Moreover, the authority relationships, the lines of dominance and submission, could also go, at least as far as his own family was concerned. For here the wish overrode reality, except that Noyes, as narcissistic and powerful as he was, could force the world, or that part of it, to heed to his demands. Then, as Father, he turned on his mother.

From the reminiscences of his sister Charlotte we get an inside view of what occurred during the winter of 1836–37. Polly Noyes's illness continued unabated, and she was often confined to her bedroom. Here in these quarters, said Charlotte, her brother John "felt most at home" while he and their mother discussed the Bible and his Perfectionism. Gradually—Charlotte was not quite certain how it all happened—she and her sister Harriet began spending their evenings up in the same room listening and reading with them. Not long thereafter their younger brother George joined them in the "small scale revival," which lasted the rest of the winter. Led by Noyes, who was alternately severe in his rebukes and compassionate in his praise, they slowly wended their way down the path of salvation from sin.

While Noyes's younger brother and sisters gladly followed his lead and confessed their Perfectionism a few months later, Polly Noyes, despite her broken body and mind, proved more resistant. She felt that John Humphrey was able to "enlighten and condemn," but failed to give peace to "her troubled mind nor renew and purify the heart." The more she fought his spiritual blandishments, the more anxious and angry Noyes became. To convert his mother, Noyes resorted to browbeating tactics. In early January 1837, Polly complained to a friend that her son's scoldings had produced a feeling of dejection and despair that she had never before experienced. Adeptly manipulating her feelings of shame and guilt, Noyes reviled his mother. He accused her of being a failure as a mother, and that he loathed her, if she did not hate herself. A crippled Polly Noyes broke down sobbing under this barrage. Once she had regained her composure and had time to reflect upon her pride and her sinful ways, Noyes again would enter her room and the whole grinding process was resumed.[2]

---

2. G. W. Noyes, ed., *Religious Experience*, p. 310. Also, "One of the Four, VI," *Oneida Circular* 12 (12 April 1875): 114.

A year later Noyes wrote his mother from Kingston, New York, reproving her for her opposition to him. He recalled the advice she used to give him when he went away to school as a small boy: be good, stay out of trouble, and remember to always obey your mother. Times and circumstances had changed, said Noyes, for in his submissive obedience to God he had undergone the same training he had experienced as a youngster. Now God was sending him to reward his mother, Noyes told Polly, for "your care over me by changing places with you and dealing with you as my little daughter." So, when she proved to be stubborn, it was his duty to "affectionately reprove" her for thinking that she knew more than her "father." "My child, be still," wrote a domineering Noyes. "You know but little, and it becomes you to be modest."

Noyes was hardly through chastening his mother. Further on in the letter he insisted that she begin to learn from her experiences and "not continually fall into the same error." Those things she saw as truths were nothing but "broken bank bills" that would never pass with him. "The true bills of God's signature," he impressed upon her, begin with 'I know,' and eventually would be accepted by every conscience. Noyes understood that this currency was still in "a disordered state," and thus there might be some excuse "for offering and receiving bad bills." However, he was doing his utmost to weed them out, and since he had on hand "a considerable amount of specie (that is, certainties)," he was confident of success. He hoped, therefore, Polly would help her "father" in these efforts, "like a dutiful daughter, and not go about to hinder and vex him." Noyes reminded her that God had put him in this highly responsible position, and prayed that she remember the days of her own motherhood, "and let your own trials teach you compassion for mine."[3]

As the summer of 1838 passed into the fall, Polly's isolation within the home became unbearable. The question before her was: how could she, who for so long had been "the acknowledged head of the family," consent to give up the position God had ordained to her as a woman? She could not, and she did her best to resist Noyes; however, his control over the younger family members was unshakeable. In her own home, Polly recalled, she was treated civilly "but with a cold reserve" by John and the younger children. To escape this suffocating atmosphere she visited some relatives in Springfield, Massachusetts, but when she returned after seven weeks, the bitter air of estrangement still hung over the house. When she remonstrated

---

3. "Noyes to His Mother," G. W. Noyes, ed., *J. H. N.—Putney Community*, pp. 27–28.

with her daughter Harriet, this once-obedient child turned on her and declared that she stood with John rather than her. Completely unnerved by this, Polly again left home, though when she came back several weeks later, the house still seemed a "furnace of fire" to her.[4]

In early December a distraught Polly turned for advice outside the family. In a letter to a member of her church, she wanted to know where her son John got his power. Did it come from within himself or was it given to him by God? Further, if it came from the Lord, was there anything in the scriptures to support it and especially prove that Noyes was the chosen one? Polly then mentioned that many of Noyes's followers believed he had the qualities and character of exalted biblical figures. His wife, for instance, thought that Noyes was a prophet because ultimately he overcame all failure and despair. Another supporter spoke of him as a veritable David. When Polly asked this person why she did not oppose Noyes, she answered that Noyes was more like God than any other person she had ever seen. Abram Smith believed that Noyes was like Paul in his dispensation— a leader who might err sometimes in his judgment but was infallible in spiritual matters. David Harrison felt Noyes was a "Leader and Commander" to the people, while Noyes's sisters, Harriet and Charlotte, considered their brother to be Christ's representative on earth. Still others spoke of Noyes in terms of being the most righteous of men, and most agreed that Noyes was to lead the way to the new dispensation.[5]

Despite this impressive array of opposition, Polly Noyes held her ground and refused to accept Noyes's claim of divine authority. By the spring of 1839, however, the constant pressure was at last too much for her to endure, and she capitulated. In the *Witness* she confessed that for the last year she had been led "through fire and flood," but the "suffering and separation" she had undergone was the only way in which she could prove to herself that she was not "governed by parental partiality and self-exaltation." Polly now temporarily acceded to Noyes his rightful position as her "teacher and father in spiritual things."[6]

Over the next several years her natural inclination to oppose her son reasserted itself. She recanted her vow and again stubbornly resisted him, only to come once more under his unrelenting attack. She accepted him again as her leader, stipulating, however, that he had "faults and infirmities" as did others. Noyes responded angrily by

4. "Mrs. Polly Noyes's Recollections," Ibid., pp. 30–31.
5. "Mrs. Polly Noyes to a Member of the Church," Ibid., pp. 31–32.
6. Ibid., p. 33.

denouncing her expression as the work of the Devil; he advised her to pray for deliverance from her "accusing spirit and . . . licentious tongue," arguing that in all matters he answered only to God. Finally, he warned her that her justification was in him and that if she was bent on destroying him, she would thereby destroy herself.

Late in 1845, as Noyes sought "slowly and silently" to establish firmer control over his Putney community and pursue his ideal mate, Mary, he also lashed out at his mother in a brief paper entitled, "Pride of Motherhood." Clearly, her pride was her primary fault, and it made her "disputatious and imperious." She would never be redeemed until her haughtiness was broken, until she could become humble enough to confess that her own character was the worst thing she had to fear. As part of redemption, Noyes took his mother to task for having "connected herself to an ungodly man," consigning at least half of her children's education to worldly matters. Noyes complained, furthermore, that as a result of her marriage, he was spiritually unable to reach and include his older sisters and brother, Horatio, in the Putney Community. But, as he proudly concluded, three of the younger children were saved by him from the carnal ways of the world.[7]

Throughout all of this it is certainly difficult to comprehend Noyes's abrasive and often cruel treatment of his mother. In order to do so it is essential to recall that in his first religious conversion an ego ideal had been constructed whose components consisted of a highly idealized self-image and omnipotent parental image. Essentially, then, for Noyes to see himself as a pure Christ-like figure, he needed the support of the other unity of his ego ideal: the pure, innocent mother figure. He had overtaken his father through purity and therefore had right over all, including his mother. This ideal "father" and the real mother would thus represent the most ideal, perfect unity, wherein the aggressive and sexual instincts were disavowed.[8] Without her support, Noyes felt he would not have been able to live up to his inflated ideals, and such a failure he could neither tolerate nor sustain.

To a lesser degree, Joanna had to face a similarly exhausting encounter with Noyes. In the spring and summer of 1837, while Noyes pressed for his mother's conversion, he decided that Joanna was ready for his Perfectionism. Like her mother, however, Joanna was a strong-

---

7. Ibid., pp. 93–98. Polly Noyes had one more period of conflict with her son, in the midst of the crisis that resulted in the breakup of the Putney Community in December 1847. Not long after that she was reconverted and joined the Community at Oneida in the spring of 1849. Ibid., pp. 98–99.

8. Rochlin, *Griefs and Discontents*, pp. 312–16.

willed woman, or as Noyes expressed it, she had "a masculine, independent temperament."[9] In his mind Joanna was closely identified with his mother, and he tried desperately to gain her acceptance and affirmation of his beliefs. But she was "too independent, too proud and self-confident" to truckle to his arrogant spiritual demands.[10] After all, in the past had she not been the one to provide him with aid and nurturance? Nevertheless, Noyes persisted. Their arguments became bitter, resembling, as sister Charlotte observed, "a life and death struggle for mastery between the favor of God and the praise of this world—between faith and unbelief." Although Joanna's arguments proved to be as cutting as any "merciless scalpel" could be, Noyes's constant proddings, diatribes, and tenacity finally won out. Joanna, like her mother, confessed Noyes as her savior.[11]

We have no documents on the father's responses to Noyes's assertion of leadership within the family. Further, no documents exist that might indicate an intense struggle between the father and son, such as Noyes had with Polly and Joanna. We do know that Noyes, Sr., continued to deplore his son's shiftlessness and had some difficulty understanding his son's actions in the outside world. "What does John mean by this flying from one thing to another?" complained the father. "I do not understand it."[12]

If the conflict between Noyes and his father was as muted and inconsequential as it seems, then one reason for this might be that through his religious commitment Noyes had, as indicated earlier, outflanked his father. Just as importantly, by the late 1830s, when Noyes had made his resolve to convert his family and put pressure on his mother and sister, the father was well into his seventies and was not in the best of health.[13] So, in reality, the father was not a domineering figure. One source indicates that alcoholism was at least partially a cause of the father's illness. During his congressional days, the elder Noyes acquired the taste for drink, a habit that he did not relinquish upon his return to Vermont in 1816. By 1837 his moderate drinking had slowly given way to intemperance. John Humphrey remembered his father shutting himself in his room after the rest of the family had gone to bed and drinking himself into a stupor. On

9. G. W. Noyes, ed., *Religious Experience,* pp. 278, 321; "One of the Four," *Oneida Circular* 12 (22 March 1875): 91.

10. G. W. Noyes, ed., *Religious Experience,* p. 320.

11. Ibid., pp. 319–27.

12. "Mrs. Polly Noyes to Noyes," Letter dated 1 October 1837, Ibid., p. 366.

13. Reference to the father's failing health may be found in "Mrs. Polly Noyes to Noyes," Letter dated 30 August 1837, Ibid., p. 359. In a letter to Harriet, Noyes also mentioned that he was caring for his father who was ill. "J. H. N. to H. A. N.," pp. 202–4.

more than one occasion, Noyes sadly commented, after hearing a fall, "I have found him helpless on the floor." In the spring of 1837, while Noyes was busy asserting his leadership over other family members, he wrote a letter to his father (signed by all the children) that was firm yet conciliatory and contained none of his usual arrogance.

It was their fondest hope that the father would not have to face "the public disgrace of drunkenness" and the rest of them endure the "mortification of a drunkard's family." While the father had on occasion checked his intemperance, more often than not he had resumed his deleterious habit "with increased momentum and decreased self-control." Drinking had given him an "unreasonable temper" that sadly contrasted with "the kindness and consistency" of his previous behavior. Moreover, the children no longer had any confidence in him as "a counsellor and guide of the family," which his "former character was wont to inspire." The letter ended with an impassioned plea, imploring the father to give up alcohol for the sake of everyone concerned.[14] Within four years Noyes's father died, but not before overcoming his drinking habit and at least perfunctorily accepting his son's Perfectionist beliefs.

Some months before his father's death in October 1841, Noyes arranged the marriages of his sisters Harriet and Charlotte, which certainly confirmed his role as father and leader of both his personal and his "utopian" families. As of 1838 the nucleus of the Putney Corporation consisted of Noyes, his wife, mother, brother George, and sisters Harriet and Charlotte. The first outsider to join them was John L. Skinner, a young Quaker teacher who had been converted by Noyes in 1837. Over the bitter protests of his family, Skinner came to Putney in 1839 to help on the *Witness*. Eventually, as his responsibilities increased so did his closeness to Noyes and his family. Exercising parental prerogatives, Noyes arranged the marriage between Skinner and Harriet in February 1841, and seven months later paired John Miller with Charlotte.[15] Thus, by the time the Putney Community was well underway, Noyes had gone far to assume both a nurturant, protective, and a stern disciplinarian role within his two families, a role that helped shape Noyes's views and solution to the problems of the family at large.

14. "Petition of the Junior Members of the Noyes Family to Their Father," G. W. Noyes, ed., *J. H. N.—Putney Community,* pp. 91–92. This is the only reference to the father's drinking problem. It is not mentioned in any of the correspondence between Noyes and his family and friends. Moreover, it is never mentioned in the later reminiscences by family members.
15. Parker, *Yankee Saint,* pp. 90–93, 95.

A writer for the *Harbinger*, strolling through the neighborhoods of New York, observed: "Our dwellings are now symbols . . . . of isolation. . . . They present not the tokens of a true human society, but of a society distracted, discordant, fragmentary, competitive." This was a well-travelled walk for antebellum social critics, and in most instances Noyes was right in step with them. He was convinced that the complexity of modern civilization would claim the family as one of its principal victims. Daily he passed rows of single homes whose sterile architecture reflected a dearth of human unity on the inside. The "narrow twenty-five feet fronts," which silently stared at each other from both sides of the street, suggested to him "poverty, selfishness, and division."[16]

Noyes recognized, along with a host of others, that industrialism had a harmful effect upon family unity.[17] The vast increase in communications, business ventures, and commerce pulled fathers out of the family circle and made them "fixtures in the store, the workshop, and the street." Men trudged home at night from work enervated, their emotional reserves impoverished. Little was left over for their families.[18] This separation not only aggravated the relationship between an exhausted husband and equally tired wife, who remained at home to take care of the children; but it also encouraged women, "left with a crumbling institution," to demand their freedom from the burdens of child rearing and the tedium of housework.[19]

The signs were clear to Noyes. Traditional marriage was proving itself a failure. If a person were to "lift the curtain of the private life

16. J. A. Saxton, "The Isolated Household," *The Harbinger* 1 (24 June 1845): 22; "Houses," *Circular* 2 (8 December 1852): 26. The relationship of Victorian architecture to cultural values is brilliantly explored in Clifford E. Clark, Jr., "Domestic Architecture as an Index to Social History: The Romantic Revival and the Cult of Domesticity, 1840–1870," *Journal of Interdisciplinary History* 7 (Summer, 1976): 33–56.
17. Some of the best work on the family in the nineteenth century is in unpublished dissertations: Kirk Jeffrey, "The Middle-Class American Family in the Urban Context, 1830–1870," (Ph.D. diss. Stanford University, 1972); Mary P. Ryan, "American Society and the Cult of Domesticity, 1830–1860" (Ph.D. diss. University of California, Santa Barbara, 1971). Also see, Ronald G. Walters, "The Family and Ante-Bellum Reform: an Interpretation," *Societas* 3 (1973): 221–31.
18. "Houses," p. 26. For similar statements from other social critics see Ora Gannett Sedgwick and Charles Lane quoted in Henry W. Sams, ed., *Autobiography of Brook Farm* (Englewood Cliffs, N.J., 1962), pp. 227, 91.
19. "Houses," p. 26. Also see "Woman's Slavery to Children," *Spiritual Magazine* 1 (8 October 1853): 109–10; "Home—A Few Words with a Magazinist," *Circular* 5 (6 March 1856): 26. For a similar view of the plight of the woman in the family see Brisbane, *Social Destiny of Man*, pp. 300, 431, 439; *Design for Utopia, Selected Writings of Charles Fourier*, trans. by Julia Franklin (New York, 1971), pp. 76–81.

of men and women under the present social system," he would uncover "a vast amount of discord," which sprung from "an attempted reversal of the true relations of the sexes." Voicing fears similar to the critic, Horace Bushnell, Noyes complained that women were attempting "to rule and lead the man—to play a dynamic part in the family organization" and society in general.[20]

As if this were not enough, the efficient "old forms of family government" were failing to secure the respect and obedience of the children.[21] In his *Familiar Letters to Young*, for example, William Alcott freely admitted that he was writing in order to encourage in the young "a due respect for the aged," especially at a time when such respect seemed to be totally disregarded if not "obliterated."[22] William Henry Channing argued that one source of this parent-child friction was to be found in the tendency of city youth to seek social satisfaction within their peer groups instead of the family. No matter where they congregated, thought Channing, they now "corrupt each other."[23] To see children socializing at parties and dances was to Lydia Maria Child "a heart-sickening sight," detrimental to their health and happiness.[24] Many critics attributed this moral decline to the fact that parents, no longer secure in their own roles, and seemingly bereft of communal supports, had come to doubt the legitimacy of their own authority.[25]

Noyes vigorously agreed with these observations. All too often in families "the spiritual relations of superior and inferior [are] actually reversed, and parents [are] ruled by their own children."[26] Noyes also lamented the fact that boys were in the streets "learning everything that is pernicious," and becoming more and more alienated from their guides. The deportment of girls was not much better. They too were deserting the family for the pleasures found in their own circle of friends.

The meaning of this pattern of events was all too evident to Noyes.

20. "National Troubles and Their Sources," *Circular* 1 n.s. (5 September 1864), p. 193. Also see Home-Talk by J. H. N.—No. 22, 'The Principles of Distribution," *Spiritual Magazine* 2 (1 December 1849): 321. On Bushnell see his *Woman's Suffrage; The Reform Against Nature* (New York, 1869).
21. Rev. Orville Dewey, "Boyhood in America," reprinted in the *Circular* 2 (27 November 1852): 16.
22. Alcott, *Familiar Letters to Young Men*, p. 194.
23. *The Harbinger* 1 (9 August 1845): 141–42.
24. Child, *Mother's Book*, p. 60.
25. John S. C. Abbott, *The Mother at Home, or the Principles of Maternal Duty* (New York, 1833), pp. 63, 65. Lydia H. Sigourney, *Letters to Mothers* (Hartford, Conn., 1838), p. 14; Horace Bushnell, *Christian Nurture* (New York, 1890), p. 66; Catharine E. Beecher and Harriet Beecher Stowe, *The American Woman's Home: or Principles of Domestic Science* (New York, 1869), p. 199.
26. Dewey, "Boyhood in America," p. 16. Also see Barron and Miller, eds., *Home-Talks*, pp. 310–14.

As the country's population increased, he reasoned, "the necessity becomes more imperative for improved arrangement for social order and control, both among the old and young."[27] As it was, "isolated interests, social disorganization, and oppressive labor," were conspiring to create a gigantic "vortex" that seemed to lure men irresistibly into "the snare of intemperance, or some form of dissipation and excess."[28] To avoid being sucked in by the strong currents of disorder and social chaos, which ultimately might lead to total dissolution and insanity, strong, if not radical, measures had to be taken.

During the nineteenth century the onus for inculcating the ascetic values that would help restore a personal and communal sense of order increasingly fell upon the very institution that many feared was crumbling: the family. And as the spate of family guidance literature after 1830 indicates, the lion's share of this burden fell to the mother.[29] But how could mothers be relied upon to undertake this important nurturing function if they "were preparing to fly the coop, some to flutter amid scenes of idle diversion, others to swoop down upon the world of men?"[30] Obviously she could not be trusted, and much of this literature was, therefore, an attempt to reinforce the woman in her role as wife and mother.

Catharine E. Beecher stated that in order to preserve the social order it was essential "that certain relations be sustained that involve the duties of subordination." All relationships involved one person who was superior and one who was inferior. There must be, she felt, "relations of husband and wife, parent and child, teacher and pupil . . . each involving the relative duties of subordination."[31] Another

27. (Oneida Association), *Mutual Criticism* (Oneida, N.Y. 1876), p. 88; *Circular* 3 (8 June 1854): 320.
28. "The Temperance Problem," *Circular* 4 (9 April 1855): 50.
29. For a survey of this literature see Anne L. Kuhn, *The Mother's Role in Childhood Education: New England Concepts, 1830–1860* (New Haven, Conn., 1947); Robert Sunley, "Early Nineteenth-Century American Literature on Child Rearing," in *Childhood in Contemporary Cultures,* ed. Margaret Mead and Martha Wolfenstein (Chicago, 1955), pp. 150–67.
30. Janet Wilson James, "Changing Ideas about Women in the United States, 1777–1825" (Ph.D. diss., Harvard University, 1954), p. 146. For nineteenth-century developments in England see J. A. and Olive Banks, *Feminism and Family Planning in Victorian England* (Liverpool, 1964).
31. Catharine E. Beecher, *A Treatise on Domestic Economy, for the Use of Young Ladies at Home and at School* (Boston, 1841), p. 2. A brilliant detailed study is Kathryn Kish Sklar, *Catharine Beecher: A Study in American Domesticity* (New Haven, 1973). The essential task for Beecher and others was to clarify the differentiation in role relationships. Once this was accomplished, it was necessary to convince and encourage the mother to use her authority wisely within the home. For further examples see "Woman's Sphere," *The American Ladies' Magazine* 8 (May 1835): pp. 262–67; "Ladies Fair," Ibid. 4 (July 1831): 289–93; Catharine E. Beecher, *Letters to the People on Health and Happiness* (New York, 1855), pp. 188–89.

author wrote that self assertion and independence in women were clearly "unfeminine" and that a woman should understand that "a passive fortitude . . . is more essential than active strength."[32]

Armed with her God-given qualities of piety, purity, submissiveness, and domesticity, the mother was told that in child rearing the authority was hers and that her foremost duty was to secure the obedience of her children. Any indecision or vacillation on her part would certainly lead to self-indulgent, insubordinate, and disobedient children. Ideally, the key to her discipline was moderation—a firm gentleness that avoided the extremes of harshness and permissiveness.[33] Mothers were further counseled that all signs of anger and violent passions were to be repressed, for such behavior could eventually disrupt the unity of the family.[34] Control over her own feelings was thus mandatory for a mother, and she was to "keep her heart and conscience pure." To Lydia Maria Child it was nothing less than "pure indolence" on the part of a mother who was "not willing to take the pains, and practice the self-denial, which firm and gentle management requires."[35]

32. Mrs. John Sandford (Elizabeth Poole), *Woman, in her Social and Domestic Character,* 6th ed. (Boston, 1842), p. 9. Also see Mrs. L. G. Abell, *Woman in her Various Relations* (New York, 1853), p. 9; Sigourney, *Letters to Mothers,* pp. 10–11; Barbara Welter, "The Cult of True Womanhood, 1820–1860," *American Quarterly* 18 (1966): 151–74; Ronald W. Hogeland, " 'The Female Appendage': Feminine Life-Styles in America, 1820–1860," *Civil War History* 17 (June 1971): 101–14.

33. Jacob Abbott, *Gentle Measures in the Management and Training of the Young* (New York and London, 1871), p. 16; Beecher, *Treatise on Domestic Economy,* p. 224; John S. C. Abbott, *Mother at Home,* pp. 27, 62–63.

34. John Abbott, *Mother at Home,* pp. 11, 13, 62; Child, *Mother's Book,* pp. 26, 46, 49–50; Beecher and Stowe, *American Woman's Home,* p. 224. Robert Elno McGlone, "Suffer the Children: The Emergence of Modern Middle-Class Family Life in America, 1820–1870," (Ph.D. diss., University of California, Los Angeles, 1971), pp. 45, 69, states that it was commonly believed that anger, jealousy, and grief might produce a miscarriage. Further, it was felt that a woman's state of mind could be passed on to the fetus. The young bride was warned that her first dispute with her husband was like the "disruption of a river's bank; the injury may be but small, but is continually increasing, until the waters rush out, inundate and devastate the country." It was a woman's duty to avoid showing anger to her husband and children. See, Arthur Freeling, *The Young Bride's Book* (New York, 1845), pp. 9–10. For the deleterious effects of a "bad temper" see "Anger," *Godey's Lady's Book* 4 (March 1834): 156; A. B. Muzzey, "Power of the Voice over Children," *Mother's Assistant* 1 (November 1841): 241–43.

35. Child, *Mother's Book,* pp. 4–5, 31; William A. Alcott, *The Young Wife, or Duties of Woman in the Marriage Relation,* 3rd ed. (Boston, 1837), p. 109. The mother was not alone in her daily efforts to inculcate a socially acceptable morality into her children. School teachers were also encouraged to use the same disciplinary methods of the mothers for the same ends. See, for example, Jacob Abbott, *The Teacher: or Moral Influences Employed in the Instruction and Government of the Young* (Boston, 1834). Also see Ruth Miller Edson, *Guardians of Tradition: American Schoolbooks of the Nineteenth Century* (Lincoln, Nebraska, 1964).

In her own life as well as the lives of her children, the ideal mother was to proscribe all manifestations of vanity, pride, and self-indulgence in dress and speech.[36] And finally, to assure the organic unity of the family and society, the mother was urged to assign her children tasks within the home, for by doing this the influence of the peer group would be subverted and the "salutary . . . happy intercourse of the old and young" would be reestablished.[37]

Although the father's departure from the home to the outside world of business was regretted, it was accepted as an undeniable fact of modern life in much of the guidance literature. As a result of his absence for a good part of the day, the ideal father was encouraged to take a supportive role to maternal authority within the home. His duty was "to provide the needful support" to the mother whenever a sterner discipline was necessary. The father was also cautioned, however, to be flexible and not authoritarian in his handling of his children.[38] In summing up the dramatic changes for the father within the home (changes that only recently have come under exacting study and analysis), de Tocqueville intuitively perceived that in the home "the master and constituted ruler have vanished; the father remains."[39]

36. It was feared that a woman's extravagance would eventually undermine the whole social order. Her indolence and demands for splendor would weaken her authority over her children, and her demands for material luxuries would put extra pressure on the father to make more money to satisfy her. In the end he would be debilitated by this "unnatural quest" and possibly driven insane. See, Abell, *Woman in her Various Relations*, pp. 263, 307–12; William A. Alcott, *The Young Woman's Guide to Excellence*, 5th ed. (Boston, 1841), p. 275.

37. Child, *Mother's Book*, pp. 61–62, 111–14. Ideally, children were expected to obey their parents. John S. C. Abbott, *The Child at Home, or the Principles of Filial Duty* (New York, 1833), p. 62, warned: "If you disobey your parents, it is impossible to tell where it will lead." Also see Jacob Abbott, *The Rollo Code of Morals; or, The Rule of Duty for Children* (Boston, 1841). Within the home, support of male-female role differentiation was also extended to the children. Girls were encouraged to be more like their mothers; in fact, they were asked to become little mothers in relationship to their brothers. The sons, on the other hand, were expected to be more intractable and aggressive than the girls. L. H. Sigourney, *Letters to Young Ladies* (New York, 1839), p. 210; Abell, *Woman in her Various Relations*, p. 154.

38. In disciplining his children the father was to remain somewhat aloof and act as a court of last resort when sterner authority was needed. See John Abbott, *Mother at Home*, pp. 13, 124; Rothman, *Discovery of the Asylum*, p. 219; Theodore Dwight, Jr., "A Father Among His Children," *Mother's Assistant* 1 (April 1841): 82; John S. C. Abbott, "Paternal Neglect," Ibid. 2 (January 1842): 1–3.

39. Alexis de Tocqueville, *Democracy in America*, ed. by Phillips Bradley (New York, 1960), 2: 205–6. For important studies that shed some light on these changes within father-son relationships see Philip J. Greven, Jr., *Four Generations: Population, Land and Family in Colonial Andover, Massachusetts* (Ithaca, N.Y., 1970); Kenneth Lockridge, *A New England Town: The First Hundred Years, Dedham, Massachusetts 1636–1736* (New York, 1970); and on a more theoretical level, Weinstein and Platt, *Wish to be Free*, pp. 137–67.

Again, there was much here that Noyes could agree with. Like many others, Noyes saw the parallels between women, southern slaves, and children, since all were placed "in a state of subordination, and have not the advantage of personal independence." Despite this sympathy for the plight of the woman in her role as a domestic slave, Noyes had a strong aversion to women usurping man's authority.[40] Not only would women's demands for their rights rend the fabric of the family, but also, on a more fundamental level, an independent woman was seen by Noyes as a competitive, even socially threatening figure. "Our hope for the future woman," it was stated in the *Circular*, "is not that she will compete successfully with man, but that she will secure his affection, and become one with him."[41] The assumption of the women's rights organizations that men and women were separate and had their "independent rights and spheres" was an egregious fallacy. In asserting her independence a woman lost her "feminine aroma."[42]

The natural order of the male-female relationships was clearly defined by Paul, and Noyes turned to the apostle's writings repeatedly for a justification of his belief that women should never be independent and competitive with men. According to Paul's dictum: "the head of every man is Christ; and the head of the woman is the man; and the head of Christ is God."[43] If man's relationship to his head, Christ, was intact, he would have the "power and inspiration to rule his own house, and command respect, subordination, and loving receptivity on the part of woman."[44] It logically followed from this that woman was incomplete until she was in harmony with man, "such as the subordinate members of the body are in with the head."[45] Noyes could not have agreed more with Longfellow's sentiment on this point:

> As unto the bow the chord is
> So unto the man is woman,
> Though she bend him, she obeys him,

40. "Woman's Slavery to Children," p. 109. Also see, "When Shall We Have Peace?" *Circular* 1 n.s. (22 August 1864), p. 177. On a cultural level see Walters, "Erotic South."
41. "Woman's Prospects," *Circular* 2 (18 June 1853): 246.
42. "A Community Journal," *Circular* 4 (18 June 1857): 87.
43. "The Law of Fellowship," *Oneida Circular* 8 (23 October 1871): 338; "Women's Slavery to Children," p. 110. For other statements wherein Noyes agreed with Paul that women were subordinate to men, see "The Woman Question," *Witness* 2 (26 November 1841): 62–63; "Report of the Society of Inquiry," Ibid. 2 (4 November 1841): 49.
44. "National Troubles and Their Source," p. 193.
45. "An Oneida Journal," *Circular* 6 (2 April 1857): 43.

> Though she draws him, yet she follows,
> Useless each without the other![46]

Once a woman had wisely decided to assume such a posture, it became the man's duty to respond by taking her hand and guiding her "back to Eden." By seeking reconciliation through Christ and God, "the problem of the settlement of individual rights will be solved."[47]

With this spiritual unity a husband and wife could regain control over their wayward children. Noyes cautioned that as much as parents may love their children, they had to reestablish their authority for the mutual benefit of the family and society. He further advised that parents must not let their happiness be dependent upon their children, because they would know this intuitively, and soon manipulate them "for their pleasure."[48]

To insure the happiness of parents, children, and society, Noyes made a significant break from the conventional advice of the guidance manuals. Instead of accepting the absence of the father from the home, Noyes wished to restore him to a preeminent role within the family circle. "A family governed by merely motherly feeling," Noyes cautioned, "is like a wheel with the hub left out."[49] A mother's natural function was to provide nurturance; she was therefore incapable of disciplining children by herself. A man's strength was required to develop a child's self-control; there had to be "masculine power and execution at the center," and the mother's philoprogenitive love must be loyally subordinate to that.[50] The first step in restoring harmony within the family, then, required that "the father must love and reverence God, and the mother must love and reverence the father." To invert this relationship would be to destroy all family unity, and "family government" would be impossible.[51]

46. "A Community Journal," *Circular* 6 (18 June 1857): 87.
47. *Oneida Circular* 8 (8 October 1871): 338.
48. (Oneida Association), *Mutual Criticism,* p. 61.
49. "Woman's Slavery to Children," pp. 109–10. Thus, for Noyes the ideal marriage and ideal family closely resembled the early Puritan family with its emphasis upon paternal authority and clearly defined submissive relationships to the father. See, James, "Changing Ideas about Women in the United States, 1776–1825," pp. 5–63; James T. Johnson, "The Covenant Idea and the Puritan View of Marriage," *Journal of the History of Ideas* 32 (1971): 107–18; Edmund S. Morgan, *The Puritan Family: Religion and Domestic Relations in Seventeenth-Century New England,* rev. ed. (New York, 1966).
50. "A Community Journal," *Circular* 12 (5 November 1863): 143. On the development of women's increasing autonomy within the nineteenth-century family see Daniel Scott Smith, "Family Limitation, Sexual Control, and Domestic Feminism in Victorian America," in *Clio's Consciousness Raised,* pp. 119–36. Noyes could not tolerate these developments.
51. *Circular* 7 n.s. (18 July 1870): 141. As long as people insisted upon regular marriages, Noyes felt that they had to abide by their "civil contracts." Only

Noyes fully recognized that even under the best of circumstances "the government of children forms one of the hardest knots in common society."[52] The unravelling of this knot depended upon recognizing that childhood was an embryonic state. God valued the child not as he presently was but as he would eventually become. Noyes stated the common belief that "our children are serving purposes all the time that are not formed in themselves, but are in their parents."[53] Thus, parents "must themselves improve, before they can transmit improvement to their offspring."[54]

To insure the correct social, moral, and spiritual behavior of their children, Noyes advised parents generally to keep the rules governing children at a minimum; too many rules confused their pliable, receptive minds. Parents should address children's reason and conscience through kindness, patience, and forbearance in correcting their faults. Ideally a parent should not let a child's misconduct continue unchecked, but confront it directly with a faith in God's power to overcome the disobedience without anger or harsh words.[55] To bolster his argument, Noyes quoted Dr. Samuel Woodward of the Worcester State Lunatic Society to the effect that half the cases of insanity that entered the hospitals were attributable to parental

---

adultery would be grounds for divorce. In his demands for a familial unity, therefore, Noyes criticized what he considered to be the trend towards freer divorce laws. He believed such laxity to be "unscriptural, illogical, and practically bad." "Marriage and Divorce," *Circular* 1 (18 April 1852): 90; (Oneida Association), *Handbook of the Oneida Community, with a Sketch of its Founder and an Outline of its Constitution and Doctrines* (Wallingford, Conn., 1867), pp. 55–61. In this pamphlet Noyes decried the divorce schemes of Robert Dale Owen and Henry James on the one hand and the Shakers with their celibacy on the other. He believed, of course, that complex marriage would be the ideal system for those who could tolerate neither ordinary marriage nor celibacy. Also see, "The Bible on Marriage," *Circular* 3 n.s. (19 March 1866): 1–3; "The Marriage Question," *Circular* 2 (5 January 1853): 58; "The Law of Adultery," *Circular* 1 (28 March 1852): 77–78.

52. "A Community Journal," *Circular* 12 (5 November 1863): 143.

53. *Circular* 7 (8 April 1858): 43. Noyes, of course, believed that one should expect to see recalcitrant, disobedient children from a regular marriage, because such marriages heightened and worsened interpersonal tension. However, having children could be a blessing in "a right state of society." Complex marriage, by making propagation a matter of choice and conscience, was an important step on the way to securing this ideal state. "Home Journals," *Circular* 5 (1 May 1856): 58. Also see Barron and Miller, eds., *Home-Talks*, pp. 54–59. On a cultural level see Bernard Wishey, *The Child and the Republic: The Dawn of Modern American Child Nurture* (Philadelphia, 1968), Pt. I, for a discussion of the growing awareness of childhood in this era.

54. Barron and Miller, eds. *Home-Talks*, p. 141.

55. "Government of Children," *Spiritual Magazine* 2 (11 August 1849): 215. Noyes added on p. 216: "If our general rule is gentleness, and long-suffering, and the acts of love when we do chastise them it will be with the greater effect."

negligence in subduing the passions and breaking the will of children while they were young. In many cases, Woodward believed that insanity was nothing less than "the fury of disobedience—the raging of a 'stuffy' child."[56] If a child continued to manifest a spunky disposition, then more stringent methods might be necessary to modify the youngster's behavior. The ideal method, said Noyes, would consist of merging the father's "exacting and truthful severity" with the mother's "indulgent tenderness."[57] Thus, overall, the best method of child rearing was probably a middle-ground "between permissiveness and authoritarian methods."[58]

Noyes viewed the restoration of parental authority as the key factor in the return of the child to his proper place within the family. The authority of the parents would especially contravene the unfortunate influence of the peer group, just as the unified family would obviate the need for the private academy or boarding school. "A boy who is sent away from home to live," Noyes wrote, vividly recalling his own childhood experiences, "will often droop and pine, and finally vomit."[59] He was in total agreement with Catharine Beecher's denunciation of such schools. "To take the unformed youth at the most excitable period of the nervous system . . . with habits of self-control the weakest, away from mothers, sisters, and home," she asserted, would surely foster "wrecks of health, morals, home habits, and all that is good and pure."[60]

Noyes also observed, moreover, that the "mating together of persons of the same age and class, young and young, and inexperienced with inexperienced," was a major source of the numerous evils that infested the current marriage system.[61] To prevent these drawbacks to marital happiness, the "horizontal fellowships" of young people had to be superseded by an "ascending-descending" order of relationships.[62] By this Noyes meant that in any relationship the

56. "Insanity," *Circular* 1 (4 January 1852): 34. Also see "The Virtue of Obedience," *Circular* 1 n.s. (13 June 1864): 100–101.

57. "A Community Journal," *Circular* 12 (5 November 1863): 143.

58. "Obedience in Children," *Circular* 6 (23 April 1857): 54. Here Noyes's ideas on controlling children reflect accurately the broader social concerns. See, for example, Barbara Finkelstein, "Pedagogy as Intrusion: Teaching Values in Popular Primary Schools in Nineteenth-Century America," *History of Childhood Quarterly* 2 (1975): 349–78.

59. "Home-Talk," *Free Church Circular* 4 (20 June 1851): 229. For Noyes's early childhood feelings of separation and loss as a result of his attending private academies, see G. W. Noyes, ed., *Religious Experience*, pp. 9–11.

60. Beecher, *Common Sense Applied to Religion, or, the People*, quoted in the *Circular* 6 (3 December 1857): 182.

61. "An Oneida Journal," *Circular* 5 (2 February 1856): 11.

62. "True Obedience," *Free Church Circular* 3 (20 December 1850): 334. Also see "Look to Your Balance Sheet," *Circular* 5 n.s. (7 September 1868): 193; "The Law of Fellowship," Ibid. 5 n.s. (23 November 1868): 281–82.

spiritually inferior of two must subordinate himself to the spiritually superior one, if there was to be any hope of self-improvement. Within the family this concept demanded that children, in their obviously "descending role," obey their spiritually superior parents. As Noyes said, descending fellowship "is identified with the ascending fellowship and gets its authority from it." All true ascending fellowship carried with it the inspiration and guidance of the superior.[63] For Noyes the ideal family was "a miniature monarchy, rather than an example of republican equality."[64]

Noyes did not intend by his advocacy of parental control to stifle the growth of the children. It was most likely proper for young children to "be led by the hand, or watched at every step; and . . . be told what words they shall speak." But this was hardly desirable for all of child rearing. A wise parent, Noyes suggested, would want to see his child "gain strength to walk by himself," so that he need not rely passively upon others.[65] All this of course was not a prescient call by Noyes for modern child rearing. Noyes and his contemporaries were more concerned with the immediate problem of how to restore a sense of self-control and unity within a society that had seemingly been reduced to chaos by the forces of modernization.[66] He referred, therefore, to the inward acceptance of patterns of dominance and submission, to the independent acceptance of rightful authority.

---

63. Barron and Miller, eds., *Home-Talks*, pp. 204–5. Noyes claimed that "Self-limitation is the principle which qualifies one for the descending fellowship." To emphasize the fact that children belong in the descending position, Noyes stated that little children "are born in a condition of extreme dependence, and brought up under parental despotism; and the younger are subject to the elder,—one brother and sister to another." "Childhood Analogous to Heaven," *Spiritual Magazine* 1 (15 July 1846): 69.
64. "Childhood Analogous to Heaven," p. 69.
65. "Gospel Liberty," *Witness* 2 (9 October 1841): 44.
66. On this point see Brown, "Modernization: A Victorian Climax." The theme of social disorder is also touched upon in Phillip S. Paludan, "The American Civil War Considered as a Crisis in Law and Order," *American Historical Review* 77 (1972): 1013–34.

7 Health:

A Matter of Life and Death

Attitudes on health, life, and death added to the swirl of antebellum social tensions. The *Knickerbocker* said in one of its essays
that although death was usually "vilified as the cause of anguish,
consternation, and despair," it would be more accurate to say that
these feelings were related "not unto death but unto life."[1] A popular
hymn entitled "Humiliation for National Sins" helps to explain why
thoughts on death became so intensified in the antebellum era:

> See, gracious God, before thy throne
> Thy mourning people bend;
> 'Tis on thy sovereign grace alone
> Our humble hopes depend.
>
> Tremendous judgments from thy hand
> Thy dreadful power display,
> Yet mercy spares this guilty land
> And still we live to pray.
>
> What numerous crimes increasing rise,
> Through this apostate land!
> What land so favoured of the skies
> Yet thoughtless of thy hand?
>
> How changed, alas; are truths divine.
> For error, guilt and shame!
> What pious members, bold in sin,
> Disgrace the Christian name![2]

1. "Editor's Table," *Knickerbocker* 16 (July 1840): 77. Also see "Heaven is
Holiness Matured," *Guide to Holiness* 36 (April 1857): 99.
2. Nagel, *This Sacred Trust*, pp. 126–27.

The sense of mourning expressed in the poem is appropriate to the experience of loss. The rise in crime ("numerous crimes"), for example, implies that the ties of a once-binding morality have been severely strained, or even snapped. Something had to be done to repair these ties or society risked being overwhelmed by immorality— being abandoned by God. It is clear that people were threatened, that a sense of continuity in and integration with the world was lost. Fearing abandonment by God, a cataclysmic fate, men sought after "moral truths," hoping to achieve again a sense of balance, purpose, and a basis for action.[3]

The response to the idea of death in antebellum America may be taken as one gauge of a person's emotional adjustment to the rapid changes of that period. Some, of course, kept pace with the changes, but many did not. People responded to events in the idioms and metaphors of their day, and for increasing numbers the disruptive social conditions signaled God's abandonment of America. From this sense of loss derived a common concern over the meaning and consequences of death. One writer who has studied the changing American attitudes toward death has suggested that in our period, "the fear that death might involve [ego] annihilation supplemented the fear of eternal punishment."[4]

Because fears of death mirrored the actual tensions of life, the theme was used to teach moral lessons, as the elegiacal strains, which filled the journals of the day, testify.[5] And nowhere is this theme

---

3. Freud can help us clarify the nature of this pervasive fear that God was on the verge of forsaking His people. To the ego, Freud wrote, living is equated to being loved—loved by the superego. In this respect the superego fulfills a similar function of "protecting and saving that was fulfilled in earlier days by the father and later by Destiny." However, if the ego finds itself in a highly threatening situation that it feels unable to overcome by its own resources, "it is bound to draw the same conclusion. It sees itself deserted by all protecting figures." *Ego and Id,* p. 48. Also see Roy Schafer, "The Loving and Beloved Superego in Freud's Structural Theory," *Psa. St. Chi.* 15 (1960): 163–88; Martin H. Stein, "Self-Observation, Reality, and the Superego," in *Psychoanalysis— A General Psychology,* pp. 275, 295; Leo A. Spiegel, "Superego and the Function of Anticipation with Comments on 'Anticipatory Anxiety,' " *Ibid.,* pp. 315–36.

4. Charles Allen Shively, "A History of the Conception of Death in America, 1650–1860." (Ph.D. diss., Harvard University, 1968), pp. 255–56. Further analysis of the attitudes of death in the nineteenth century may be found in Lewis O. Saum, "Death in the Popular Mind of Pre-Civil War America," in David E. Stannard, ed., *Death in America* (Philadelphia, 1975), pp. 30–48; Ann Douglas, "Heaven Our Home: Consolation Literature in the Northern United States, 1830–1880," *Ibid.,* pp. 48–68.

5. Short stories, poems and brief essays filled the pages of such journals as *Godey's, Ladies' Repository, American Ladies' Magazine, Knickerbocker,* and countless others.

more forcefully portrayed than in the death scene of little Eva in Harriet Beecher Stowe's *Uncle Tom's Cabin*. In Eva's bedroom we are fully aware that death is nearby. But this pale messenger is submerged and even at times lost in the sight, smell, and breath of life. The windows, for instance, were hung with curtains "of rose-colored and white muslin," which drew out nicely the rose patterns in the floor matting. Light and fragile curtains of "rose-colored gauze" with silver stripes hung over Eva's bed to protect her against the annoying bite of mosquitoes as well as the more deadly sting of death. The bed frame, chairs, and lounges were made of bamboo "wrought in particularly graceful and fanciful patterns," while in the center of the room an equally elegant table held a Parisian vase, shaped like a water lily and filled daily with flowers. Across the room on the marble mantle of the fireplace stood a "beautifully wrought statuette of Jesus" gently receiving little children. On the walls one could see two or three paintings of children in a variety of poses and activities, and as the eye slowly drifted back to Eva it could not help but take in the alabaster bracket above her bed, which held "a beautifully sculptured angel . . . with drooping wings, holding out a crown of myrtle-leaves." In short, as Stowe wrote, "the eye could turn nowhere without meeting images of childhood, of beauty, and of peace."

In this hushed and tranquil setting, Eva, much like the spiritual messenger above her head, would act to dispel the fears of death, lessen the pain of mourning, and urge others to walk the path of a Christian life. Eva quieted the "groans and lamentations" of her father, and the family servants gathered around, reminding them that she was shortly going to heaven, and that in time they too could join her. "It is for you, as much as me," she said. But "if you want to go there, you must not live idle, careless, thoughtless lives. You must be Christians."

Near the end, Eva's ebbing strength did not reveal itself in a pale, "ghastly imprint" upon her face. Instead, her countenance was flush with "a high and almost sublime expression," which seemed to reflect "the dawning of immortal life in that childish soul." And her own inner quietude and resolve lent support to her distraught father. Through the example of his dying daughter, St. Clare found a strange calm coming over him, something like a hushed spirit "amid the bright, mild woods of autumn, when the bright hectic flush is on the trees, and the last lingering flowers by the brook."[6]

That feelings of separation and loss could be camouflaged in the

6. Harriet Beecher Stowe, *Uncle Tom's Cabin*, Riverside Library (Boston and New York, n.d.), pp. 317–18, 322, 327, 329.

browns and greens of Nature's woods and in the bright hues of her flowers was, of course, a widely held belief in the America of Emerson and Thoreau. The rural cemetery movement articulated, among other things, the desire of the living to have roots in the soil and a sense of permanence and continuity in a world of flux. Orville Dewey, a prominent New York minister, thought he saw in the graves of dead fathers and the homes of living sons a line of continuity that linked past, present, and future.[7] Others were not so sure. The social tensions put a tremendous strain on the links in this chain of generations, threatening to snap it altogether. The *Guide to Holiness* suggested that death involved "the suffering of the present and the untried experience of the future," giving voice to the inevitable fear of the disruption of continuity.[8]

The rural cemetery, nestled in the comforting arms of Nature, was used in the service of continuity, providing people with a sense of integration. Death in a natural setting such as the beautifully landscaped Mount Auburn Cemetery or the Worcester Rural Cemetery would impress upon the mind that "in the mighty system of the universe, not a single step of the destroyer, Time, but is made subservient to some ulterior purpose of reproduction, and the circle of creation and destruction is eternal."[9]

The rural cemetery, little Eva, popular journals, all fragments of ideology, imparted reassuring messages to the living. In his address at the dedication of lush, sylvan Mount Auburn, Justice Joseph Story pointedly observed that "the rivalries of the world will here drop from the heart . . . the restlessness of ambition will be rebuked; vanity will let fall its plumes." In fact, Mount Auburn was "but the threshold and starting point of an existence," not the home of death and dissolution.[10] Death held precepts and examples for the living, as Levi Lincoln told his audience in an address at the Worcester Cemetery. "The sweetest memorials of the dead are to be found in

---

7. "Death's Teachings," *Knickerbocker* 17 (June 1841): 530.
8. "The Holy has Rest from Doubts and Fears in Relation to Its Final Acceptance," *Guide to Holiness* 19 (1851): 32.
9. *New England Magazine* quoted in Stanley French, "The Cemetery as Cultural Institution: The Establishment of Mount Auburn and the 'Rural Cemetery' Movement," *American Quarterly* 26 (1974): 47. Also see Thomas Bender, "The 'Rural' Cemetery Movement: Urban Travail and the Appeal of Nature," *New England Quarterly* 47 (1974): 196–211. K. R. Eissler, *The Psychiatrist and the Dying Patient* (New York, 1955), p. 92, says that the feeling that the past and present are meaningful and continuous holds the unconscious conviction that "identity will also extend into the future." Moreover, it is "a consoling reassurance that the ego is protected against the possibility of . . . present and future dissolution."
10. "Consecration Dell," *Ladies' Repository* 9 (September 1831): 257.

the admonitions they convey, and the instructions they give, to form the character and govern the conduct of the living."[11]

Noyes also addressed himself to the problem, hardly surprising since it was associated with separation and loss, mourning and personal control. Many of his associations with death had negative connotations: sin, habit, doubt, self-condemnation, and all social attributes of individualism. Noyes, however, also pictured death free from personal or social conflict. When a person had committed himself to a righteous life, death became a peaceful kind of oneness; a kind of sleep where unity with Christ obviated the "deep mourning" that accompanied all other types of separation.[12] To experience Christ's death as one's own was a reward and not a deprivation, because it led to a perfect unity where time was stopped and death stayed. Death was thus a transformation, yet with continuity. No need for mourning here, for the ideal had not been lost; to the contrary, it has been attained.[13] Noyes concluded as much when he claimed that he would never die "in fact or form," after his New York episode in 1834.[14]

Along with so many others, however, Noyes continued to feel "the want of protection in respect to health." In a world "ravaged by disease, in which decay marks the largest part of life," and where each day a person was exposed to infirmities and death, it was no wonder that the mind sought "a resting place of hope—a covering real or imaginary" where one could remain healthy and strong.[15] The mind was so delicately balanced that it would not take much to disrupt it, and one found consolation where one could.

Noyes never fully accepted the doctrines of physiology because they seemed to deny the centrality of man's spiritual life. But he did agree that in matters of eating and drinking, self-control was paramount. "The stomach and bowels are intimately connected with the

11. French, "Cemetery as Cultural Institution," p. 46.
12. For Noyes's equation of sleep with death see Barron and Miller, eds., *Home-Talks*, pp. 110–12; "Glad Tidings for the Dead and Dying," *Circular* 2 (29 June 1853): 258. George H. Pollock, "On Anniversary Suicide and Mourning," in *Depression and Human Existence*, p. 373, states that "death is primarily perceived as a separation and an instinctual and narcissistic frustration. It can reawaken old concerns dealing with need gratification, rage, guilt, unfulfillment, or idealization." With this statement in mind, one can easily understand why Noyes wished to control death.
13. George H. Pollock, "On Mourning, Immortality, and Utopia," *J. Am. Psa. Assn.* 23 (1975): 339.
14. G. W. Noyes, ed., *J. H. N.—Putney Community*, p. 63. Noyes's identification with Christ was, as indicated, a means of overcoming feelings of loss and abandonment. See Loewald, "Internalization, Separation, Mourning and the Superego," p. 487.
15. "Coverings," *Spiritual Magazine* 2 (1 August 1847): 88.

brain, and thus are specially subject to the action of the mind." Any excessive eating was bound to agitate the "self-inspecting faculty" of the mind, blunt the perceptive powers, and breed decay and death. Noyes many times recalled being "sorely tempted to give up my bowels to runaway merriment," but his will power prevailed and he refused to be "sucked in."[16] Thus, Noyes concurred with Edward Hitchcock of Amherst College that the health and purity of the soul were increased immeasurably by withholding "from the stomach a few ounces of improper or unnecessary food."[17] Eating and drinking in moderation, Noyes declared, were not only "a sacrifice to God," but they guaranteed to man a physical and spiritual unity; or, as Noyes phrased it, "We sanctify that which we take into ourselves."[18]

Health and food served Noyes as metaphors in his religious conversions and in explaining the omnipotence of his Perfectionism. As he stated, there were two parts to the act of eating: one was "mastication," which was highly pleasurable; the other was "digestion" and "distribution" of the food, which was not as enjoyable but far more important. Mastication, then, resembled the insecure and incomplete conversions practiced by the regular Protestant denominations while the thoroughness of digestion was equated with the security and completeness of his conversion to Perfectionism.[19] Moreover, a person might feast upon "probabilities, suppositions, and approximations to truth," Noyes said, but all "such food of the mind and heart" was harmful and unhealthy. While these poisonous uncertainties were ingested, a man's life would eventually become "diseased, and grow into a morbid state." Men therefore, must "concentrate vital energy in the heart and not the stomach." Noyes would have accepted a school of physiology readily enough if it had been harnessed to a faith in Christ, and could have devoted itself "to the work of raising men to absolute, i.e., immortal health."[20]

16. "Correspondence," *Spiritual Magazine* 2 (11 August 1849): 222–23; Home-Talk by J. H. N.—No. 83, "The Heart and the Mind," *Circular* 1 (22 February 1852): 64. For Noyes's opinions of physiology see Home-Talk by J. H. N.—No. 95, "A Glimpse at Physiology," Ibid. 1 (9 May 1852): 103; "Thoughts on Grahamism," Ibid. 2 (9 March 1853): 131.

17. Edward Hitchcock, "Blessings of Temperance in Food," *National Preacher* 9 (November 1834): 93. In addition to censuring the use of alcohol, coffee, tea, and tobacco, Noyes had harsh words for meat and its deleterious effects. "The Bible on Alimentiveness," *Witness* 2 (30 September 1842): 148–49; "Sobriety," Ibid. 2 (1 April 1842): 101.

18. "Table-Talk by J. H. N.—No. 11," *Circular* 1 (18 April 1852): 92; "Table-Talk by J. H. N.—No. 32," Ibid. 1 (26 September 1852): 188.

19. "Experiencing Religion," *Spiritual Magazine* 2 (1 July 1847): 49–51.

20. "Anastatic Physiology," *Circular* 2 n.s. (29 May 1865): 81. Also see Barron and Miller, eds., *Home-Talks*, pp. 209–11; "The Higher Hygiene," *Circular* 5 n.s. (10 August 1868): 161.

Noyes had a growing interest in conquering disease and death by faith, though he was still some distance from fully accepting it and applying it. His ideas on this subject were not especially unique; indeed, he faced a great deal of competition. Ralph Waldo Emerson, in his paeans to oneness, emphasized that aspect of Transcendentalism calling for the merger of man's mind with the Creator's. Emerson urged men not to sit idly by, passively recording the joy of fusion; rather, men should actively change "every jot of chaos which threatens to exterminate us . . . into the wholesome force."[21] Emerson and his Transcendental friends were, of course, too intellectual and abstruse for the common man, but, there were a variety of other mind-cure doctrines that commanded attention.

Spiritualism had a pervasive influence in the mid-nineteenth century, and its greatest exponent was Andrew Jackson Davis with his interpretations of Swedenborgian doctrines.[22] Davis promised that through "spiritual intercourse" all men would some day be joined into "one Brotherhood," wherein everything would be pure, just, and harmonious. "Streams of good and healthy inspirations" would wash away all weakness, error, corruption, and even death.[23] Similarly, the Fowlers and other phrenologists, who combined their science with physiology and religion, also offered a way of overcoming feelings of loss and social anxiety.[24]

There are too many differences between these systems of thought for exploration here; I shall focus rather on their shared attributes, particularly their concern with mental health. Each system offered

---

21. Emerson quoted in Donald Meyer, *The Positive Thinkers: A Study of the American Quest for Health, Wealth, and Personal Power from Mary Baker Eddy to Norman Vincent Peale* (Garden City, N.Y., 1965), p. 80.

22. A very brief introduction to Davis may be found in Alice Felt Tyler, *Freedom's Ferment: Phases of American Social History from the Colonial Period to the Outbreak of the Civil War,* Harper Torchbooks (New York, 1962), pp. 78–82. A more detailed account of Davis and his thought is in Robert W. Delp, "Andrew Jackson Davis: Prophet of American Spiritualism," *Journal of American History* 54 (1967): 43–56; Delp, "Andrew Jackson Davis's *Revelations,* Harbinger of American Spiritualism," *The New York Historical Society Quarterly* 55 (1971): 211–34.

23. Tyler, *Freedom's Ferment,* p. 79; Delp, "Andrew Jackson Davis's *Revelations,* p. 213. An excellent article placing spiritualism within its nineteenth-century context is R. Laurence Moore, "Spiritualism and Science: Reflections on the First Decade of the Spirit Rappings," *American Quarterly* 24 (1972): 474–500.

24. A solid book on this subject is John D. Davies, *Phrenology, Fad and Science: A Nineteenth-Century American Crusade* (New Haven, Conn., 1955). The best source on the interconnection between religion, phrenology, and physiology is O. S. Fowler, *Religion; Natural and Revealed: or, The National Theology and Moral Bearings of Phrenology and Physiology,* 10th ed. (New York, 1844).

the individual a feeling of security through mental and spiritual fusion with a force larger than the self.[25] Each system, moveover, stressed the cultural values of activism: one gained inner strength through merger, but then one must take the responsibility for the continued improvement of his own health and of the society at large.[26] Noyes's belief in mind cure had much in common with these other various systems, especially in the omnipotence and grandeur of their design.

In the spring of 1840 Noyes visited David Harrison and found him gravely ill. He persuaded his bed-ridden friend to quit taking the doctor's medicine, offering instead some "large doses of faith with moderate doses of brandy and wine." After a day's time Harrison was better and within a week he was on his feet.[27] Noyes was gratified but also cautious in ascribing great healing powers to himself, although like many mind curists he believed in the power of thought to cure sickness, which he defined as an evil spirit.[28]

In 1842–43, at the same time that Noyes was attempting to enforce a stricter regimen within his Putney group and agonizing over the state of marriage, he was enmeshed in the prolonged struggle to clear his name and defend his beliefs in the village of Belchertown. Noyes's anxieties manifested themselves at length in a boil and a severe sore throat. In pain, Noyes wrote his wife that he did not wish to turn to faith healing until he could thoroughly justify it within himself. "Let us put on the whole armor of Bible physiology," he told her, "before we attempt much offensive warfare against the medical profession."[29] Despite his efforts at regaining control by means of thought and faith, Noyes's sore throat continued to wear him down. On 1 January 1843, he ceased all public speaking and rarely attended meetings for over a year.[30]

In the spring of 1843 Harrison's illness recurred, and he died within a month. Badly shaken by this loss, Noyes again found it necessary

25. For Emerson it was the Oversoul or Nature. On Davis and the merger with a cosmic universe similar to Fourier's, see Delp, "Andrew Jackson Davis's *Revelations,*" p. 213; on God's merger with man in phrenology see Fowler, *Religion; Natural and Revealed,* pp. 17, 22, 25.

26. This point is made by Meyer, *Positive Thinkers,* pp. 80–81, in reference to Emerson. Also see pp. 120–22 in Meyer's work. In addition, Gail Thain Parker, *Mind Cure in New England: From the Civil War to World War I* (Hanover, N.H., 1973).

27. G. W. Noyes, ed., *J. H. N.—Putney Community,* pp. 63–64.

28. Parker, *Mind Cure in New England,* makes this point throughout her book, and we have already seen how Noyes put a great deal of emphasis upon the mind having absolute control over the passions.

29. G. W. Noyes, ed., *J. H. N.—Putney Community,* p. 64.

30. Ibid. The point here is that faith cure was part and parcel of Noyes's Perfectionism and omnipotence of ideas. When that omnipotence was shattered, so too was the ability to control the impulses that produced disease and death.

to affirm to himself that true believers relied upon God and "spiritual medicines" rather than doctors and drugs. He admitted to a correspondent, however, that the subject of faith healing had been buried too deeply in skepticism and doubt. Strenuous efforts were needed to get it back to the accepted position it held in the Primitive Church. A worried Noyes declared to fellow Perfectionist, Eli Wadsworth, that in the present order of things Satan enticed the unwary to push ahead too fast and too far. Salvation from sin, or an absolute security of mind, was the first step of a true believer while salvation from disease and death was the last. Suffering and death, meanwhile, were to be employed as a means of perfecting the spirit. Faith was the primary concern, Noyes reminded Wadsworth, and physical concerns were secondary. Once a person had learned the "faith of endurance," he was ready to apply "the faith of resistance" to disease and death. In the near future Noyes felt that God would be calling him to the faith of resistance, and everything seemed to point toward a restoration of primitive Christianity.

In early 1845, Noyes was writing in the *Perfectionist* that the reign of death was "an evil second only to the reign of sin." The gospel promised redemption not only of the soul but the body as well. Over the past few years Noyes's own illness, compounded by the sickness and death of friends, had forcefully impressed upon his mind "the close relation between salvation from sin and salvation from disease and death." While Noyes disavowed any immunity from disease and death, he was convinced that God, at that very moment, was "making war on death in connection with the gospel of salvation from sin."[31] Thus, just as Noyes would conquer sin through his perfection and total self-control, so too would disease and death fall prey to the omnipotence of his thought. Through self-control a kind of immortality would be granted, a world of fulfillment and continuity, rather than death, conflict, and nothingness.

By the fall of 1845, Noyes felt his Putney Community was taking on a healthier atmosphere, as his theories advanced on all fronts, and he subdued his mother and he grew more attached to Mary Cragin. It was no mere coincidence, therefore, that as Noyes was finding a more secure environment, battles against disease through faith cures spread throughout the Community. "The first requisite of health is a *healthy atmosphere*," said Noyes addressing his followers. "We must insulate ourselves from the world and the devil, by reflection, and by abstinence from evil communications and unnecessary intercourse."[32] The

31. Ibid., pp. 65–67.
32. "Hints on the Means of Health," *Perfectionist* 3 (15 August 1843) : 50.

climax came when Noyes cured himself of the sore throat that had plagued him for the past three years. "When the symptoms were at their worst," he recalled victoriously, "Jesus Christ advised me to neglect my disease, and act as though I was well," which he faithfully did.[33]

Spiritually and physically strengthened by his recovery, Noyes's optimism spread in several directions. He began his attacks upon competitors within the mental health field. Andrew Jackson Davis was hotly abused for his "pathological affairs" of the mind that merely led to a temporary salvation and cure instead of a permanent one.[34] In 1845 and 1846 Noyes corresponded with George Bush, one of the leading exponents of Swedenborgian theory in America. Throughout their many exchanges Noyes denounced Swedenborg for relegating Paul and Christ to secondary status in the drama for salvation, while arrogating for himself a position next to God.[35] Furthermore, Swedenborg's ideas on sexual morality, as seen in his doctrine of conjugal love, was an invitation to the worst forms of sexual indulgence and promiscuous behavior.[36]

By June 1847 the Putney Community had adopted the resolution that the Kingdom of God had come. One of the reasons for this exuberance was the apparent conquering of death by several Community members over the past year. "Some of us have lived a long time in the jaws of death," reported the *Spiritual Magazine*, "and also in the jaws of resurrection; dying daily and rising daily."[37] Mary Cragin was one of those who experienced these mental and spiritual states. Sometime in the spring of 1847, not long after the Community had come together "in family unity," Mary suffered an attack of a virulent illness, which she ascribed to "various secondary causes." Noyes himself recognized the severity of her crisis and agreed that her poor health was of "an obstinate and threatening character." Submerged in despair, Mary surrendered herself completely to Christ as her "physician for the body as well as the soul." After giving herself to Christ, Mary came to realize that unbelief was "the first cause of disease and death," and that she must have "a healthy spirit in order to have a healthy body."

Noyes was profoundly upset by the afflictions of his recently chosen

33. "The True Issue," *Spiritual Magazine* 2 (15 October 1847): 154.
34. For Noyes's attacks on Davis, see Home-Talk by J. H. N.—No. 61, "Davis's Superior Condition," *Free Church Circular* 4 (6 May 1851): 145–53.
35. Most of these exchanges are conveniently reprinted in G. W. Noyes, ed., *J. H. N.—Putney Community*, pp. 170–85.
36. Ibid., pp. 180–85.
37. "Has the Kingdom of God Come?" pp. 65–68.

spiritual mate, and he examined more closely than ever the meaning of sickness and death. Noyes reaffirmed his belief in faith cure, as a result of his reflections, and openly announced his "independence of the medical systems of this world," claiming for Christ, "the office of physician to our Community." Noyes then treated Mary, who recalled that after a great deal of "bodily suffering and mental conflict with the powers of darkness," she was at last able to confess Christ as her savior "from the power of unbelief." The sickness immediately left her and she was restored to health, able and eager to prove to others that Christ's resurrection had taken place within her. With a healthy Mary at his side, Noyes was ready to undertake his most celebrated case of faith cure.

Mrs. Harriet Hall of Putney had been blind and bedridden for a number of years. In 1843, after she had been converted to Noyes's Perfectionism, she was carried to his home, where he successfully cured her by faith. With her eyesight restored and legs strengthened, Harriet walked out of Noyes's home only to relapse into her previous state shortly thereafter. In 1845 she married Daniel Hall, an openly vociferous critic of Noyes and his beliefs. Yielding to her husband, Harriet confessed her doubts about Noyes and grew nearly as skeptical of him as her husband was. Fortunately, her brother and two sisters were followers of Noyes and persuaded her to allow him to undertake a second faith cure.

Noyes fully understood that Harriet's relationship to a disbelieving husband and father, representatives of a larger number of scoffers in Putney, made her case a special one. In fact, he felt himself "challenged to a public contest with death," and he was determined not to attend to her until he was in "the fulness of faith." At the moment, however, he was busy ministering to Mary and realized that it would be impossible to "carry victory over unbelief" to others until he had accomplished it within his own Community. On the twenty-first of June (1847), Noyes successfully lifted Mary "from the grave of unbelief," and now he was certain that this was the time to raise Harriet Hall.

The next day, as Noyes and Mary entered Harriet's darkened room, the sight of a helpless Harriet brought back fresh, anxious memories to Mary, who was "struck with horror at the mighty power of unbelief." The thought occurred to Mary that poor Harriet was "in the same grave" from which she had recently been raised, but that she would be willing to reenter that black terrain of unbelief if by so doing it would help Harriet recover. As these thoughts crossed her mind, Mary was "conscious of a general sickness" unlike anything she had ever experienced before. She quickly regained her composure, nevertheless, and listened attentively with Harriet as Noyes expounded on the meaning of faith.

Noyes talked for half an hour and then turned to Mary, asking her to testify to her recent struggles with disease and death. As Mary began to recount her victory over unbelief, suddenly she was overcome by a sea of darkness. Her eyes grew dim and hazy, she lost her hearing, and she was made incoherent by a palsied tongue. Vaguely she recalled that she desperately wanted to leave the room, but felt Noyes's stronger will forbidding it. With all emotional avenues of escape blocked, Mary sank "lower and lower into a dreadful, dark abyss."

Slowly, in recovery, Mary found herself sitting in a chair and Noyes's loud voice commanding her to look at him. "His tones," she later testified, "thrilled me like a shock of electricity, and soon as I looked at him life triumphed over death." Arising from the chair, Mary was filled with the power of faith, which seemed to pulsate through her veins, and she turned to Harriet and said: "This is the most effectual preaching you can have; I have tasted of death, and behold the power of resurrection."

After talking with Harriet for a brief period, "the same horror of unbelief began to paralyze" Mary again. She attempted to gain control over it but was defenseless until once more she caught Noyes's eye. She gazed steadily at him until she "partook of his strength," and the work of the devil was cast out. Even though she felt "stupid and sleepy" for the remainder of the three hours they spent with Harriet, Mary continued to help Noyes with his faith cure. Along with him she placed herself into closer spiritual communication with Harriet by taking hold of her hands, and shortly thereafter Noyes felt that the power of unbelief was broken. Feeling much the same, Harriet admitted that "something good" was taking place inside her.

Things had worked well for Noyes up to this point, but beyond that he had no clear idea what else was to be done for Harriet. She was apparently getting better, and since this was his first effort at curing an outsider, Noyes "shrank from anything like over-boldness or experimenting." He thought at first that he had better go home, but Harriet pleaded that he stay until she could go with him. Perplexed, Noyes paced the floor trying to decide what to do, when abruptly "an omnipotent will began to infuse itself" into his consciousness, and he laid his case before God. Soon the Lord indicated His will, and "the way was naturally and easily opened" for Noyes to lead Harriet out of her spiritual and mental prison into the "full consciousness of the authority and cooperation of God."

Noyes at once ordered Harriet to sit up in bed, which she did easily. He then commanded her to get up, and he took her by the hand to a chair. "Without pain and with great delight," Harriet was now able to look out the window, and she marvelled at the sights that were once closed to her eyes. It was soon determined that a restored Harriet Hall should accompany Noyes and Mary to the Community. As Noyes put it, "I . . . felt an omnipotent will going forth from my heart that she should go home with me; which she did."[38]

Harriet's cure encouraged the Community to expect equally dramatic victories over disease, and they were not shy in broadcasting Noyes's "miracle" to the rest of Putney. In August a resident of the town, Mr. Knight, asked the Community if they would help his daughter Mary, who was apparently suffering from an advanced case of tuberculosis. With her father's approval, she was eventually moved into one of the Perfectionist's houses, where several of the Community's leading members undertook to cure Mary. In the meanwhile Noyes and his wife had departed for central New York in order to attend some Perfectionist conventions.

Mary Knight shortly became the focal point of contention between the Community and the village of Putney. As her health fluctuated from one day to the next, the Community tried to isolate her from her relatives and all other outsiders. The war against unbelief was waged, Mary Cragin taking a leading role. She told Mary Knight bluntly that while the rest of the village had been resigned to her death, the Perfectionists had faith in Christ and life and that it was up to her to choose between the two worlds. Naturally, she chose the latter, and when visitors were permitted to see her, Mary openly testified that she was well.

But not all was well either with Mary or the townspeople. Dr. John Campbell, once a warm supporter of Noyes and his Perfectionism, was enraged when he learned of the methods used to cure Mary. He angrily denounced them for going too far too fast, claiming they had lost their senses and deriding their assertion that the Kingdom of God had come. A bitter argument with John Miller only served to harden Campbell's opposition to the Community. Mary Knight continued to weaken through the course of the dispute, and in September she died. As one Community member wrote to Harriet Noyes: "The final result was not as we anticipated"; clearly there was "some mystery" in the whole affair. His faith in Christ and Noyes was still unshaken, however. He knew that the Community would prevail over

38. All quoted material found in G. W. Noyes, ed., *J. H. N.—Putney Community,* pp. 240–47. Also see Home-Talk by J. H. N.—No. 135, "Sensible and Insensible Diseases," *Circular* 1 (24 October 1852): 203–04, where he talks about a faith in God enabling a person to control the disease within himself.

all, even though, as he admitted, in Putney the people's "rage is great" against them.[39]

Noyes luckily had no direct part in the failure of Mary Knight's faith cure. Nevertheless, he did have a few thoughts on its significance to the Community, which he expressed in a letter to John Miller. While Noyes believed that God had authorized them to attempt the faith cure, He had not given them permission to predict the final recovery. "Faith for present action is one thing," Noyes wrote, "and faith for prophesy is another." Noyes had neatly sidestepped any responsibility for Mary's death at the same time that he tried to uplift the fallen spirits of the Community and protect its integrity. Even though God had not given him the right to undertake Mary's cure, Noyes was willing to let others attempt it; perhaps God had given them more faith than He had shown Noyes. Failure indicated otherwise, but the Community had nothing to fear, said Noyes. "God has given us a lesson, and if we are good scholars the jeers of the world will not hurt us." There was plenty of time to carry on the work of the Lord; a single battle did not determine the whole war. God remained immutable and the Community's "partnership with him is not broken or weakened." The Putney Perfectionists would emerge victorious in the end; defeat and confusion would be the lot of their enemies.[40]

Noyes wrote that letter coolly and dispassionately from central New York; he was not on hand to feel the heat of Putney's anger. His enemies were unifying, and their unity presented a direct threat to the life of his Putney Community. For example, in 1847 the Community had successfully converted Helen and Emma Campbell and Lucinda Lamb, three young women from two of Putney's leading families. However, these conversions did not go unquestioned or unchallenged, as a reading of the few letters remaining testifies. In one, John Miller tried to assure Mrs. Campbell that his feelings for her daughters were solely motivated by spiritual concerns. "If you or they supposed that I had any other motive," declared Miller, then "you have altogether undervalued my friendship."[41]

Things were quite a bit touchier with Lucinda Lamb's father, who had openly expressed his opposition to many of Noyes's theories and was planning to take his daughter out of the Community. Noyes hoped to prevent this, suggesting that his youngest brother George marry Lucinda. This, of course, said Harriet Skinner, "would be a perfect countercheck to the plans of the enemy, and place Lucinda

39. G. W. Noyes, ed., *J. H. N.—Putney Community,* pp. 267–69.
40. "Noyes to Miller," Ibid., p. 270.
41. "John R. Miller to Mrs. Achsah R. Campbell," Ibid., p. 227.

independent of her parents under John's instruction." The plan failed, but Noyes did get off a final parting shot at Mr. Lamb. In a lengthy letter to him Noyes insisted that he did not actively seek Lucinda but that she had been thrust upon him by the Lord. As a result it was Noyes's duty to accept her, and in so doing he would more fully define their relationship.

As her natural parent, Mr. Lamb was "the father of her body," but God was her spiritual father. While Mr. Lamb may have had the legal right to take his daughter away, God possessed "the absolute right and irresistible power" to control her spirit and "fix her heart on the Kingdom and followers of his Son." Christ himself predicted that there would be a collision between these two claims of ownership, and, as one close to the Son and the Father, Noyes would do all that he lawfully could to maintain God's claim against Mr. Lamb's. As God's representative on earth it was Noyes's duty to persuade Lucinda to renounce her father's world for that of God's, as it was embodied in the Putney Community. Noyes finished the letter by warning Mr. Lamb that his efforts to take Lucinda would only succeed in alienating her even further from him and his wife. The best solution to the problem, thought Noyes, was to have all three join the Community where they would find "a religion that has power to heal divisions and bind hearts together for eternity."[42] The Lambs never took Noyes up on his offer; on the contrary, by the summer of 1847, opposition to Noyes and his followers was rapidly swelling.

Given the faith cure of Harriet Hall, the ill-fated end of Mary Knight, and the practices of male continence and complex marriage, it is not difficult to see why Noyes's theories and practices had threatened Putney's morality. In particular, however, the question of autonomy was a volatile one in the nineteenth century, and Noyes was open to charges that the Svengalian control he imposed upon his followers, and which he exhibited in his mind cures, made mental slaves out of his believers. Moreover, in this period of physiological truth, the mind and body were not seen as separate; it was axiomatic that the mind, or thought, could control the appetites. If this were true, then Noyes's mental control over others carried undertones of sexual control and manipulation. This was not lost upon the village of Putney, where Noyes's fight over Lucinda and his mind cure of Harriet involved the daughter of one man and the wife of another.[43] In a fundamental way,

42. "Harriet H. Skinner to George Cragin," Ibid., p. 231; "Noyes to Mr. Lamb," Ibid., pp. 231–234.
43. All mental curists ran the risk of being charged with a Svengalian control and influence. Parker, *Mind Cure in New England,* pp. 9, 42, 53–54, 92, 131–32, 136, 149.

therefore, Father Noyes and his Putney family presented a formidable challenge to the traditional family and, by extension, to the village of Putney as a whole. Noyes was openly willing to turn daughter against parents as with Lucinda, while there was always the danger of turning wife against husband as with Harriet Hall. All of these fears converged and erupted when word of Noyes's new sexual morality—male continence and complex marriage—was spread throughout the town. In the fall of 1847, Noyes was arrested and later indicted by the county court for adultery.

Shortly after Noyes's arrest, his sister Harriet wrote their mother explaining the situation in Putney. "If you look this way now-a-days," she said, "you may conceive of us as walking unbounded, unharmed in the midst of a fiery furnace," because Christ was still with them.[44] Noyes, however, did not get by unscorched. At one point he reported that his mind was reeling in a chaos with no hope forthcoming from any direction. It seemed that no matter how strong his faith in God, Satan "in the shape of law and brutality" would prevail.[45] Yet the continued support of his followers and the generally favorable attitude of his sister, Mary Mead, helped Noyes sustain his confidence and belief in himself.[46] Nevertheless, the storm around him did not lift, and with the possibility of mob violence in Putney, Noyes fled in November, leaving the other Community members to fend for themselves.

Despite this turn of events Noyes continued to believe in the essential correctness of his beliefs; nor, except for a few trying moments, did his followers lose faith in him. Unlike the Mormon leader Joseph Smith, Noyes did not meet an untimely end at the hands of an angry mob; God had spared him. United in belief, it was not hard to rationalize the fate of the Putney Community, which appeared more and more "like one of God's sagacious military maneuvers, which will blind and deceive the enemy." This, after all, was precisely what Putney Perfectionists expected from their God; every attempt the enemy made to harm and oppress them was "completely over-ruled" by God's efforts to improve them.[47]

From New York, Noyes sent back words of encouragement to Putney. Men had the right to be ruled by God and live under the rules of this new morality. Women, furthermore, had the right to "dispose of their sexual nature" by "attraction instead of by law and routine," and to have children only when they wished to. Everyone had the

44. "Harriet H. Skinner to Her Mother," G. W. Noyes, ed., *J. H. N.—Putney Community*, p. 282.
45. Ibid, p. 293.
46. Ibid., pp. 292–300.
47. "George Cragin to Mrs. Harriet A. Noyes," Ibid., p. 306.

right, he added, to seek his happiness in the purity of association. These were certainly the most cherished of all human rights and a life was well-spent in fighting for them.[48] Their position, Noyes reminded his followers, was approved spiritually by the fact that God stood with them. Believers were secured intellectually by their theories of sexual rights and relations, and physically by good health and faith healings, which promised them an ultimate victory over death. They had forsaken the old morality, Noyes concluded, but he still felt sure that the glory of God and heaven was one day to be theirs.[49]

48. Parker, *Yankee Saint,* p. 142.
49. Ibid.

8 *Noyes:*

The Democratic Theocrat

We have seen all the anxieties and wishes which prompted Noyes's turn to Perfectionism, his solutions to the tensions besetting the family and sexual relationships, and his concerns about health. Such wishes and anxieties were also embedded in his outlook on current political institutions and the individual's relationship to political authority.

Noyes wrote in the summer of 1835 that the old American morality had collapsed. Everything, it seemed, was running headlong into catastrophe. The once-cherished values no longer bound people with sufficient force. To all appearances the present generation was vigorously "shaking the pillars of the temples their fathers built" and "the spirit of insubordination was taking over."[1]

Religious Perfectionism was one contingent response to this sense of unrest, and its emphasis upon millennial expectations and appeals to the individual conscience to extirpate all sin, had a profound effect upon society and its institutions. William Goodell, a well-known abolitionist, explained as well as anyone what the social and individual consequences of millennial Christianity would be. According to him the conversion of the world would come to involve the complete "moral renovation" of social institutions "as well as of the individuals of whom society is composed." When the world was converted to Christ and governed by His principles, sin would be destroyed and replaced by brotherly love and truth. "The character of Christ will become," Goodell predicted, "the character of individuals, of communities, of states, and of nations."[2]

1. *Perfectionist* 2 (31 August 1835): 3.
2. Goodell quoted in Perry, *Radical Abolitionism*, p. 46.

As John L. Thomas tells us, with its demands for "total commitment and immediate reform," Perfectionism radically changed the diverse reform movements. It split the American Peace Society into warring factions and led to the creation of the New England Non-Resistance Society in 1838. Additionally, it disrupted and helped to fragment the temperance movement, and most profoundly contributed to the rise of immediate abolition.[3] Just how closely connected religious Perfectionism, abolition, and non-resistance were can be observed in the later career of Noyes's quondam friend, James Boyle. In 1837 Boyle had written William Lloyd Garrison, arguing that all institutions that impeded the arrival of Christ's kingdom had to be done away with. In the next two years Boyle grew close to Garrison, became an antislavery agent in Ohio, and wrote lengthy letters on perfectionism, which were published in the *Liberator* and the *Non-Resistant*, the journal of the newly-formed society.[4]

This orientation to Perfectionism, abolition, and non-resistance also involved—as it had with Noyes—a strong sense of the need for self-control and autonomy. We can observe this in the rhetoric of many abolitionists and non-resistants, and while it is true that no one or two figures represent the whole of either movement, the words of Garrison seem to capture the emotional flavor and spirit which many others were experiencing.

Garrison had come to appreciate fully the doctrines of Perfectionism, and as 1837 came to a close, he poured out his ideas in the *Liberator*. Garrison had concentrated in the past upon the plight of the Southern slaves; now, however, he was concerned with a universal emancipation "from the dominion of man, from the thraldom of self, from the government of brute force, from the bondage of sin." All men should be brought "under the dominion of God, the control of an inward spirit, the government of the law of love, and into obedience and liberty, of Christ."[5]

Garrison, in addition to conquering physical and emotional slavery, dedicated himself to the cause of "PEACE," a word that had a special connotation. Out of his millennial expectations, Garrison surmised

3. John L. Thomas, "Romantic Reform in America, 1815–1865," *New Perspectives on the American Past,* ed. Stanley N. Katz and Stanley I. Kutler (Boston, 1969), 1: 471.

4. Perry, *Radical Abolitionism,* pp. 65, 72; Cross, *Burned-Over District,* pp. 189–90.

5. From the *Liberator,* 15 December 1837, quoted in Fredrickson, ed., *Garrison,* p. 48. Some years later still, Garrison wrote that, "Some speak of anarchy in connection with non-resistance. But this principle teaches those who receive it to be just, and upright, and kind, and true, in all the relations of life. It is the men of violence who furnish anarchists." Garrison quoted in Perry, *Radical Abolitionism,* p. 53.

that the time was not far off when the kingdom of God would supplant all earthly forms of government. As he confidently predicted, the Lord's kingdom "shall never be destroyed, but it shall 'BREAK INTO PIECES AND CONSUME ALL OTHERS'." Brotherly love and righteousness would govern this kingdom, not mental and physical coercion. Its laws would not be written down on some mere scrap of paper but "upon the hearts of its subjects—they are not conceived in the wisdom of man, but framed by the spirit of God: its weapons are not carnal, but spiritual." Under such circumstances it was incumbent upon the true Christian to separate himself immediately from corrupt political authority and confront wicked government with spiritual weapons.[6]

The mid-1830s, then, were pivotal years in the development of immediate abolition and the creation of the non-resistance movement, cutting across equally important years in Noyes's personal life. Noyes suffered various blows to his Perfectionist self-image in those years; the Battle-Axe Letter, it will be remembered, was one response to those blows. The fear of passivity, the feared loss of autonomy and control, which those experiences represented, spread to strong feelings of alienation from existing institutions. His need to respond helped clarify his thoughts on the corruptness of existing political authority.[7]

Not long after he had written his explosive Battle-Axe Letter to David Harrison in January 1837, Noyes stood before a small gathering of Perfectionist believers in Putney and announced his "Declaration of '76."[8] Noyes declared at once his independence from a government drunk with tyrannic power and brutally insensitive to the plight of Negroes and Indians. In late March, Noyes decided to go to Boston in order to present his radical ideas to the celebrated Garrison. Noyes saw Garrison there alone, in his office, and he did not waste any time launching into a harangue against the government, denouncing it as totally immoral, controlled by the slave power, "the instrument of every kind of villainy and oppression," and wholly antagonistic to peace and spiritual brotherhood. He left Garrison with the reminder that the time was ripe for a revolt of the North from "the unholy

6. Fredrickson, ed., *Garrison,* p. 49.

7. Anxiety associated with feelings of separation and loss may come to include such abstractions as an attachment to institutions, liberty, an ideal, and so forth. See, David Peretz, "Development, Object Relations, and Loss," in *Loss and Grief: Psychological Management in Medical Practice,* ed. by Bernard Schoenberg, *et al.* (New York, 1970), pp. 5–8; Erna Furman, *A Child's Parent Dies: Studies in Childhood Bereavement* (New Haven and London, 1974), pp. 34–40; Rochlin, *Griefs and Discontents,* p. 39; Weinstein and Platt, *Psychoanalytic Sociology,* p. 102.

8. "Perfectionism not Pro-Slavery," *Perfectionist* 3 (1 October 1843): 61.

compact," not simply in the interest of the abolition of slavery but of the entire regeneration of society.[9] Some few days after this personal interview Noyes sent Garrison a long letter elaborating upon these beliefs.[10]

Noyes declared to Garrison that he was renouncing his allegience to the government of the United States, and was forthrightly claiming all authority for Jesus Christ. This "wild deed" was motivated by a government that, in Noyes's view, had been changed into a "bloated, swaggering libertine"—in losing control over itself, it had run amok not only over the rights of its citizens but over the Bible as well. Noyes had asked himself the question that many others were asking at the same time: what would be his relationship, as a Christian, to the political embodiment of the Antichrist? He concluded that he must either withdraw from everyone and everything or find some way to live without being hypocritical or sharing in the nation's sins.

To renounce active cooperation with an aggressive and wicked government was one thing; but, as Noyes acknowledged, to put an end to that government was another. All efforts to reform it appeared to be useless, not only because it was corrupt to the core, but also because remonstrance and civil agitation had proved, to borrow a modern term, counterproductive. The only alternatives Noyes saw open to him in the spring of 1837 was either to remain in a state of conscience slavery within the system or to "commence war" upon it by a declaration of independence and "other weapons suitable to the character and son of God."

The signs of the times, Noyes explained to Garrison, clearly pointed to the millennium. America was ripe for a revolution similar to that which shook France, minus, however, the infidelity that marked that catastrophic event. Because Noyes was sure that the Bible would accomplish this deed in the United States, in the end Christ, rather than an atheistic Napoleon, would rule the world. The coming social and religious convulsion would resemble the resurrection; it would not

9. Parker, *Yankee Saint,* pp. 48–49. The influence of Noyes upon Garrison's thinking has been vastly overrated by historians. See Russel B. Nye, *William Lloyd Garrison and the Humanitarian Reformers* (Boston and Toronto, 1955), p. 105; John L. Thomas, *The Liberator, William Lloyd Garrison: A Biography* (Boston and Toronto, 1963), pp. 227–35; Wyatt-Brown, *Lewis Tappan,* pp. 186–87. Recently, James Brewer Stewart, "Peaceful Hopes and Violent Experiences: The Evolution of Reforming and Radical Abolitionism, 1831–1837," *Civil War History* 17 (1971): 293–309, correctly minimizes Noyes's influence.

10. This letter may be found in Wendell Phillips Garrison and Frances Jackson Garrison, *William Lloyd Garrison, 1805–1879, The Story of His Life Told by His Children* (New York, 1885), 2: 145–48. This letter was taken from the *American Socialist* article printed on 12 June 1879. For an earlier version of the letter, which was dated 22 March 1837, see "Perfectionism Not Pro-Slavery," p. 61; Parker, *Yankee Saint,* pp. 49–51.

be "the struggle of death, but the travail of childbirth"—the birth of a new world. And Noyes left little doubt where he stood in terms of this rebirth of innocence. The conservative benevolent societies, such as those led by Lyman Beecher, would raise the religious consciousness of the people and control social disorder within the conventional morality and the existing institutional framework.[11] Noyes would not: "My hope of the millennium begins," he cried, "where Dr. Beecher's expires—viz., AT THE OVERTHROW OF THIS NATION."

Noyes cautioned Garrison, in conclusion, that abolitionism ran the risk of suffering the same fate as colonization unless it were made subservient to the "UNIVERSAL EMANCIPATION FROM SIN." Since Garrison was the most reknowned abolitionist, he had the duty to persuade others to join the cause of holiness. Men less imbued with the spirit of Christ might abondon Garrison, but he would be left as Jonah had been left by the whale: "the world, in vomiting you up, will heave you upon the dry land."[12]

During the spring and summer of 1837, Noyes continued to reach out to other reformers for both an expression and affirmation of his views. He struck up a correspondence with Gerrit Smith, the abolitionist, and even suggested that they might join hands in fighting slavery. This idea went for nought, although Noyes was encouraged by Smith's statement that his wife had long favored some of the ideas of Perfectionism. In April, Noyes wrote to Finney on the subject of salvation from sin. Finney replied that from all he had heard, Noyes was on the right track, though he had carried some of his ideas too far. Finney was apparently too busy to engage in a regular correspondence with anyone; but he assured Noyes that he would be interested in talking to him. Finally, he told Noyes that he had no fear of any doctrine of holiness since he had been preaching such ideas for years.[13]

This was all the encouragement Noyes needed; within a short span of time he was at Finney's doorstep in New York. Their meeting was short but amicable, and certainly stood in naked contrast to his pre-

---

11. On Beecher see J. Earl Thompson, Jr., "Lyman Beecher's Long Road to Conservative Abolitionism," *Church History* 42 (1973): 89–109. On conservative reform, see W. David Lewis, "The Reformer as Conservative: Protestant Counter-Subversion in the Early Republic," in *The Development of an American Culture*, ed. by Stanley Coben and Lorman Ratner (Englewood Cliffs, N.J., 1970), pp. 64–91; Clifford S. Griffen, *Their Brothers' Keepers: Moral Stewardship in the United States, 1800–1850* (New Brunswick, N.J., 1960); Charles I. Foster, *An Errand of Mercy: The Evangelical United Front, 1790–1837* (Chapel Hill, N.C., 1960).

12. All quotes from Garrison and Garrison, *William Lloyd Garrison*, 2: 145–48.

13. Letter of Finney to Noyes, dated 3 April 1837, reprinted in G. W. Noyes, ed., *Religious Experience*, pp. 333–35.

vious experience in 1834, when Noyes was not even permitted to see Finney. After Noyes left, he felt animated by the hope of gaining for himself and his doctrines "that public confidence without which testimony is powerless."[14] Noyes was riding high. From Garrison, Smith, and Finney he had received the impression that Perfectionism was beginning to exert a powerful influence upon all reform movements and upon the public imagination.

Noyes kept a sharp watch subsequently on political developments, shrewdly noting that an "elevation and refinement of the popular ideal of a ruler" had given rise to the demand that an elected leader possess the highest ideals and principles. Anyone who gave any serious thought to this matter, Noyes thought, would naturally aspire "to a very high standard; so high, indeed, as to be beyond the reach of merely human attainment." It was evident to Noyes that only one person could satisfy this high ideal: Christ.[15]

As the political turmoil over slavery increased during the 1830s and 1840s, Noyes's sympathies lay clearly with those political groups and parties acting to delimit or extirpate "the peculiar institution," praising the efforts of the Liberty Party in the 1840s, for example. In the national elections throughout the decades of the 1840s and 1850s, he denounced both major political parties and nominated Jesus Christ as President of the World.[16] He warmly applauded, in the 1850s, William Seward's higher law doctrine as presaging the coming of a new Christian morality.[17] Noyes enthusiastically joined the verbal battles over the divisive Kansas-Nebraska Act of 1854. While the North was hardly innocent in the matter, he assigned most of the blame to the decadent South. Noyes answered that the North was simply not yet

14. Ibid., p. 335.
15. "The National Want," *Circular* 5 (4 September 1856): 130.
16. For Noyes's support of the Liberty Party see "Protestant Abolition," *Perfectionist* 3 (15 November 1843): 73. For his nomination of Christ for the Presidency, which abolitionists such as Garrison were doing, see "Presidential," *Circular* 1 (11 August 1852): 158; "The Theocratic Nomination," Ibid. 1 (4 July 1852): 134. For readings on the pervasiveness of millennial thought in America, see Ernest Lee Tuveson, *Redeemer Nation: The Idea of America's Millennial Role* (Chicago, 1970); Ira V. Brown, "Watchers of the Second Coming: The Millenarian Scholarship in America," *Mississippi Valley Historical Review* 39 (December 1952): 441–48; David E. Smith, "Millenarian Scholarship in America," *American Quarterly* 17 (1965): 533–49; J. F. MacLear, "The Republic and the Millennium," in *The Religion of the Republic* (Philadelphia, 1971), pp. 183–216.
17. "Christ's Policy," *Circular* 1 (21 December 1851): 25. Noyes praised the higher law doctrine because he felt it would lead to his ideal of a theocratic republicanism. Also see "Seward and Calhoun," *Free Church Circular* 3 (13 April 1850): 88. On Seward, see Major L. Wilson, "The Repressible Conflict: Seward's Concept of Progress and the Free-Soil Movement," *Journal of Southern History* 38 (1971): 533–56.

spiritually pure and innocent enough to rebuke the South.[18] In 1857 he assailed the wicked government for its complicity in the infamous Dred Scott decision.[19]

From his highly moral stand on these issues one might have expected Noyes to be in the ranks, if not the forefront, of an activist, radical movement. The Bible-toting John Brown could not have agreed more with Noyes's statement that the Lord's book "instead of being on the side of old institutions," was "on the side of radicalism."[20] But where Brown, Garrison, and a host of other abolitionists could translate their radical vision into a call for action, Noyes could not.[21] For one thing, he had to maintain the boundaries of his Putney and Oneida Communities, and he could hardly have done so had he permitted his followers to become emotionally involved in "external" issues.

For another reason, any abolitionist had to expect retaliatory abuse, verbal and physical, for his moral and political assaults. Noyes, however, could not risk attacking authority directly, because he was too fearful of the kind of punishment abolitionists had to endure. Instead of direct confrontation, therefore, Noyes advocated a personal, moral reform that would gradually lead to the social, curative one.[22] His great objection to all the multifarious schemes of reform was that they concentrated solely upon bettering social institutions instead of destroying "the morbid life within men that craves excitement."[23] For men to reform society they first had to unite themselves with Christ, and from this inner bond an external perfection would emerge.[24]

As the rhetoric became more vitriolic and the action more violent during the antebellum years, Noyes began to shy away from the implications of his earlier radical statements. Although his new morality,

18. "The Supremacy of the South," *Circular* 3 (27 May 1854): 298.

19. "Slavery Nationalized," *Circular* 4 (19 March 1857): 34. On the election of 1856 between Fremont and Buchanan, Noyes wrote that he was content to let the machinery of government continue creaking and groaning until it collapsed. "The Elections," *Circular* 5 (14 August 1856): 118.

20. "The Bible as a Banner of Reform," *Circular* 2 (15 January 1853): 69.

21. In the fall of 1839 Noyes was backing away from the radicalism of his Declaration of '76 and his letter to Garrison. He now suggested that civil governments were ordained by God for "good and important purposes" in the present state of mankind. While they existed they should be respected and submitted to, but yet one should not regard them as made for the righteous but rather for the lawless and disobedient. For the righteous, the civil government was like a straight jacket for an insane man. "Correspondence with Torrey," *Witness* 1 (25 September 1839): 76.

22. "The Primary Reform," *Perfectionist and Theocratic Watchman* 4 (28 December 1844): 77.

23. "How to Overcome Evil," *Circular* 4 (31 May 1855): 73; "Infidelity Among Reformers," *Circular* 2 (22 December 1852): 45.

24. For example, see Home-Talk by J. H. N.—No. 6, "What is Truth?" *Spiritual Magazine* 1 (15 August 1847): 97–98; Home-Talk by J. H. N.—No. 200, "Godly Spontaneity," *Circular* 2 (11 May 1853): 203.

justified by the teachings of Paul and Christ, had radical if not anarchial implications, Noyes would not draw the logical conclusions. He wrote at length to persuade his critics that the gulf between the "letter-law and spirit-law" was not as great as it seemed; in fact, Paul's doctrine contained numerous safeguards against "antinomianism which the liberty maniacs know nothing about."[25]

In his own defense Noyes asserted that there were two kinds of antinomianism. One in fact did confer a freedom from the civil law. In order to control the personal sense of fragmentation and anxiety that would result from such freedom, however, Noyes claimed that a new morality based on the spirit-law could be just as rigorous in its moral demands as the old civil law had been. "The idea of the law's coming to an end," he wrote, "is frightful only when disjointed from that which Paul constantly connects with it, namely consequent righteousness."[26] Anyone who forsook both the spiritual and civil laws entered into a state of moral degradation that eventually led to decay and death.[27]

By the mid-1850s, Noyes was arguing that Christ and Paul were thoroughly conservative men of peace who sought not violence and destruction, but progress through spiritual change.[28] Within his morality, however, the definition of conservatism took on a special meaning, which seemed to belie his fears of confrontation and conflict. In Noyes's view, to be a conservative in reference to the traditions and customs that claimed the Bible as their justification was to be evil and false, because such traditions were "human and diabolical productions" that only obscured the word of God. True conservatism, in contrast, sought to create "the *principal* good, even at the expense of destroying inferior interests"; the person who sought to preserve the pristine morality of the Bible, even though in so doing he "subverts the Church" and other institutions, was a true conservative.

To Noyes, the problem with the current batch of reformers could be found in their arguments with "the representatives of existing institutions," where they unwittingly allowed themselves to be placed

---

25. G. W. Noyes, ed., *Religious Experience,* p. 369. For further examples of the conservative nature of Paul see J. H. Noyes, *The Berean,* pp. 188–99, 201–17; "Paul's Views of Law—No. 1," *Witness* 1 (22 January 1840): 98–99; "Paul's Views of Law—No. 2," Ibid. 1 (7 February 1840): 113–14.

26. "Two Kinds of Antinomianism," *Perfectionist and Theocratic Watchman* 5 (28 June 1845): 30. Also see J. H. Noyes, "Anti-Legality not Antinomianism," *The Berean,* pp. 218–22. For a discussion of the anxieties involved (and courses of action possible) when it is perceived that a given morality is no longer binding, see Platt and Weinstein, "Alienation and the Problem of Social Action"; in *The Phenomenon of Sociology,* ed. by Edward A. Tiryakian (New York, 1971), pp. 284–310.

27. G. W. Noyes, ed., *Religious Experience,* p. 30.

28. "Who Are True Conservatives?," *Circular* 5 (1 May 1856): 57.

in an "anticonservative" position. The established leaders had a strong grip on moral legitimacy, and it was easy for them to stand before the people as "the acknowledged conservators of order, government, good breeding, stability." As long as they occupied positions of authority, Noyes reasoned, they could not be overthrown—no matter how "glaring may be their errors and corruptions," no matter "how skillfully those errors and corruptions may be exposed." Consequently, it was necessary for reformers to take stock of the spiritual battle in which they were engaged, adopt the older, higher morality of the Bible, and "prove themselves more conservative than their adversaries, or they will labor in vain."[29]

Noyes's continuing fears that violence might lead to social and personal chaos played an important role in his changing view of Garrison in particular and abolitionism in general. He lamented the fact that abolitionism had usurped center stage among the various reform movements, because as the other movements receded into the background, abolitionism became "separate from, and independent of religion, exalting it into rivalry with, and hostility to, the system of the Bible."[30] The violence surrounding Garrison and his colleagues was reprehensible. While Garrison's motives and objectives may have at one time been praiseworthy, his actions had been "unchristian and even anti-christian" ever since the collapse of the American Anti-Slavery Society in the early 1840s.[31] In the words of Lewis Tappan, Garrison and his followers had sunk low "in the moral thermometer," and Bronson Alcott condemned Garrison as the "most intolerant of men."[32] Noyes added to this clamor by censuring Garrison for surrounding himself with a "clique of Anti-Bible men, semi-infidels, and Jacobinal organizers," who were attempting to "subvert the present institutions of society without introducing better to fill their places."[33]

In the mid-1840s, Noyes's disfavor included the come-outers, whose desire for personal liberation led them to renounce institutional attachments. He had few kind words for Nathaniel Peabody Rogers; and Stephen S. Foster, Perfectionist and abolitionist, was scolded for his "church-rapes," which were "truly deeds of physical violence and

29. "Conservatism," *Circular* 2 (4 December 1852): 21.
30. "Fourierism," *Circular* 2 (22 December 1852): 41.
31. "Anti-Slavery," *Perfectionist and Theocratic Watchman* 5 (12 July 1845): 34; "Protestant Abolitionism," p. 73. Noyes was not alone in this view of Garrison and his wing of the abolitionist movement. See Stanley M. Elkins, *Slavery: A Problem in American Institutional and Intellectual Life* (Chicago and London, 1964), p. 183; Allan Nevins, *Ordeal of the Union: Fruits of Manifest Destiny, 1847–1852* (New York and London, 1947), 1: 146.
32. Wyatt-Brown, *Lewis Tappan*, p. 248. Shepard, ed., *Journals of Bronson Alcott*, p. 191, quoted in Perry, *Radical Abolitionism*, pp. 84–85.
33. "Blind Zeal," *Perfectionist* 3 (1 January 1844): 87–88.

illegality; as brickbat-mobbing, or fighting with fire-arms."[34] The right way to effect reform, thought Noyes, was to turn to the spiritual truth of the Bible and, with it as a guide, progress "from tradition and forms" into the teaching of God and Christian life. The wrong way was to "burst out" into the "external void" without spiritual guidance. The come-outers employed this method as they "fled from the religion of the churches into infidelity, or semi-infidel schemes of liberty under the mask of reform."[35] A terrifying outgrowth of this anti-Christian radicalism was John Brown's raid. Where Emerson and Thoreau extolled it as the quintessential act of a transcendental individual, Noyes decried the violence and again urged that men must be raised to the level of Christ and God before social change was to have any meaning.[36]

In the decade or so prior to the Civil War, Noyes found much to fight against, but to engage in violence and rebellion threatened to undermine all his efforts at self-control. Noyes resolved this contradiction by turning to a familiar solution: he chose passive resistance, a safe middle ground wherein passivity, by religious commitment independent of any political base, could be translated into a form of activity. Noyes was opposed to combativeness no matter what form it took, be it social or inner emotional turmoil or lengthy quarrels with someone else. In whatever shape combativeness might reveal itself, it threatened to impair the health of the individual. Some reformers, upon occasion, might march under God's banner to fight evil, and flail away in all directions until they conquered it. But a close inspection of their motives would reveal "that such manifestations of strength" really derived from selfish, egoistic sources; they were "of a legal nature—opposed to the natural and easy method of gospel growth." The moment any kind of quarreling began, life became stunted in selfish concerns instead of blossoming in spiritual unity.[37]

34. "The Worst Enemies of Reform," *Perfectionist* 3 (15 October 1843): 68. For information on Rogers and Foster see, Perry, *Radical Abolitionism*, pp. 117–28, 162–63, 182, 185–86, 205. In addition, on Foster see "The Perfectionist Radical: Stephen Symonds Foster," in Jane H. Pease and William H. Pease, *Bound With Them in Chains: A Biographical History of the Anti-slavery Movement* (Westport, Conn., 1972), pp. 191–217; on Rogers see Robert Adams, "Nathaniel Peabody Rogers: 1794–1846," *New England Quarterly* 20 (1947): 365–76.

35. "Right and Wrong Come-out-ism," *Perfectionist and Theocratic Watchman* 4 (1 June 1844): 23.

36. *Circular* 8 (17 November 1852): 170. Also see Gilman M. Ostrander, "Emerson, Thoreau, and John Brown," *Mississippi Valley Historical Review* 39 (1953): 713–26; John J. McDonald, "Emerson and John Brown," *New England Quarterly* 44 (1971): 377–96. After Brown suffered a martyr's death, Noyes, like so many other Northerners, changed his opinion of him.

37. "Strength Wasted in Combativeness," *Circular* 5 (18 September 1856): 234.

Faced with social injustice, a person thus might choose to fight, or he might suppress his conscience "and settle down into gouging and being gouged." Noyes had no liking for either of these alternatives. His answer to this dilemma was, rather, "to retire from the jurisdiction of the state." But even this path could not be taken in a "high-minded, combative state, nor in a sensual state; but only in a spirit of meekness like that of Christ."[38] When Christ withdrew from the world, He still kept up communication with it, acting upon it through this disciples. In other words, it was not necessary either to fight or submit, "you can *die*; and the advantage of being dead, is that you are neither quarreling or submitting," but as death was to Christ, you were "retiring to another city," which was His chosen method.[39]

Unlike Garrison and his followers, Noyes thought it was senseless to arouse and antagonize people. It actually required more courage, he believed, "to be quiet, and blow peace in the face of an enemy, than to fight him."[40] This kind of passive action Noyes considered to be a "higher grade of manliness."[41] In the end, the uplifting salvation for both the individual and his society would come not through violence, but through what Noyes called "baiting." To him the act of saving man was analogous to fishing, in that both required patience and correct action. A leader, that is, must sacrifice himself, offer himself as "bait" by dangling in the water on a hook, waiting for the larger fish to bite. The person who strove to emulate Christ and Paul must have "the patience, heroism, nonresistance and endurance" necessary to save others from their follies.[42]

Noyes's solution to the dilemma of social injustice and political power through non-resistance was formulated in the security of Putney and Oneida, which made it all the easier for him. But his solution also had its roots in the broader resolution of authority conflicts that he had established in his religious conversions. Noyes was quick to note that the Bible had "a feminine side, but it is also, and even predominately, masculine," with "meekness, humility, and patience" being married to "vigor, justice, and warlike energy."[43] In word if not act, therefore, Noyes could agree with Maria W. Chapman who argued that passive non-resistance may be one thing, but active non-resist-

38. "Philosophy of Non-Resistance, No. 3," *Free Church Circular* 4 (20 June 1851): 234.
39. Ibid., pp. 234, 237, 238.
40. "Philosophy of Non-Resistance," Ibid. 4 (20 May 1851): 206.
41. Ibid.
42. "Philosophy of Non-Resistance, No. 2," Ibid. 4 (6 June 1851): 220.
43. "Our Beligerent Principles," *Perfectionist and Theocratic Watchman* 5 (22 March 1845): 3.

ance was another. "We mean to *apply* our principles," she reported to a meeting of the New England Non-Resistance Society. "We mean to be bold for God. Action!—Action—thus shall we overcome the violent. Not by their own weapons—but it behooves us to preach." Chapman then went on to say that no one could dictate to her where, how, or when she should speak, because she would do it as her reason and conscience told her.[44] Noyes, of course, was unwilling and emotionally unable to bear the public consequences of such action; but, in his Communities he could have the best of both worlds. In these nurturing environments, separate from yet close to the mainstream of society, activity could be encouraged without fear of public rebuke.

Noyes's theories of non-resistance placed him, then, somewhat between the right and left wings of the non-resistance movement. Along with Adin Ballou, the founder of the Hopedale Community, Noyes strongly emphasized the Christian basis of non-resistance, while the more radical Garrison and Henry Clarke Wright later attempted to free non-resistance beliefs from "a stifling dependence on Biblical authority."[45] When one combined peaceful principles with the "anticipations of ultimate and legitimate vengeance," declared Noyes, the result was not to eradicate from the mind all "the natural sentiments of anger against wrong doing, and desire of retribution," but to bring them under control and direct them to God. Man must turn his feelings from "the lawlessness of individual violence" and channel them into the "governmental authority" of the Lord. To suffer injury and abuse as a passive non-resister was an act of courage and unflinching confidence in the supremacy and justice of God's government, as well as one's own self-control. The purpose of Biblical non-resistance, then, was not to snuff out "the salutary energy of destructiveness," but to control those feelings until one could justify their expression in a war ordained by God.[46]

Noyes's rather inflexible position aided him in avoiding a major obstacle that stymied most non-resistant pacifists; that is, how could God's seeming approval of the wars conducted by the Jews in the

---

44. Perry, *Radical Abolitionism*, p. 247. "Our Political Position," *Perfectionist* 3 (1 January 1844): 87, states that "the son in protesting and refusing obedience, appeals from the government of the father, to the government of God, and necessarily assumes the independent right of judging for himself whether the command of the father comes in competition with God."
45. Peter Brock, *Radical Pacifists in Antebellum America* (Princeton, N.J. 1968), pp. 142–43. On Ballou see Perry, *Radical Abolitionism*, pp. 130–57. Also see Lewis Perry, "Versions of Anarchism in the Anti-Slavery Movement," *American Quarterly* (1968): 768–82.
46. "Our Belligerent Principles," pp. 3–4; "Bible Principles of Peace and War," *Circular* 1 n.s. (29 August 1864): 185–86; "The North and the South— The End of the War," Ibid. 1 n.s. (18 July 1864): 137–38.

Old Testament, and their draconian penal code, be justified in light of Christ's prohibition of all kinds of violence in the New Testament? Ballou provided the conservative answer that the new dispensation superseded all others in questions of truth and human duty. Garrison and Wright argued more radically that all such ideas and arguments should be discarded in favor of the view that the Jewish prophets were just as bloodthirsty as the current military and political leaders.[47]

If Christ's teachings were incompatible with the actions of the Jewish patriarchs, Noyes did not recognize it. He included both in his ideas for attaining a peaceful world order. The war that Moses and Joshua made upon Canaan was justified and seen as consistent with the peaceful principles of the New Testament. The legitimacy of that war, it was stated in the *Circular*, stood upon the same ground that sanctioned the war that "God will make on the wicked at the final judgment."[48] Wars would end, said Noyes, not through peace congresses, not through the efforts of the Quakers, and not through the labors of peace societies and non-resisters, as long as their efforts were directed primarily at exposing the "horrors of war and immorality of using carnal weapons." For Noyes and his followers there was no sharp moral distinction between carnal and spiritual weapons. The right to use any weapon to inflict injury and death could only be derived from God. "War can only be justified . . . by the direct authority and inspiration of God. War without this is no better than a private, murderous brawl." Furthermore, the distinction between an offensive and defensive war was a specious one to Noyes. God had a right "to make either and men have as good a right to serve him in one as in the other."[49] As the *Circular* bluntly put it during the course of the Civil War, there was such a thing as a just war even though they at Oneida did not wish to participate in it. "We have no such clearly defined scruple of conscience about War, as the Shakers and Peace Reformers have; but we certainly think that our best function is not fighting."[50]

Although Noyes was careful to keep his Oneida Community out of the war, for the most part he supported the cause of the North in word and spirit if not body and arms. The basis of his support lay in his belief of the North's spiritual supremacy. Noyes was convinced in any event that the "New England life has been the home of progressive spirituality," starting with the Puritans and continuing all the way

47. Brock, *Radical Pacifists*, pp. 145–46.
48. "Bible Principles of Peace and War," pp. 185–86.
49. J. H. Noyes, "Peace Principles," *The Berean*, pp. 446–51; "Peace and War," *Perfectionist* 3 (15 January 1844): 89.
50. "About the War," *Circular* 1 n.s. (February, 1864), p. 7.

through the present revivals.[51] It was this submission to God that allowed the North to become "the medium of the Spirit of Christ and the representative of his kingdom."[52]

Noyes further derived from this spiritual superiority an intriguing analysis of the overriding causes of the war. He saw the war as essentially a struggle between two separate cultures: the North, masculine, aggressive, and competitive; the South, feminine, passive and dependent. Noyes believed that the nation, like everything else, had a dual nature; it was both male and female—"man and wife, Uncle Sam and Aunt Sam." The North was the man of the family having yielded its heart "to another and higher husband." The North had a passive, receptive "female attitude toward Christ," which ultimately gave it the power to assume a "male attitude toward the South."[53] The conflict arose from the South's attempt to control the North, in effect, an attempt to subvert the divine order of male-female relationships.[54]

The terms, of course, are familiar: Noyes's resolution of the problem of autonomy played a significant role not only in the formation of his Communities but also in his perceptions of American democracy. During the nineteenth century the concepts of democracy, republicanism, and protestantism became inextricably linked and thought of as one.[55] From their many shared attributes, one component commands our attention here: an emphasis upon individual initiative and autonomy. No one was more sensitive to this than Noyes, who decried the fact that America bred men to be independent. According to Noyes,

51. "Basis of Northern Supremacy," *Circular* 1 n.s. (6 June 1864): pp. 89–91.

52. Ibid., p. 90. Although Noyes favored the North, he did not do so blindly. He criticized it for not living up to its spiritual superiority, for giving in to the fighting spirit instead of conquering the South through the spirit of Christ, and for the fact that it was controlled by the money-spirit. "Means of Conquest —Why the North Has Failed," *Circular* 1 n.s. (25 July 1864): 145–46; "When Shall We Have Peace," Ibid. 1 n.s. (23 August 1864): 177; "The North and the South—The End of War," p. 138.

53. "Means of Conquest—Why the North Has Failed," p. 145; "The Duality of the American People," *Circular* 1 n.s. (30 May 1864): 81; "Uncle Sam's Quarrel," Ibid. 1 n.s. (2 May 1864): 51.

54. "The Duality of the American People," pp. 81–82; "Uncle Sam's Family Quarrel," pp. 65–66. "Is it not to the fact," Noyes asked somewhat incredulously, that the North-South conflict emanated from the "discord and anarchy in the social relations of the men and women who form the nation?" "National Troubles and Their Source," *Circular* 1 n.s. (5 September 1864): 193–94.

55. On this point see Timothy L. Smith, "Protestant Schooling and American Nationality, 1800–1850," *Journal of American History* 53 (1967): 679–95; Edson, *Guardians of Tradition*. As de Tocqueville pointed out: "The Americans combine the notions of Christianity and of liberty so intimately in their minds that it is impossible to make them conceive the one without the other"; quoted in George E. Probst, ed., *The Happy Republic: A Reader in Tocqueville's America* (New York, 1962), p. 222. For a similar statement by Chevalier, see Probst, p. 241.

people in America defended republicanism and thought that they should enjoy "individual liberty," but they were wrong. Man, he said, was simply never intended to govern himself, and when man arrogated this responsibility, he was denying God.[56]

Nor was Noyes alone in this opinion. In emphasizing the failures of nineteenth-century democracy, James G. Birney, the abolitionist, felt that no greater delusion was ever "hatched from any cockatrice's egg, than what is commonly boasted of as the *Democratic* principle. . . . We must insist upon the control of Wisdom. The wisest and strongest we must seek out and welcome to their proper places, that is, we must turn to God and Jesus."[57] Beriah Green, who had been the first president of the American Anti-Slavery Society, insisted that in its "origin and authority" the presently constituted civil government was the workmanship of God and thereby "must be a reflection of his throne." Anything short of that could "no wise, for no purpose be a Government."[58] Noyes thought so too, and he turned his back on democracy because it had "no value whatsoever as a permanent institution," the individualism it fostered was "inevitably a weak, sickly, unruly and degraded position."[59] To continue to live under the current form of democracy, thought Noyes, was to expose one self to "social and political dissolution." Democracy, that is to say, shared some common attributes with death: both contained loss and disorganization. In each a spirit of selfishness separated men from God and the "body from the soul," with the result that "the body decays and crumbles to dust." Death and democracy were thus "the consummation of the disorganizing principle."[60]

Unable to implement the demands for autonomy within himself and unable to tolerate the tension arising from his ambivalent feelings regarding autonomy and passivity, Noyes demanded an inner and outer world of simple unity and perfection, a realm devoid of complexity and ambiguity. What had to be done, he said, was "to organize—condense; *begin* with organizing our ideas and spiritual nature; then our social relations." The results of this consummate organization would be "perfect unity and perfect life."[61] To realize these ends,

56. "Human Governments; Civil and Ecclesiastical—No. 1," *Perfectionist* 2 (17 October 1835): 13. Also see Home-Talk by J. H. N.—No. 24, "Becoming as Little Children," *Spiritual Magazine* 2 (22 December 1849): 337–43; "Communism," *Circular* 1 (1 February 1852): 50.
57. Birney quoted in Perry, *Radical Abolitionism*, p. 172.
58. Green quoted in Ibid., p. 171.
59. Home-Talk—No. 23, "Universal Dependence," *Spiritual Magazine* 2 (1 December 1849): 324–26.
60. "Union With Christ," *Spiritual Magazine* 2 (18 September 1849): 248; Home-Talk—No. 11, "Thoughts on Liberty," Ibid. 2 (11 August 1849): 213.
61. "Thoughts on Liberty," p. 213.

Noyes felt that independence and liberty had to be separated from each other; true freedom for him was only possible in that ideal world where wills merged and became one. Noyes argued often and at great length that to become "possessed by another's will in such complete oneness as to make us act obediently without any double consciousness" was the greatest glory and highest form of liberty. Surely, it was far better to be under the benign rule of God, thought Noyes, than to be on one's own in a world of discordant democracy.

By placing his will under God, a person might in a sense be dependent and submissive, said Noyes. Unlike sons who were jealous of their father's authority, however, those who submitted to God would be freed from all such degraded feelings and would find happiness in renouncing their independence for the security of harmonious organization.[62] Noyes further suggested that this emotional subjugation and apparent passivity allowed a person to be active and assertive in life. Indeed, in his solution to this active-passive dilemma, Noyes fully realized that there was "a Revolution wrapped up in the ideas presented here, greater than the French or American Revolution. The greatest revolution the world has ever seen will grow out of these ideas."[63] Unfortunately, the legally constituted governments of the world, whether they be democratic or despotic, had fallen far short of the necessary submission and obedience to God.

Noyes thought it imperative, then, that a new socio-political order be created, which would embody a new morality. In this new order justice and compassion would be united, and so Noyes envisoned that the church, instead of being an adjunct to the state, was "to BE the State; and this Church-State was to be the only government over the whole world."[64] Further, Noyes concluded that not only was the earliest government of man a theocracy, but so too would be the final one during the millennium. In the long interim the one government that commanded praise was the New England Puritan's. Even though part of Noyes identified with Anne Hutchinson's "religion of the heart," which posed a threat to the standing order, his strongest sympathies lay with the stern yet benign theocracy of the Puritan fathers.[65]

In Noyes's scheme of things the "purely Theocratic" aspect of the

---

62. "What is Death?", *Spiritual Magazine* 1 (15 July 1846): 69. On this point also see "Thoughts on Liberty," p. 215.
63. "Becoming As Little Children," p. 339. Also see "Our Ultimate Object," *Perfectionist* 3 (1 April 1843): 15.
64. "The Unity of the Kingdom of God," *Perfectionist and Theocratic Watchman* 4 (13 July 1844): 33.
65. "The Trial of Mrs. Hutchinson," *Witness* 1 (3 January 1840): 84; "Remarks on the Trial of Mrs. Hutchinson," Ibid. 1 (22 February 1840): 131.

government would be "spiritual and didactic, rather than legislative." This element would indeed suffuse the whole spirit of the people and in this manner indirectly influence the course of legislation. In a "mature Theocracy" the voice of the people would be expressed "by a vote in some form, as freely as if the government were merely human."

In effect what Noyes wished to do was combine the ideas of democracy and theocracy. He saw no contradiction in this, for as he said in his grandiose way, "Extremes meet in every thing that is perfect."[66] On the one occasion when Noyes actually proposed an alternative to the current system, he demanded that the corrupt national legislature, which distorted the will of the people, be discarded. In its place he urged the creation of a periodical paper as the sole medium through which laws were to be proposed, discussed, and enacted.

Noyes then suggested that the whole people could in this way be convened into a permanent legislative assembly. Every citizen would have the right to propose and debate bills, with all points-of-view being printed in the paper for each and every citizen to contemplate before voting. The responsibility for the stability and continuity of this system of government rested with the sagacious, disinterested leadership of the paper's publisher, who would be an elected official. In the leader's God-inspired guidance, and the eager participation of every citizen, Noyes saw the best of all possible worlds—"a theocratic democracy." Under this system "the will of all" would be expressed, and everyone would be "infused with the spirit of Christ."[67]

In sum, demands for personal autonomy to be expressed in the competitive marketplace were not permissible. True freedom rested in spiritual conversion; people devoted to God's will as expressed through Noyes would feel no envy, no greed, no malice. Thus, in this perfect world, beyond separation, there was no contradiction between authority and freedom. Secure in this unchallenged perfection, it was axiomatic to him that "solidarity and liberty are at harmony with each other."[68]

Beginning with "a bare nucleus of ecclesiastical order" in Putney, Noyes attempted to secure the "full *liberty*" of each individual. One article in the Society of Inquiry's constitution declared that all acts of

66. "A New Form of Government," *Perfectionist and Theocratic Watchman* 4 (15 June 1844): 26.
67. Ibid. On the nature of the *gemeinschaft* as the personality of united natural wills see Ferdinand Tonnies, *Community & Society*, trans. and ed. Charles P. Loomis (New York, 1963), pp. 103–70 and passim.
68. Home-Talk by J. H. N.—No. 75, "The Liberty of Union," *Circular* 1 (4 January 1852): 36.

the Society depended upon the unanimous votes of the members present. Ideally, the Society was not permitted to "domineer over the will or conscience of one of its members," and thus a majority was not able to vote away the rights of the minority members as was done in regular society.[69] There would be no tyranny of the majority in Putney!

Noyes stated many years later that he meant the Community to be "a thoroughly regulated family," where all the members would be as one and where truth would "reign in all the affections." Moreover, it would be a family without any "independent, reckless spirits," and each member would gladly "stand below a wiser in his or her place, and love to submit to those who are above."[70] But as Noyes was to discover, it was not an easy task to keep his small group of followers on a unified spiritual track. In 1842 he had had to expel two Community members who married without his approval.[71] Threatened by this insubordination, Noyes realized that faithful obedience had to flow from within or all order and stability would be lost. To make sure that this did not occur, Noyes wrote a long paper extolling the virtues of theocracy. Under this governmental system the authority of God and Christ was transmitted to Their representative on earth, who, naturally, was Noyes. Correspondingly, Noyes delegated authority to his disciples, who in his name conducted the daily affairs of the Community. After this paper was read to the Community, the members unanimously affirmed Noyes's divine authority and their own need to obey him.[72]

To protect the integrity of the Community by assuring its conformity to his morality, Noyes introduced the system of mutual criticism, first at Putney and later at Oneida. Under this system of communal control, which underwent various technical changes over the years, an individual's thoughts, feelings and actions were dissected before a committee or even before the whole Community.[73] Criticisms usually stressed a member's bad traits (those thoughts or acts that detracted from family unity), and an individual could be put through a shameful, humiliating experience. Noyes was the only person not subjected to the repeated agony of exposure and censure. As he explained, it was not natural for "a family to criticize their leader," and on those few occasions when it did occur, it "was always kind of a farce." It would be natural for his followers to criticize him when Christ or Paul or any member of the Primitive Church returned to

69. "The Putney Corporation," *Circular* 3 n.s. (27 August 1866): 191.
70. "Home, Sweet Home," *Circular* 5 n.s. (19 October 1868): 241.
71. G. W. Noyes, ed., *J. H. N.—Putney Community*, pp. 51–52.
72. Ibid., pp. 53–54
73. "Free Criticism," *Circular* 1 n.s. (4 April 1864): 17–18.

earth, as they surely would do. Then the members of the Community could tell them what they thought of him, and Noyes promised that at that time "I will drop my officiality and offer myself to criticism."[74]

This mutual criticism, which replaced any written codes or laws, was consistent with Noyes's need for strict obedience to his authority. And, arising as it did from his special brand of religious morality, the *Circular* did not hesitate to suggest that society at large might benefit from this system of control. On all institutional levels—home, school, or politics—mutual criticism could be used to "inculcate respect for authority."[75] Moreover, the system contained within itself all that was ideal in other forms of government. It was theocratic in that "Truth was King," and the system recognized God as the source of truth. It was the Father's spirit alone that gave true criticism its power. Then, too, it was aristocratic since those who were closest to God would be the best critics and have the most power. Finally, it was democratic because it was open to all, and each could rise spiritually within it.[76]

In fact, mutual criticism was cohesive because it was cathartic. The experience bound people emotionally as it elevated them. As one person wrote:

> Every trait of my character that I took any pride or comfort in seemed to be cruelly discounted and after, as it were, turned inside out and thoroughly inspected, I was metaphorically, stood on my head, and allowed to drain till all the self-righteousness had dripped out of me. John H. Noyes wound up the criticism, and said many kind things. I don't know what they were. Perhaps it was only his personal magnetism or the magnetism of the spirit he represented. But there was not a word or a thought of retort left in me. I felt like pouring out my soul in tears, but there was too much pride left in me yet to make an exhibition of myself. The work had only begun.[77]

74. "Community Politics," *Circular* 2 (25 June 1853): 255.
75. "Society Needs Free Criticism," *Circular* 1 n.s. (20 February 1865): 385–86; "King Criticism," *Circular* 2 n.s. (8 May 1865): 57.
76. (Oneida Association), *Mutual Criticism*, p. 94. Noyes's first experiences with openly shared criticism were at Andover. For brief but clear accounts of how this system worked, see Parker, *Yankee Saint*, pp. 215–26; Carden, *Oneida*, pp. 71–77. The boundary-maintenance aspects of mutual criticism were noted by Stow Persons, "Christian Communitarianism in America," in Donald Drew Egbert and Stow Persons, eds., *Socialism and American Life* (Princeton, N.J. 1952), 1: 148; Fogarty, "Oneida: A Utopian Search for Religious Security," pp. 208–10.
77. The author of this quote, Allan Estlake, did not join the Community but remained sympathetic to it. After coming to terms with the mental anguish of this experience, Estlake felt it had improved his character and that "I would gladly give many years of my life if I could have just one more criticism from John H. Noyes." Estlake, *The Oneida Community: A Record of an Attempt to Carry out the Principles of Christian Unselfishness and Scientific Race-Improvement* (London, 1900), pp. 66–68.

Noyes of course had insight into these processes; in his time and in his way he could heal. Life, he used to say, was like a ball "wound up with the threads of our passing experience." All past thoughts and deeds, whether good or bad, were tightly wrapped in the recesses of the mind. There they lay, ours alone, constraining in an unseen way current thought and action. As Noyes aphoristically put it, "We live, what our past lives have been."[78] Mutual criticism, therefore, was to help unravel that ball, force the individual to face his anxieties, and with the aid of his friends become a more active, productive member of the Community.

Naturally, not everyone in his Putney group accepted the blunt criticisms or what they felt to be Noyes's increasing authoritarianism. During 1843 and 1844 nine adults, along with their children, left the Community, many because they could not bear Noyes's harsh criticisms. One man departed after Noyes reproved him "for light-mindedness and a worldly spirit," and another had been scolded for his "indolence, pride, and independence." A woman was criticized by the group for her "unkind and disrespectful treatment" of her husband.[79] At any rate, by 1845, through a process of sifting and winnowing, Noyes was molding a group of faithful disciples, who in the years ahead would be asked to accept his more adventurous theories of male continence and complex marriage.

One aspect of Noyes's contingent response was thus the repudiation of competitive autonomy through a community-based familial order. Such a response was attractive to some because it addressed itself to various fears and experiences. But, as noted, it could only work for Noyes if he retained control. The outside political world was too large for him to manipulate and control; so, Noyes preserved his image intact by not really challenging, by not risking the larger attack. He risked nothing by criticism, he muted society's ire by not organizing a political attack (while keeping faith with his own morality); he did not risk his self-esteem in any failed attack of a political nature. To the contrary, he enhanced esteem by keeping most of the members of his community in tow.

It should also be stressed that Noyes had no political solution except for some random people. There could have been no general appeal for his religio-familial basis of political authority. His refusal to challenge openly was not successful; because he would not go out for people, no significant body of people would turn to him either. More-

78. (Oneida Association), *Third Annual Report of the Oneida Association: Exhibiting Its Progress to February 20, 1851* (Oneida Reserve, N.Y., 1851), pp. 21–22.
79. G. W. Noyes, ed., *J. H. N.—Putney Community,* pp. 123–25.

over, his desire to establish a *"thoroughly regulated family"* was, in a sense, anachronistic. It was too late in that society for *gemeinschaft* solutions, to create a world where the personal and social ramifications are tied together. Noyes attempted this through his mutual criticism, but this was inapplicable to outsiders and the larger community. Finally, whereas Noyes's criticisms did confront and present alternatives to the existing political structure, the repressive arm of that structure did not strike back. Noyes, in fact, was pretty much ignored on this level. He had no authority in the wider arena and could not present an effective challenge. He was, however, attacked for the sexuality because he threatened the basis for political action in the wider community, and that no one liked.

Conclusion

From 1848 on, Oneida's struggle for survival, its successes and failures, occupies the center stage, while the daily actions and feelings of Noyes recede well into the background. The events at Oneida have been fully chronicled and bear no repeating here.[1] Historians have also fully explored Noyes's changing views, particularly on economic competition, as Oneida slowly adapted itself to an industrial America during the 1850s to the 1870s.[2] What has not been fully appreciated, though, are the changes in Noyes's Perfectionist thought that provided the rationale for Oneida's accommodations to American society. Indeed, as one reads through the Community periodicals of the 1850–70 period, one can easily get the impression that Noyes's Perfectionism remained static. Reprints of his speeches and sermons from decades earlier fill the pages and seem to imply a stagnation of his thought. But a close reading of these periodicals indicates, I think, that Noyes's Perfectionism underwent subtle but important shifts.

While the early physical contours of the Oneida Community grew out of the spade work of his followers, the blue prints, which lent Oneida its uniqueness, emanated from Noyes's fertile mind as it responded to the rapid social change, and tried to master the implications of personal, competitive autonomy. Noyes, in seeking a solution that would prove both integrative for himself and others, had to make compromises with reality by seeking and creating a world where the

1. Fogarty, "Oneida: A Utopian Search for Religious Security," pp. 202–27; Carden, *Oneida*; May Louise Sobel, "An Experiment in Perfectionism: The Religious Life of the Putney and Oneida Communities" (Ph.D. diss., Boston University, 1968).
2. Fogarty, "Oneida: A Utopian Search for Religious Security"; Robert S. Fogarty, "The Oneida Community, 1848–1880: A Study in Conservative Christian Utopianism" (Ph.D. diss., University of Denver, 1968).

standards and expectations of the day had no place, unless ideally they were wrapped in a world of diminished conflict, greater unity, and Perfectionist ideals. Such a solution may in part express Noyes's personal, inner strivings, but one must remember that another part of him was responding to real problems, which is why people were able to recognize his authority. He was, through his vision of utopia, promising consolations (inner and outer harmony) on the basis of real experiences of loss, not solely or even predominantly in terms of neurotic fantasies and certainly not in terms of fantasy alone.

As other Americans attempted to cope with the profound changes, the ever-increasing complexity of society, and the tensions within their own homes, it was proudly noted that Oneida combined in one organization "the various functions of Education, Religion, Industry, and Domestic Life." The outside world, in contrast, separated the church from the school, the school from the place of business, and the family was isolated from them all. At Oneida these various institutions were "consolidated and interlocked . . . within the limits of that one best locality, HOME."[3] Noyes, in other words, shared with numerous other utopians the belief that the Community was the family writ large. Charles Lane, of the Fruitlands experiment, asserted in the *Dial* that "the question of Association and of marriage are one." If, as it was commonly believed, "the individual or separate family" was the true order of God, then communal life was necessarily a false one. But, if the "Associative Life" was the true one, then it followed that the monogamous family was a false arrangement.[4] Noyes agreed, but for him there was no real question which was the true and which was the false order. "The object and end of association in all its forms," he wrote in his *History of American Socialisms*, "is to gather men, women, and children into larger and more permanent HOMES than those established by marriage."[5]

Once this home, Oneida, had been firmly established, Noyes at last succeeded in providing himself with a measure of emotional security that he briefly enjoyed in his Putney Community. And he had company in rediscovering a sense of stability. Many other Americans, who had undergone experiences of alienation and inflated hopes of perfecting institutions during the 1830s and 1840s, rechanneled their expectations in the next decade into the preservation of the Union, its institutions, and a Protestant morality.[6] Perfectionism, by the 1850s,

3. *Handbook of the Oneida Community, with a Sketch of its Founder and an Outline of its Constitution and Doctrine* (Wallingford, Conn., 1867), p. 17.
4. Charles Lane, "Brook Farm," *Dial* 4 (1844): 355–56.
5. John Humphrey Noyes, *History of American Socialisms* (New York, 1961), p. 292.
6. John Higham, *From Boundlessness to Consolidation: The Transformation of American Culture, 1848–1860* (Ann Arbor, 1969).

was significantly modified within the established churches. Suffering was no longer regarded as a prerequisite for salvation, and men were encouraged to employ their Perfectionism for the benefits of society. One writer in the *Guide to Holiness* urged that Perfectionist aspirations be used to establish asylums for the poor, hospitals for the ill, "and retreats for the various classes of the forlorn and distressed among mankind."[7] On other fronts the transcendental communion with Nature was dissolving. Spiritual lessons were to be learned elsewhere, and as many transcendentalists emerged from the woods, they found a sense of purpose and direction in the cause of the North and the Civil War.[8] In light of all this, it is probably correct to view the period of the 1850s and the Civil War as a time of catharsis and purgation of the national character. But this period also marked for many a psychic readjustment on all levels of personality, wherein ideals were lowered to "realistic expectations."[9]

Significantly for Noyes and his Oneida Community, his newly found inner strength eventually led to modifications in his thought and behavior. Within the confines of his Brooklyn home and at Oneida, Noyes gradually felt less threatened by outside critics and foes.[10] Feeling secure, Noyes declared in 1853 that during the Second

7. N. Bangs, "Christian Perfection," *Guide to Holiness* 24 (February 1853): 38. Also, First Purified, Then Free," Ibid. 35 (January 1859): 37; Peters, *Christian Perfection,* pp. 133–80.

8. Robert C. Albrecht, "The Theological Response of the Transcendentalists to the Civil War," *New England Quarterly* 38 (1965): 21–34; George F. Fredrickson, *The Inner Civil War: Northern Intellectuals and the Crisis of the Union,* Harper Torchbooks (New Haven and Evanston, 1965); Leo Stoller, *After Walden: Thoreau's Changing Views of Economic Man* (Stanford, Cal., 1957).

9. There is a growing body of literature on continued growth and change (beyond adolescence) and the concomitant changes within the systems id, ego, and superego. See, Burton N. Wixen, "Object-Specific Superego Responses," *J. Am. Psa. Assn.* 18 (1970): 835–37. Joseph Sandler, "On the Concept of the Superego," *Psa. St. Chi.* 15 (1960): 156–57, states that the superego is "only supported by the ego as long as it functions, in its turn, to support the ego; and situations do exist in which the ego and will totally disregard the standards and precepts of the superego, if it can gain a sufficient quantity of narcissistic support elsewhere." One sees "this impressive phenomenon in the striking changes in ideals, character, and morality which may result from the . . . feeling of identity with the group." If this narcissistic support is sufficient enough, and group ideals permit a gratification of wishes, then a character transformation can result. Also see Roy Schafer, *Aspects of Internalization* (New York, 1968), pp. 176–77; Rudolph M. Loewenstein, "On the Theory of the Superego: A Discussion," in *Psychoanalysis—A General Psychology,* p. 312.

10. Noyes easily brushed aside an attack on him and his policies in the early 1850s by Hubbard Eastman, *Noyesism Unveiled: A History of the Sect of Self-Styled Perfectionists; with a Summary View of Their Leading Doctrines* (Battleboro, Vt., 1849). During its existence as a utopian community from 1848 to 1880 Noyes did not devote much time at Oneida. For a good deal of the time he was in New York or Wallingford. Although he was at Oneida for much of the period from 1854 to 1864, he left at the end of this time to live in New York City, where he stayed until 1868.

Coming death had been consumed and that the dispensation through suffering had also come to an end. Men were weak and passive, he said, as long as they felt suffering was necessary for spiritual improvment.[11] If there were any pain involved in attaining perfection, it would be brief and soon forgotten in the pleasures that a growth in Christ offered. Noyes realized that in his past experiences God had put him into "terrible circumstances" and great suffering, even to the point where he had barely been able to sustain himself, in order that he might accept Christ. Those days were over; God no longer was "compelled to treat me that way any more," he asserted. The merger with Christ was to be experienced as "a natural, healthy, happy growth"; prolonged and painful suffering was not conditional.[12] Thus, instead of becoming *like* the father (in the usual resolution of the oedipal conflict), Noyes *was* the Father at Oneida. There his world of perfection found support and legitimacy, which meant he no longer had to fear retaliation. On one level of his thought, therefore, Father Noyes became equal to the Father, and having achieved this plane, God became helpful and not punitive.

Other related aspects of Noyes's views on salvation also underwent subtle but important shifts. To assure oneself of salvation from sin, Noyes now argued that man must not wait passively for Christ and God, but must actively seek Them. While tension and anxiety hung over people and threatened to enclose them "like a net," Noyes assured his followers that God was above the net, able to protect man from being emotionally annihilated. Man's own strength, however, determined if he were able to reach God's hand. To illustrate this activism in salvation, which was certainly a contrast to his earlier experiences with conversion, Noyes adopted the words of Christ: "MINE OWN ARM BROUGHT SALVATION unto me."[13]

11. Home-Talk by J. H. N.—No. 179, "Grace Better Than Suffering," *Circular* 2 (9 March 1853): 131. Thus, while suffering had once been an ideal for Noyes, it no longer was highly prized, which demonstrates a growth in ego strength in relationship to the other psychic structures. That is, the ego appears to be no longer threatened by a powerful, punitive superego. As Wixen ("Object-Specific Superego Responses," p. 835) points out, changes in morality can sometimes be seen when a person becomes much loved by another (and we might add: finding acceptance, love, and stability in the external environment whether it be the security provided by a person, persons, or institutions). In these cases the superego is then not as necessary as before to provide love and well-being; and in the case of Noyes, hate and destruction. On changes within the ego ideal and its influence upon the superego, see Blos, "Genealogy of the Ego Ideal," p. 86; Schafer, "Ideals, Ego Ideal, and Ideal Self," p. 161.

12. "Grace Better Than Suffering," p. 132.

13. Home-Talk by J. H. N.—No. 139, "Salvation By Our Own Arm," *Circular* 2 (24 November 1852): 11. The reader is reminded to contrast Noyes's fears of the net (see p. 55) and loss of control during his New York experience with

Noyes also modified his beliefs on the nature of sin; no longer was it an either/or proposition to him. He agreed with "imperfectionists" that in the past as well as in the present there existed in the primitive church "a class properly called *believers* or *disciples* (not sons of God) who, though not free from sin," were devoted followers of Christ and were to be counted as members of His church.[41] In addition, where good and evil had formerly been rigidly separated by him, and where he once identified himself and his world with goodness and purity, Noyes now softened his views and accepted a world that was both good and evil. If a person wished to be content in life, said Noyes, he had to be "reconciled with the universe," which was "a combination of good and evil." It was senseless for anyone to wish things otherwise. "We must not long for a universe that is free from evil. It can not be. It is not so, and . . . God can not make it so."[15]

There were other indications that Noyes's Perfectionism was becoming toned down. Earlier, as we have seen, his relationship to the primitive church emphasized a highly idealized perfection, differing morality, and separation from all worldly institutions. By the mid-1850s, however, Noyes was claiming that the established churches were to be considered auxiliaries or extensions of the church in heaven. He said, in fact, that "the present church is to form a glorious temple which shall surround the Primitive Church."[16] And, as Noyes grew more comfortable in his acceptance of the world, so too did the relationship of his Oneida Community change. As one member recalled about the early years, the Community was an ideal for all others to emulate since it presented "a true outline of Heavenly institutions" and furnished "invaluable help to future builders" whenever the outside world was "advanced enough to tolerate them and their work." Oneida, indeed, was an "imperfect miniature of the kingdom of Heaven on earth."[17]

Such pronouncements as this were muted in the mid-1850s in favor of those with less Perfectionist zeal and more toleration of the world as it existed. It was impossible for any group of people to secrete them-

---

the control he demonstrates here. Further, this statement on sacrifice should be contrasted with his earlier one, wherein he sacrificed his right arm for the glory of God. Now Noyes was admitting that it was no longer necessary to endure great suffering (and possible castration) to become saved. It should also be pointed out that Noyes was writing from the security of Brooklyn, while Oneida was in its period of severe tensions. Thus, Noyes was writing to encourage his followers and to express his new positions.

14. *The Berean*, p. vii.

15. "God's Contentment," *Circular* 5 n.s. (20 July 1868): 137.

16. Home-Talk by J. H. N., "Thoughts Suggested by a Dream," *Circular* 4 (19 April 1855): 49; J. H. Noyes, *American Socialisms*, pp. 656–57.

17. Henry Seymour, *The Oneida Community: A Dialogue* (n.d.), p. 22.

selves from the rest of the world, said Noyes in the *Circular*. At Oneida, resurrection politics now dictated that they move out into society and, with certain restraints, "enjoy all the good things that God has made."[18] Noyes was but a single marcher in the vast nineteenth-century parade, and now the tune and tempo of the march had changed. "We are a long crowd marching up the avenue of improvement," declared Noyes in 1865. Those of lesser social vision must not attempt "to stop or trample" those who walked ahead, and likewise, those who led the march "must not despise or provoke those that are behind." All must move in a spirit of brotherhood, as an army of God headed for His kingdom. But the enlightened members of society who led the parade should not be in a hurry to march across "the bridge from things as they are to things as they ought to be," cautioned Noyes. Even though they be infused with the spirit of God, they were to shun fanaticism and the "prosleyting spirit." Change was to come not in "whirlwinds and thunders, but in the still small voice of good deeds." An unmitigated disaster would result if reformers attempted to rush people into the communal spirit and feeling before they had "deliberately traversed the previous stage of Perfectionism."[19]

In the early 1840s, as utopias were sprouting throughout the American countryside, Orestes Brownson observed that "the two rocks on which the Reformer is in danger of being wrecked, are Communism and Individualism." In his attempts to avoid colliding into the one, he runs the risk of striking the other, "for the passage between them is narrow and difficult."[20] In the 1840s and 1850s Noyes had skillfully negotiated that treacherous passage by means of his Perfectionism, offering a new morality based upon the compatability of communism and individualism. And Noyes stressed the point that this compatability was only possible by adhering to his kind of religion: an "earnest kind, which comes by recognized afflatus, and controls all external arrangements."[21] Devoted men of one religious faith were thus more likely to respect organized authority and each other than were men in regular society who had to contend with a variety of religious denominations and beliefs. Although Noyes understood that his kind of

18. "Largest View of Communism," *Circular* 3 n.s. (23 April 1866): 41; Home-Talk by J. H. N.—No. 70, "Asceticism Not Christianity," Ibid. 1 (23 November 1851): 11–12.

19. "Do You Think the World is Prepared for Communism?" *Circular* 2 n.s. (19 June 1865): 105. Also see "Prospectus," *Oneida Circular* 13 (9 March 1876): 73; "Why We Do Not Proselyte," Ibid. 12 (30 August 1875): 276; "What is Coming?" *Circular* 4 n.s. (25 November 1867): 291; "Decadence of Marriage," *Oneida Circular* 13 (3 February 1876): 36.

20. Brownson, "The Community System," p. 134; "Individuality in Association," *Harbinger* 1 (4 October 1845): 264–66.

21. J. H. Noyes, *American Socialisms*, p. 656.

religion might be "worthless" in the diverse and complex outer society, he knew that it was "the indispensable element of success in close Association."[22] But Noyes's own shifts in thought, and the toning down of his Perfectionism, in time helped to erode this kind of religion. By the 1870s religion was interpreted to mean "the rational apprehension of the existence of the spiritual world and the love of truth that will make us eager to explore that world and prompt to accept and act upon all discoveries in that world"; a definition which certainly contrasted with the ideal Perfectionism of the early years.[23]

While the gulf between Noyes and the outside world narrowed, it never closed completely; his last sociosexual experiment, "stirpiculture," certainly testifies to that.

By the 1860s, having imbibed the doctrines of Darwin and Galton, Noyes believed it was time to extend his millennial hopes of perfection beyond the first generation of Oneidians.[24] Aside from the general social and intellectual climate of the times, which encouraged the belief that a rational control of intercourse could lead to a perfection of the race, other immediate factors helped to form his decision to begin a genetics experiment.[25] By the late 1860s Oneida had become a prosperous community, and it alarmed Noyes to think that they might be straying from their religiosity. Then too, by the time Noyes implemented the experiment he was only a few years from his sixtieth birthday, which meant that he had to contend with separation and loss anxieties associated with the tasks of old age, and contemplate such meaningful issues as life and death, past and future.[26] What better way to preserve one's ideal of perfection and gain immortality than by creating perfect offspring.

In 1869, Noyes, secure in his role as Community Father, inaugurated his program of scientific propagation, which he named "stirpiculture."[27] As in the circumstances of the early biblical fathers, Noyes

22. Ibid.
23. "A New Definition of Religion," *American Socialist* 2 (18 January 1877): 20.
24. "Scientific Propagation," *Circular* 2 (27 March 1865): 10–11; "Stirpiculture," Ibid. (3 April 1865): 17. The connection between the millennium and scientific propagation was made in "The Hope of the Millennium," Ibid. 7 (23 May 1870): 73–74. Also see "A Millennial Discovery," Ibid. 3 (18 June 1866): 109, where he claims that male continence "opens the way for improvement of the race by scientific propagation."
25. Walters, ed., *Primers for Prudery,* pp. 147, 154–55.
26. Noon Discourses by J. H. N., No. XXVI, "Old Age A Species of Dementia," *Circular* 4 n.s. (26 August 1867): 185.
27. At this time Galton had not yet coined the term "eugenics." Noyes selected the term "stirpiculture" from the Latin "stirps," which meant "stock" or "root." When he combined "stirps" with "culture," the term signified "race-culture." "Stirpiculture, 2," *Circular* 2 n.s. (10 April 1865): 26.

considered a "mating of close relatives" necessary, but as the population grew and the blood remained pure, the mating of close relatives would not be as urgent as before. In the early stages though, he emphasized the need for a "breeding in and in," that is, "a mating between very near relatives, as there was in Adam's family."[28] If there was to be sexual and propagative suppression, declared Noyes, "it must not be by castration and confinement, as in the case of animals, or even by law and public opinion," since most men were morally bound, but by the free choice of those who obeyed a new and higher morality. As Noyes enthusiastically pointed out, once Christ had ascended to heaven, He "had the passions of an ordinary lover," and was morally free to do as He saw fit.[29]

Noyes was not advocating incest. He explained that by close relatives he meant the spiritual affinity that was to be found in all ascending fellowships, and that in order to produce perfect stock, mating should take place among these people. "Obedience and receptivity to inspiration," and not sexual pleasures, were the essential elements of stirpiculture.[30] In this "system of regulated promiscuity," as one might expect, Noyes's spiritual authority made it incumbent upon him to produce as many morally perfect children as possible.[31] He certainly was not derelict in his duty, fathering ten of the "stirpicults"; five boys, four girls, and a stillborn.[32]

As Anthony Comstock began to cast his long shadow over American morality, and the purity crusade gained momentum in the late 1860s and 1870s, Noyes's comments on sex and family life fell on reddened ears.[33] The country must be free to experiment with "all sorts of families, and not be confined to what may be called the one-horse

28. John Humphrey Noyes, *Essay on Scientific Propagation* (Oneida, N.Y., 1872), pp. 12, 16.
29. "Mary of Bethany. The Romance of the Cross," *Circular* 3 n.s. (24 September 1866): 217–19.
30. "Stirpiculture," p. 17. A suggestive article in this context is Martin D. Weich, Jr., "The Terms 'Mother' and 'Father' as a Defense Against Incest," *J. Am. Psa. Assn.* 16 (1968): 783–90.
31. Anita Newcomb McGee, "An Experiment in Human Stirpiculture," *American Anthropologist* (1891): 320. For further information see Hilda Herrick Noyes and George Wallingford Noyes, "The Oneida Community Experiment in Stirpiculture," *Eugenics, Genetics, and the Family,* Scientific Papers of the Second International Congress of Eugenics, 1921 (Baltimore, 1923), 1: 374–86; William M. Kephart, "Experimental Family Organization: A Historico-Cultural Report on the Oneida Community," *Journal of Marriage and Family Living* 25 (August, 1963): 261–71; Carden, *Oneida*, pp. 61–65.
32. For more information see Ely Van de Warker, "Gynecological Study of the Oneida Community," *American Journal of Obstetrics and Disease of Women and Children* 17 (1884): 755–810.
33. David J. Pivar, *Purity Crusade: Sexual Morality and Social Control, 1868–1900.* (Westport, Conn., 1973).

family," he asserted. Just as Americans had learned to accept the railroad as part of modernity, they should try to tolerate a variety of sexual and marital arrangements in order to discover "which combinations are best for producing family blessings." Members of the Oneida Community, practicing complex marriage and the selective breeding of the stirpiculture experiment, were in the vanguard of this experimentation and were "presenting the world with that liberty at our own cost—the liberty to think, try experiments, and discuss the great subject."[34]

Even though nineteenth-century America was becoming more pluralistic, it was not ready to listen to Noyes and was hardly willing to condone his theories. While the Mormons in Utah were feeling the wrath of Congress, Noyes and Oneida were also attacked, albeit on a more local level.[35] Their Comstock was Professor John W. Mears of Hamilton College, whose sermons and letters to newspapers stirred widespread opposition to Oneida.[36] He condemned the Community as an institution "avowedly at war with the foundation principles of our domestic and civil order, a set of men banded together for the purpose of practicing shameful immoralities." To make matters even worse, the leaders of the Community then enticed the younger and less-experienced members into their illicit practices. While the Mormons had been hounded out of Illinois for thier polygamy, Mears was disturbed to think that an equally outrageous Oneida "luxuriates at ease in the heart of New York State."[37]

So, once again Noyes and his Community were under attack. Certainly he had shown that he was no threat to established political power, and, as others have indicated, by the 1850s he was capable of making an accommodation on economic competition. As Mears's words clearly reveal, the attack came because of the threat to the incest barrier in Noyes's sexual theories and experiments. The sexual lines Noyes pursued threatened to undermine the repressions necessary for successful economic and political activity in the wider community. There were still these dependent longings to be guarded against, and thus Noyes was berated on the sexual level much more so than on other institutional levels where he operated and had an effect (or tried to).

34. "Our Contribution," *Circular* 5 n.s. (21 September 1868): 209.
35. Charles A. Cannon, "The Awesome Power of Sex: The Polemical Campaign Against Mormon Polygamy," *Pacific Historical Review* 43 (1974): 61–82.
36. On Mears and his activities against Oneida, see Constance Noyes Robertson, *Oneida Community: The Breakup, 1876–1881* (Syracuse, N.Y., 1972), pp. 76–90; Parker, *Yankee Saint,* pp. 268, 279, 281, 285.
37. Parker, *Yankee Saint,* p. 268.

The details of Oneida's breakup and Noyes's retreat to Niagara Falls do not concern us here, but what he attempted to accomplish does. He had tried to deal with the disruptive circumstances of a rapidly changing society through a unique vision of *gemeinschaft*, a community based on devotion, sentiment, obedience, and hierarchy. In short, Noyes tried to raise a religio-familial principle to a cultural and social level. But American enterprise had no tolerance for that kind of emotional network, as indeed his own community did not once it developed into a more complex, differentiated community. The American stress on the individual depended on the containment of precisely those emotional strivings that Noyes wished to exploit, that is, passivity, dependence, and familial lines of submission. Thus, Noyes, as a religious leader, could be tolerated but his thought could never serve as a model for the general population. Noyes, though, could recruit and surely did help various floundering souls who sought familial solutions. As his final isolation in Niagara Falls indicates, however, the idea of his community could not be carried politically or economically further than that. When he died in 1886, public sentiment and sweeping revivals had yet to legitimate complex marriage or any other of Noyes's religio-familial solutions to perplexing social change.

Bibliography

This bibliography does not pretend to list each source consulted in the preparation of this study. A more extensive list may be found in the notes to this book and in my doctoral dissertation, "The Development of a Utopian Mind: A Psychoanalytic Study of John Humphrey Noyes, 1828–1869" (Stony Brook, 1973).

NOYES AND ONEIDA

Unpublished Works

Fogarty, Robert S. "The Oneida Community, 1848–1880: A Study in Conservative Christian Utopianism." Ph.D. dissertation, University of Denver, 1968.

Oneida Family Register. MSS listing names and personal data on the first 111 people who joined Oneida. Historical collection, Mansion House Library, Kenwood, N.Y.

Sobel, May Louise. "An Experiment in Perfectionism: The Religious Life of the Putney and Oneida Communities." Ph.D. dissertation, Boston University, 1968.

Periodicals (listed by date of publication)

The Perfectionist. New Haven, Conn. Vols. 1–11. 1834–35.

The New Covenant Record. New Haven, Conn. Vol 2. 1835–36.

The Witness. Ithaca, N.Y., and Putney, Vt. Vols. 1–2. 1837–42.

The Spiritual Moralist. Putney, Vt. Vol. 1. 1842.

The Perfectionist. Putney, Vt. Vol. 3. 1843–44.

The Perfectionist and Theocratic Watchman. Putney, Vt. Vols. 4–5. 1844–46.

The Spiritual Magazine. Putney, Vt., and Oneida, N.Y. Vols. 1–2. 1846–50.

Free Church Circular. Oneida Reserve, N.Y. Vols. 3–4. 1850–51.

The Circular. Brooklyn and Oneida, N.Y., and Wallingford, Conn. Vols. 1–12. 1851–64; Vols. 1–7, New Series. 1864–70.

The Oneida Circular. Oneida, N.Y. Vols. 8–13. 1871–76.

Daily Journal. Oneida, N.Y. 1863.

Daily Journal of the Oneida Community. Oneida, N.Y. Vols. 1–3. 1866–67.

The O. C. Daily. Oneida, N.Y. Vols. 4–5. 1867–68.

The American Socialist. Oneida, N.Y. Vols. 1–4. 1876–79.

Community Books and Pamphlets

Barron, Alfred and Miller, George Noyes, eds. *Home-Talks by John Humphrey Noyes.* Vol. 1. Oneida, N.Y.: Oneida Community, 1875. Only Vol. 1 was published.

(Oneida Association). *Bible Communism: A Compilation of the Annual Reports and Other Publications of the Oneida Association and its Branches.* Brooklyn, N.Y.: Office of *The Circular*, 1853.

Cragin, George, ed. *Faith Facts; or a Confession of the Kingdom of God and the Age of Miracles.* Oneida Reserve, N.Y.: Leonard and Co., 1850.

(Oneida Association). *First Annual Report of the Oneida Association.* Oneida Reserve, N.Y.: Leonard and Co., 1849.

Handbook of the Oneida Community, with a Sketch of its Founder and an Outline of its Constitution and Doctrines. Wallingford, Conn.: Office of *The Circular*, 1867.

Handbook of the Oneida Community: Containing a Brief Sketch of its Present Condition, Internal Economy and Leading Principles. No. 2. Oneida, N.Y.: Oneida Community, 1871.

Handbook of the Oneida Community, 1875. Oneida, N.Y.: Office of the *Oneida Circular*, 1875.

(Oneida Association), *Mutual Criticism.* Oneida, N.Y.: Office of *The American Socialist*, 1876.

Noyes, George Wallingford, ed. *John Humphrey Noyes: The Putney Community.* Oneida, N.Y.: By the Author, 1931.

———, ed. *Religious Experience of John Humphrey Noyes, Founder of the Oneida Community.* New York: MacMillan Co., 1923.

Noyes, John Humphrey. *The Berean: A Manual for the Help of Those who Seek the Faith of the Primitive Church.* Putney, Vt.: Office of the *Spiritual Magazine*, 1847.

———. *Confessions of John H. Noyes. Part I: Confession of Religious*

Experience: Including a History of Modern Perfectionism. Oneida Reserve, New York: Leonard and Co., 1849. Part II was never published.

_____. *Dixon and His Copyists: A Criticism of the Accounts of the Oneida Community in "New America." "Spiritual Wives" and Kindred Publications.* Wallingford, Conn.: Oneida Community, 1872.

_____. *The Doctrine of Salvation from Sin, Explained and Defended.* Putney, Vt.: By the Author, 1843.

_____. *Essay on Scientific Propagation.* Oneida, N.Y.: Oneida Community, 1872.

_____. *Male Continence.* Oneida, N.Y.: Office of the *Oneida Circular*, 1872.

_____. *Male Continence; or Self-Control in Sexual Intercourse.* Oneida, N.Y.: Office of *The Circular*, n.d.

_____. *Salvation from Sin: The End of Christian Faith.* Wallingford, Conn.: Oneida Community, 1866.

_____. *"The Way of Holiness." A Series of Papers Formerly Published in the Perfectionist, at New Haven.* Putney, Vt.: J. H. Noyes and Co., 1838.

Noyes, Theodore R. *Report on the Health of Children in the Oneida Community.* Oneida, N.Y., 1878.

(Oneida Association). *The Oneida Community: A Familiar Exposition of its Ideas and Practical Life.* Wallingford, Conn.: Office of *The Circular*, 1865.

_____. *Second Annual Report of the Oneida Association: Exhibiting its Progress to February 20, 1850.* Oneida Reserve, N.Y.: Leonard and Co., 1850.

_____. *Third Annual Report of the Oneida Association: Exhibiting Its Progress to February 20, 1851.* Oneida Reserve, N.Y.: Leonard and Co., 1851.

Secondary Sources

Achorn, Erik. "Mary Cragin: Perfectionist Saint." *New England Quarterly* 28 (1955): 490–518.

Bernstein, Leonard. "The Ideas of John Humphrey Noyes, Perfectionist." *American Quarterly* 5 (1953): 157–65.

Carden, Maren Lockwood. *Oneida: Utopian Community to Modern Corporation.* Baltimore: Johns Hopkins Press, 1969.

Eastman, Hubbard. *Noyesism Unveiled: A History of the Sect of Self-Styled Perfectionists; with a Summary View of Their Leading Doctrines.* Battleboro, Vt.: By the Author, 1849.

Edmonds, Walter D. *The First Hundred Years: 1848–1948.* Oneida, N.Y.: Oneida Ltd., 1948.

Ellis, Havelock. *Sex in Relation to Society. Vol. VI: Studies in the Psychology of Sex.* Philadelphia: F. A. Davis Co., 1911.

Ellis, John B. *Free Love and Its Votaries; or American Socialism Unmasked.* New York: United States Publishing Company; San Francisco: A. L. Bancroft and Co., 1870.

Estlake, Allan. *The Oneida Community: A Record of an Attempt to Carry out the Principles of Christian Unselfishness and Scientific Race-Improvement.* London: George Redway, 1900.

Fogarty, Robert S. "Oneida: A Utopian Search For Religious Security." *Labor History* 14 (1973): 202–27.

Hinds, William Alfred. *American Communities.* Oneida, New York: Office of the *American Socialist*, 1878.

Kephart, William M. "Experimental Family Organization: An Historico-Cultural Report on the Oneida Community." *Journal of Marriage and Family Living* 25 (1963): 261–71.

Lockwood, Maren. "The Experimental Utopia in America." In *Utopias and Utopian Thought*, edited by Frank E. Manuel, pp. 183–98. Boston: Beacon Press, 1966.

McGee, Anita Newcomb. "An Experiment in Stirpiculture." *American Anthropologist* 4 (1891): 319–25.

Noyes, Corinna Ackley. *The Days of My Youth.* Kenwood, N.Y.: By the Author, 1960.

Noyes, Hilda Herrick and Noyes, George Wallingford. "The Oneida Community Experiment in Stirpiculture." In *Eugenics, Genetics, and the Family.* Vol. 1, pp. 374–86. Scientific Papers of the Second International Congress of Eugenics, 1921. Baltimore: William and Wilkins Co., 1923.

Parker, Robert Allerton. *A Yankee Saint: John Humphrey Noyes and the Oneida Community.* New York: G. P. Putnam's Sons, 1935.

Robertson, Constance Noyes. *Oneida Community: The Breakup, 1876–1881.* Syracuse, N.Y.: Syracuse Univ. Press, 1972.

Sandeen, Ernest R. "John Humphrey Noyes as the New Adam." *Church History* 40 (1971): 82–90.

Sibley, Mulford Q. "Oneida's Challenge to American Culture." In *Studies in American Culture*, edited by Joseph J. Kwiat and Mary C. Turpie, pp. 41–62. Minneapolis: Univ. of Minnesota Press, 1959.

Van de Warker, Ely. "Gynecological Study of the Oneida Community." *American Journal of Obstetrics and Diseases of Women and Children* 17 (1884): 755–810.

Worden, Harriet M. *Old Mansion Memories.* Oneida, N.Y., 1950.

SOURCES RELATING TO THE NINETEENTH CENTURY

Unpublished Works

Gaddis, Merrill Elmer. "Christian Perfection in America." Ph.D. dissertation, Chicago University, 1954.
Jeffrey, Kirk. "The Middle-Class American Family in the Urban Context, 1830–1870." Ph.D. dissertation, Stanford University, 1972.
Nissenbaum, Stephen Willner. "Careful Love: Sylvester Graham and the Emergence of Victorian Sexual Theory in America, 1830–1840." Ph.D. dissertation, University of Wisconsin, 1968.
Ryan, Mary P. "American Society and the Cult of Domesticity, 1830–1860." Ph.D. dissertation, University of California, Santa Barbara, 1971.

Periodicals

The American Ladies' Magazine. Boston. 9 vols. 1828–36.
American National Preacher. New York. 31 vols. 1826–57.
Boston Quarterly Review. Boston. 5 vols. 1838–42.
Consecrated Life and Guide to Holiness. Boston, New York, and Philadelphia. Vols. 1–47. 1839–65.
Democratic Review. Washington and New York. Vols. 1–29. 1837–51.
The Dial. Boston. 4 vols. 1840–44.
Godey's Lady's Book. Philadelphia. Vols. 1–23. 1830–41.
The Harbinger. Boston. 8 vols. 1845–49.
The Knickerbocker. New York. Vols. 1–65, vol. 66, nos. 1–4.
Massachusetts Quarterly Review. Boston. 3 vols. 1847–50.
Whig Review. New York. 16 vols. 1845–62.

Contemporary Books and Pamphlets

Abbott, Jacob. *Gentle Measures in the Management and Training of the Young.* New York and London: Harper and Brothers, 1871.
_____. *The Rollo Code of Morals; or, The Rules and Duties for Children.* Boston: Crocker and Brewster, 1841.
Abbott, John S. C. *The Child at Home, or the Principles of Filial Duty.* New York: American Tract Society, 1833.
_____. *The Mother at Home, or the Principles of Maternal Duty.* New York: Crocker and Brewster, 1833.
Alcott, William A. *Familiar Letters to Young Men.* Buffalo: Geo. H. Derby and Co., 1850.

———. *The Physiology of Marriage.* Boston: John P. Jewett and Company, 1859.

———. *The Young Man's Guide.* 11th ed. Boston: Perkins and Marvin, 1837.

Atkinson, Brooks, ed. *The Complete Essays and Other Writings of Ralph Waldo Emerson.* The Modern Library. New York: Random House, 1950.

Beecher, Catharine E. and Stowe, Harriet Beecher. *The American Woman's Home: or Principles of Domestic Duty.* New York: J. B. Ford and Co., 1869.

Beecher, Catharine E. *Letters to the People on Health and Happiness.* New York: Harper and Brothers, 1855.

———. *A Treatise on Domestic Economy, for the Use of Young Ladies at Home and at School.* Boston: Marsh, Capen, Lyon, and Webb, 1841.

Beecher, Henry Ward. *Seven Lectures to Young Men.* Indianapolis: Thomas B. Cutler, 1844.

Brisbane, Albert. *Social Destiny of Man; or Association and Reorganization of Industry.* Philadelphia: C. F. Stollmeyer, 1840.

Bushnell, Horace. *Christian Nurture.* New York: Charles Scribner's Sons, 1890 (First published in 1847).

Child, Lydia Maria. *Letters from New-York.* New York: C. S. Francis and Co., 1844.

———. *The Mother's Book.* Boston: Carter, Hendee, and Babcock, 1831.

Drysdale, George. *The Elements of Social Science; or Physical Sexual, and Natural Religion.* London: E. Truelove, 1867.

Finney, Charles Grandison. *Lectures on Systematic Theology.* Edited by J. H. Fairchild. Oberlin, Ohio: E. J. Goodrich, 1887.

———. *Views of Sanctification.* Oberlin: James Steele, 1840.

Fowler, O. S. *Religion; Natural and Revealed: or The Natural Theology and Moral Bearings of Phrenology and Physiology.* New York: Fowler and Welles, 1844.

Graham, Sylvester. *Chastity, in a cause of Lectures to Young Men; intended also, For the Serious Consideration of Parents and Guardians.* 2nd ed. New York: Fowler and Welles, n.d.

Grimké, Sarah M. *Letters on the Equality of the Sexes and the Condition of Women.* Boston: Issac Knapp. 1838.

Love, Marriage and Divorce and the Sovereignty of the Individual. Source Book Press, 1972.

Mahan, Asa. *Scripture Doctrine of Christian Perfection.* . . . 11th ed. Oberlin: James M. Fitch, 1850.

Parker, Theodore. *Lessons From the World of Matter and the World of Man.* Edited by Rufus Leighton. Boston: American Unitarian Assoc., n.d.

_____. *Sins and Safeguards of Society.* Edited by Samuel B. Stewart. Boston: American Unitarian Assoc., n.d.

_____. *The Transient and Permanent in Christianity.* Edited by George Willis Cooke. Boston: American Unitarian Assoc., 1908.

Shepard, Odell, ed. *The Journals of Bronson Alcott.* Boston: Little, Brown, and Co., 1938.

Sigourney, Lydia H. *Letters to Mothers.* Hartford: Hudson & Skinner, 1838.

_____. *Letters to Young Ladies.* New York: Harper and Brothers, 1839.

Todd, John. *The Young Man: Hints Addressed to the Young Men of the United States.* 4th ed. Northampton: Hopkins, Bridgman and Co., 1850.

Walters, Ronald G., ed. *Primers for Prudery: Sexual Advice to Victorian America.* Spectrum Book. Englewood Cliffs, N.J.: Prentice-Hall, 1974.

Books and Articles—Secondary Sources

Allmendinger, David F. Jr. *Paupers and Scholars: The Transformation of Student Life in Nineteenth-Century New England.* New York: St. Martin's Press, 1975.

Arieli, Yehoshua. *Individualism and Nationalism in American Ideology.* Baltimore: Penguin Books, 1966.

Banner, Lois W. "Religion and Reform in the Early Republic: The Role of Youth." *American Quarterly* 23 (1971): 677–95.

Bestor, Arthur. *Backwoods Utopias: The Sectarian Origins and the Owenite Phase of Communitarian Socialism in America, 1663–1829.* 2nd ed. Philadelphia: Univ. of Pennsylvania Press, 1970.

_____. "Patent-Office Models of the Good Society: Some Relationships Between Social Reform and Westward Expansion." *American Historical Review* 58 (1953): 505–26.

Betts, John R. "Mind and Body in Early American Thought." *Journal of American History* 54 (1968): 787–805.

Bridges, William E. "Warm Hearth, Cold World: Social Perspectives on the Household Poets." *American Quarterly* 21 (1969): 764–79.

Brock, Peter. *Pacifism in the United States: From the Colonial Era to the First World War.* Princeton: Princeton Univ. Press, 1968.

184   *Bibliography*

Brown, Richard D. "Modernization: A Victorian Climax." In *Victorian America*, ed. Daniel Walker Howe, pp. 29–44. Philadelphia: Univ. of Pennsylvania Press, 1976.

Cross, Whitney R. *The Burned-Over District: The Social and Intellect-History of Enthusiastic Religion in Western New York, 1800–1850*. Harper Torchbooks. New York: Harper and Row, 1965.

Davies, John D. *Phrenology, Fad and Science: A Nineteenth-Century Crusade*. New Haven: Yale Univ. Press, 1955.

Davis, David Brion. "Some Ideological Functions of Prejudice in Ante-Bellum America." *American Quarterly* 15 (1963): 115–25.

———. "Some Themes of Counter-Subversion: An Analysis of Anti-Masonic, Anti-Catholic, and Anti-Mormon Literature." *Mississippi Valley Historical Review* 47 (1960): 205–24.

Delp, Robert W. "Andrew Jackson Davis: Prophet of American Spiritualism." *Journal of American History* 54 (1967): 43–56.

———. "Andrew Jackson Davis's *Revelations*, Harbinger of American Spiritualism." *The New-York Historical Society Quarterly* 55 (1971): 211–34.

Demos, John and Virginia. "Adolescence in Historical Perspective." *Journal of Marriage and the Family* 31 (1969): 632–43.

Egbert, Donald Drew and Persons, Stow, eds. *Socialism and American Life*. 2 vols. Princeton: Princeton Univ. Press, 1952.

Elson, Ruth Miller. *Guardians of Tradition: American Schoolbooks of the Nineteenth Century*. Lincoln: Univ. of Nebraska Press, 1964.

Fredrickson, George M. *The Inner Civil War: Northern Intellectuals and the Crisis of the Union*. Harper Torchbooks. New York and Evanston: Harper and Row, 1965.

Gordon, Michael and Bernstein, Charles M. "Mate Choice and Domestic Life in the Nineteenth-Century Marriage Manual." *Journal of Marriage and the Family* 32 (1970): 665–74.

Grimsted, David. "Rioting in Its Jacksonian Setting." *American Historical Review* 72 (1972): 361–97.

Gutman, Herbert G. "Work, Culture, and Society." *American Historical Review* 78 (1973): 531–88.

Heimert, Alan. "Moby-Dick and the American Political Symbolism." *American Quarterly* 15 (1963): 498–534.

Hiner, N. Ray. "Adolescence in Eighteenth-Century America." *History of Childhood Quarterly* 3 (1975): 253–80.

Howe, Daniel Walker. "Victorian Culture in America." In *Victorian America*, ed. by Daniel Walker Howe, pp. 3–28. Philadelphia: Univ. of Pennsylvania Press.

Jeffrey, Kirk. "The Family as Utopian Retreat from the City: The

Nineteenth-Century Contribution." In *The Family, Communes, and Utopian Societies*, edited by Sallie TeSelle, pp. 21–39. Harper Torchbooks. New York: Harper and Row, 1972.

Kett, Joseph F. "Adolescence and Youth in Nineteenth-Century America." *Journal of Interdisciplinary History* 2 (1971): 283–98.

———. "Growing Up in Rural New England, 1800–1840." In *Anonymous Americans: Explorations in Nineteenth-Century Social History*, edited by Tamara K. Hareven, pp. 283–98. Englewood-Cliffs, N.J.: Prentice-Hall, 1971.

Kuhn, Anne L. *The Mother's Role in Childhood Education: New England Concepts, 1830–1860*. New Haven: Yale Univ. Press, 1947.

Lewis, R. W. B. *The American Adam: Innocence, Tragedy, and Tradition in the Nineteenth Century*. Phoenix Book. Chicago: Univ. of Chicago Press, 1971.

Ludlum, David. *Social Ferment in Vermont, 1791–1850*. New York: AMS Press, 1966.

Marty, Martin E. *Righteous Empire: The Protestant Experience in America*. New York: The Dial Press, 1970.

Marx, Leo. *The Machine in the Garden: Technology and the Pastoral Ideal in America*. Paperback edition. New York: Oxford Univ. Press, 1968.

Mathews, Donald G. "The Second Great Awakening as an Organizing Process, 1780–1830." *American Quarterly* 21 (1969): 24–43.

Meyer, Donald. *The Positive Thinkers: A Study of the American Quest for Health, Wealth and Personal Power from Mary Baker Eddy to Norman Vincent Peale*. Garden City, New York: Doubleday and Company, 1965.

Meyers, Marvin. *The Jacksonian Persuasion: Politics and Belief*. Vintage Books. New York: Random House, 1960.

Miller, Perry. *The Life of the Mind in America: From the Revolution to the Civil War*. New York: Harcourt, Brace and World, 1965.

Moore, R. Laurence. "Spiritualism and Science: Reflections on the First Decade of the Spirit Rappings." *American Quarterly* 24 (1972): 474–500.

Nagel, Paul C. *This Sacred Trust: American Nationality, 1798–1898*. New York: Oxford Univ. Press, 1971.

Noyes, John Humphrey. *History of American Socialisms*. New York: Hillary House Publishers, 1961.

Paludan, Phillip S. "The American Civil War Considered as a Crisis in Law and Order." *American Historical Review* 77 (1972): 1013–34.

Perry, Lewis. *Radical Abolitionism: Anarchy and the Government of God in Antislavery Thought.* Ithaca: Cornell Univ. Press, 1973.

Pessen, Edward. *Jacksonian America: Society, Personality, and Politics.* Homewood, Ill.: The Dorsey Press, 1969.

Pivar, David J. *Purity Crusade: Sexual Morality and Social Control, 1868–1900.* Westport, Conn.: Greenwood Press, Inc., 1973.

Richards, Leonard L. *"Gentlemen of Property and Standing": Anti-Abolition Mobs in Jacksonian America.* New York: Oxford Univ. Press, 1970.

Rosenberg, Carroll Smith. "Beauty, the Beast and the Militant Woman: A Case Study in Sex Roles and Social Stress in Jacksonian America." *American Quarterly* 23 (1971): 562–84.

———. "The Hysterical Woman: Sex Roles and Role Conflict in 19th-Century America." *Social Research* 39 (1972): 652–78.

———, and Rosenberg, Charles. "The Female Animal: Medical and Biological Views of Woman and Her Role in Nineteenth-Century America." *Journal of American History* 60 (1973): 332–56.

Rosenberg, Charles E. *The Cholera Years: The United States in 1832, 1849, and 1866.* Chicago: Univ. of Chicago Press, 1962.

———. "Sexuality, Class and Role in 19th-Century America." *American Quarterly* 25 (1973): 131–54.

Rothman, David J. *The Discovery of the Asylum: Social Order and Disorder in the New Republic.* Boston and Toronto: Little, Brown and Co., 1971.

Sanford, Charles L. *The Quest for Paradise: Europe and the American Moral Imagination.* Urbana: Univ. of Illinois Press, 1961.

Smith, Timothy L. *Revivalism and Social Reform: American Protestantism on the Eve of the Civil War.* Harper Torchbooks. New York: Harper and Row, 1965.

Somkin, Fred. *Unquiet Eagle: Memory and Desire in the Idea of American Freedom, 1815–1860.* Ithaca: Cornell University Press, 1967.

Sunley, Robert. "Early Nineteenth-Century American Literature on Child Rearing." In *Childhood in Contemporary Cultures,* edited by Margaret Mead and Martha Wolfenstein, pp. 150–67. Chicago: Univ. of Chicago Press, 1966.

Taylor, William R. *Cavalier and Yankee: The Old South and the American National Character.* New York: George Braziller, 1961.

Thomas, John L. "Antislavery and Utopia." In *The Antislavery Vanguard: New Essays on the Abolitionists.* Edited by Martin Duberman, pp. 240–69. Princeton: Princeton Univ. Press, 1965.

———. "Romantic Reform in America." In *New Perspectives on the American Past.* Vol. 1, edited by Stanley Katz and Stanley I.

Kutler, pp. 466–91. Boston: Little, Brown and Co., 1969.

Thompson, J. Earl Jr. "Abolitionism and Theological Education at Andover." *New England Quarterly* 47 (1974): 238–61.

Tuveson, Ernest Lee. *Redeemer Nation: The Idea of America's Millennial Role.* Chicago: Univ. of Chicago Press, 1968.

Tyler, Alice Felt. *Freedom's Ferment: Phases of American Social History from the Colonial Period to the Outbreak of the Civil War.* Harper Torchbooks. New York: Harper and Row, 1962.

Walters, Ronald G. "The Erotic South: Civilization and Sexuality in American Abolitionism." *American Quarterly* 25 (1973): 177–201.

Welter, Barbara. "The Cult of True Womanhood, 1820–1860." *American Quarterly* 18 (1966): 151–74.

Wilson, R. Jackson. *In Quest of Community: Social Philosophy in the United States, 1860–1920.* Paperback edition. New York: Oxford Univ. Press, 1970.

SOURCES FROM THE SOCIAL SCIENCES

Arlow, Jacob A. "The Consecration of the Prophet." *Psychoanalytic Quarterly* 20 (1951): 374–97.

_____. "Ego Psychology and the Study of Mythology." *Journal of the American Psychoanalytic Association* 9 (1961): 371–93.

Bak, Robert C. "Being in Love and Object Loss." *International Journal of Psychoanalysis* 54 (1973): 1–8.

Barnett, Joseph. "Dependency Conflicts in the Young Adult." *Psychoanalytic Review* 58 (Spring, 1971): 111–24.

Beres, David. "Ego Autonomy and Ego Pathology." *Psychoanalytic Study of the Child* 26 (1971): 3–23. New York and Chicago: Quadrangle Books.

Berkowitz, Louis. "The Devil Within." *Psychoanalytic Review* 55 (1968): 28–36.

Bibring, Edward. "The Mechanism of Depression." In *Affective Disorders: Psychoanalytic Contributions to Their Study,* edited by Phyllis Greenacre, pp. 13–46. New York: International Universites Press, 1953.

Blatt, Sidney J. "Levels of Object Representation in Anaclitic and Introjective Depression." *Psychoanalytic Study of the Child* 29 (1974): 107–53. New Haven: Yale University Press.

Blos, Peter. "The Epigenesis of the Adult Neurosis." *Psychoanalytic Study of the Child* 27 (1972): 106–34.

_____. "The Genealogy of the Ego Ideal." *Psychoanalytic Study of the Child* 29 (1974): 43–86.

Brenner, Charles. "Depression, Anxiety and Affect Theory." *International Journal of Psychoanalysis* 55 (1974): 25–32.

———. "On the Nature and Development of Affects: A Unified Theory." *Psychoanalytic Quarterly* 43 (1974): 532–56.

Edgcumbe, Rose and Burgner, Marion. "Some Problems in the Conceptualization of Early Object Relationships: Part I: The Concept of Need Satisfaction and Need-Satisfying Relationships." *Psychoanalytic Study of the Child* 27 (1972): 283–312.

———. "Some Problems in the Conceptualization of Early Object Relationships. Part II: The Concept of Object Constancy." *Psychoanalytic Study of the Child* 27 (1972): 315–31.

Eissler, Kurt R. "Death Drive, Ambivalence, and Narcissism." *Psychoanalytic Study of the Child* 26 (1971): 25–75.

Engel, George L. "Anxiety and Depression-Withdrawal: The Primary Affects of Unpleasure." *International Journal of Psychoanalysis* 43 (1962): 89–96.

Evans, William N. "The Eye of Jealousy and Envy." *Psychoanalytic Review* 62 (1975): 481–92.

Feldman, Sandor S. "Blushing, Fear of Blushing, and Shame." *Journal of the American Psychoanalytic Association* 10 (1962): 368–85.

Festinger, Leon; Riecken, Henry W.; and Schachter, Stanley. *When Prophecy Fails*. Minneapolis: Univ. of Minnesota Press, 1956.

Freedman, David A. "The Genesis of Obsessional Phenomena." *Psychoanalytic Review* 58 (1971): 367–82.

Freud, Anna. *The Ego and the Mechanisms of Defense*. Rev. ed. *The Writings of Anna Freud*, vol. 2. New York: International Universities Press, Inc., 1966.

———. "Obsessional Neurosis: A Summary of Psycho-Analytic Views as Presented at the Congress." *International Journal of Psychoanalysis* 47 (1966): 116–22.

Freud, Sigmund. *The Ego and the Id*. Translated by Joan Riviere, revised and edited by James Strachey. The Norton Library. New York: Doubleday and Company, Inc., 1957.

———. "Obsessive Acts and Religious Practices." *The Standard Edition of the Complete Psychological Works of Sigmund Freud*, edited by James Strachey, 9: 117–27. London: Hogarth Press, 1959.

Gay, Volney Patrick. "Psychopathology and Ritual: Freud's Essay 'Obsessive Actions and Religious Practises.' " *Psychoanalytic Review* 62 (1975): 493–507.

Gitelson, Maxwell. "Therapeutic Problems in the Analysis of the

'Normal' Candidate." *International Journal of Psychoanalysis* 35 (1954): 174–83.

Greenacre, Phyllis. "A Study on the Nature of Inspiration. Part I: Some Special Considerations Regarding the Phallic Phase." *Journal of the American Psychoanalytic Association* 12 (1964): 6–31.

Greenson, Ralph R. "The 'Real' Relationship Between the Patient and the Psychoanalyst." In *The Unconscious Today: Essays in Honor of Max Schur*, edited by Mark Kanzer, pp. 213–32. New York: International Universities Press, 1971.

Grotjahn, Martin. "Ego Identity and the Fear of Death and Dying." *Journal of the Hillside Hospital* 9 (1960): 147–55.

Jacobson, Edith. *Depression: Comparative Studies in Normal, Neurotic, and Psychotic Conditions.* New York: International Universities Press, 1971.

_____. "The Regulation of Self-Esteem." In *Depression and Human Existence*, edited by E. James Anthony and Therese Benedek, pp. 169–80. Boston: Little, Brown and Co., 1975.

_____. *The Self and the Object World.* New York: International Universities Press, 1964.

Jaffe, Daniel S. "The Masculine Envy of Woman's Procreative Function." *Journal of the American Psychoanalytic Association* 16 (1968): 521–48.

Jarvis, Wilbur. "Some Effects of Pregnancy and Childbirth on Men." *Journal of the American Psychoanalytic Association* 10 (1962): 689–700.

Joffe, Walter G. "A Critical Review of the Status of the Envy Concept." *International Journal of Psychoanalysis* 50 (1969): 533–44.

Joffe, W. G. and Sandler, Joseph. "Comments on the Psychoanalytic Psychology of Adaptation, with Special Reference to the Role of Affects and the Representational World." *International Journal of Psychoanalysis* 49 (1968): 445–53.

Kanter, Rosabeth Moss. "Commitment and Social Organization: A Study of Commitment Mechanisms in Utopian Communities." *American Sociological Review* 33 (1968): 499–517.

Kaplan, Donald M. "On Shyness." *International Journal of Psychoanalysis* 53 (1972): 439–52.

Karch, Fred. E. "Blushing." *Psychoanalytic Review* 58 (1971): 37–50.

Katz, Jay. "On Primary Gain and Secondary Gain." *Psychoanalytic Study of the Child* 18 (1963): 9–50.

Kernberg, Otto F. "Barriers to Falling and Remaining in Love." *Jour-

nal of the American Psychoanalytic Association 22 (1974): 486–511.

―――. "Factors in the Psychoanalytic Treatment of Narcissistic Personalities." *Journal of the American Psychoanalytic Association* 18 (1970): 51–84.

―――. "A Psychoanalytic Classification of Character Pathology." *Journal of the American Psychoanalytic Association* 18 (1970): 801–20.

Kohut, Heinz. *The Analysis of the Self: A Systematic Approach to Psychoanalytic Treatment of Narcissistic Personality Disorders.* The Psychoanalytic Study of the Child Monograph No. 4. New York: International Universities Press, 1971.

Kris, Ernst. *Psychoanalytic Explorations in Art.* New York: Schocken Books, 1967.

Lampl-de Groot, Jeanne. *The Development of the Mind: Psychoanalytic Papers on Clinical and Theoretical Problems.* New York: International Universities Press, 1965.

Levin, Sidney. "The Psychoanalysis of Shame." *International Journal of Psychoanalysis* 52 (1971): 355–62.

Lewis, Helen B. *Shame and Guilt in Neurosis.* New York: International Universities Press, 1971.

Loewald, Hans. W. "The Experience of Time." *Psychoanalytic Study of the Child* 27 (1972): 401–10.

―――. "Internalization, Separation, Mourning, and the Superego." *Psychoanalytic Quarterly* 21 (1962): 483–504.

―――. "The Superego and Ego Ideal: Superego and Time." *International Journal of Psychoanalysis* 43 (1962): 264–68.

Loewenstein, Rudolph M. "Developments in the Theory of Transference in the Last Fifty Years." *International Journal of Psychoanalysis* 50 (1969): 583–87.

―――. "On the Theory of the Superego: A Discussion." In *Psychoanalysis—A General Psychology: Essays in Honor of Heinz Hartmann,* edited by Rudolph M. Lowenstein, *et al.,* pp. 298–314. New York: International Universities Press, 1966.

Lubin, Albert J. "A Boy's View of Jesus." *Psychoanalytic Study of the Child* 14 (1959): 155–68.

Mahler, Margaret S. "Notes on the Development of Basic Moods: The Depressive Affect." In *Psychoanalysis—A General Psychology: Essays in Honor of Heinz Hartmann,* edited by Rudolph M. Loewenstein, *et al.,* pp. 152–67. New York: International Universities Press, 1966.

Mendelson, Meyer. *Psychoanalytic Concepts of Depression.* Springfield, Ill.: Charles C. Thomas, 1960.

Miller, Jule P. Jr. "The Psychology of Blushing." *International Journal of Psychoanalysis* 46 (1965): 189–91.

Modell, Arnold E. *Object Love and Reality: An Introduction to a Psychoanalytic Theory of Object Relations.* New York: International Universities Press, 1968.

———. "A Narcissistic Defense Against Affects and the Illusion of Self-Sufficiency." *International Journal of Psychoanalysis* 56 (1975): 275–82.

Noy, Pinchas. "A Revision of the Psychoanalytic Theory of the Primary Process." *International Journal of Psychoanalysis* 50 (1969): 155–77.

———. "Symbolism and Mental Representation." *The Annual of Psychoanalysis: A Publication of the Chicago Institute for Psychoanalysis.* 1: 125–57. New York: Quadrangle/The New York Times Book Co., 1973.

Ostow, Mortimer. *The Psychology of Melancholy.* New York: Harper and Row, 1970.

———. "Psychological Defense against Depression." *Depression and Human Existence*, edited by E. James Anthony and Therese Benedek, pp. 395–410. Boston: Little, Brown and Co., 1975.

Peretz, David. "Development, Object-Relationships, and Loss." In *Loss and Grief: Psychological Management in Medical Practice*, edited by Bernard Schoenberg, et al., pp. 3–19. New York: Columbia Univ. Press, 1970.

———. "Reaction to Loss." In *Loss and Grief: Psychological Management in Medical Practice*, edited by Bernard Schoenberg, *et al.*, pp. 20–35. New York: Columbia Univ. Press, 1970.

Piers, Gerhart and Singer, Milton B. *Shame and Guilt: A Psychoanalytic and a Cultural Study.* New York: W. W. Norton and Co., 1971.

Pinderhughes, Charles A. "Somatic, Psychic, and Social Sequelae of Loss." *Journal of the American Psychoanalytic Association* 19 (1971): 670–95.

Platt, Gerald M., and Weinstein, Fred. "Alienation and the Problem of Social Action." In *The Phenomenon of Sociology*, edited by Edward A. Tiryakin, pp. 284–310. New York: Appleton-Century-Crofts, 1971.

Pollock, George H. "Anniversary Reactions, Trauma, and Mourning." *Psychoanalytic Quarterly* 29 (1970): 347–69.

———. "On Anniversary Suicide and Mourning." In *Depression and Human Existence*, edited by E. James Anthony and Therese Benedek, pp. 369–92. Boston: Little, Brown and Co., 1975.

———. "On Mourning, Immortality, and Utopia." *Journal of the American Psychoanalytic Association* 23 (1975): 334–60.

———. "On Time and Anniversaries." In *The Unconscious Today: Essays in Honor of Max Schur*, edited by Mark Kanzer, pp. 233–57. New York: International Universities Press, 1971.

———. "On Time, Death, and Immortality." *Psychoanalytic Quarterly* 40 (1971): 437–45.

Rangell, Leo. "The Decision-Making Process: A Contribution from Psychoanalysis." *Psychoanalytic Study of the Child* 26 (1971): 425–49.

Reich, Annie. "A Character Formation Representing the Integration of Unusual Conflict Solutions into the Ego Structure." *Psychoanalytic Study of the Child* 13 (1958): 309–23. New York: International Universities Press.

———. "Masturbation and Self-Esteem." In *Annie Reich: Psychoanalytic Contributions*, pp. 312–33. New York: International Universities Press, 1973.

———. "Pathologic Forms of Self-Esteem Regulation." *Psychoanalytic Study of the Child* 15 (1960): 215–32.

Rochlin, Gregory. *Griefs and Discontents: The Forces of Change.* Boston: Little, Brown and Co., 1965.

———. *Man's Aggression: The Defense of the Self.* Boston: Gambit, 1973.

Rose, Gilbert J. "Narcissistic Fusion States and Creativity." In *The Unconscious Today: Essays in Honor of Max Schur*, edited by Mark Kanzer, pp. 495–505. New York: International Universities Press, 1971.

Salzman, Leon. *The Obsessive Personality: Origins, Dynamics, and Therapy.* New York: Science House, 1968.

Sandler, Joseph. "The Background of Safety." *International Journal of Psychoanalysis* 41 (1960): 352–56.

———, and Rosenblatt, Bernard. "The Concept of the Representational World." *Psychoanalytic Study of the Child.* 18 (1962): 128–45.

———; and Holder, Alex; and Meers, Dale. "The Ego Ideal and the Ideal Self." *Psychoanalytic Study of the Child* 18 (1963): 139–58.

———. "On the Concept of the Superego." *Psychoanalytic Study of the Child* 15 (1960): 128–62.

———. "Psychological Conflict and the Structural Model: Some Clinical and Theoretical Implications." *International Journal of Psychoanalysis* 55 (1974): 53–61.

Schafer, Roy. *Aspects of Internalization.* New York: International Universities Press, 1968.

_____. "Ideals, the Ego Ideal, and the Ideal Self." In *Motives and Thought: Psychoanalytic Essays in Memory of David Rapaport,* edited by Robert R. Holt. Psychological Issues, Monograph 18/19, pp. 131–74. New York: International Universities Press, 1967.

_____. "The Loving and Beloved Superego in Freud's Structural Theory." *Psychoanalytic Study of the Child* 15 (1960): 163–88.

_____. "On the Theoretical and Technical Conceptualization of Activity and Passivity." *Psychoanalytic Quarterly* 38 (1968): 173–96.

Schmale, Arthur H. "A Genetic View of Affects: With Special Reference to the Genesis of Helplessness and Hopelessness." *Psychoanalytic Study of the Child* 19 (1964): 287–313.

_____. "Depression as Affect, Character Style, and Symptom Formation." In *Psychoanalysis and Contemporary Science.* An Annual of Integrative and Interdisciplinary Studies, edited by Robert R. Holt and Emanuel Peterfreund, 1: 327–49. New York: MacMillan, 1972.

_____, and Engel, George L. "The Role of Conservation-Withdrawal in Depressive Reactions." In *Depression and Human Existence,* edited by E. James Anthony and Therese Benedek, pp. 183–96. Boston: Little, Brown and Co., 1975.

Schur, Max. "The Ego in Anxiety." In *Drives, Affects, and Behavior,* edited by Rudolph M. Loewenstein, pp. 67–103. New York: International Universities Press, 1953.

Seidenberg, Robert. "Fidelity and Jealousy: Socio-Cultural Considerations." *Psychoanalytic Review* 54 (1967): 583–608.

_____. "The Trauma of Eventlessness." *Psychoanalytic Review* 59 (1972): 95–108.

Shapiro, David. *Neurotic Styles.* New York and London: Basic Books, 1965.

Spiegel, Leo A. "Superego and the Function of Anticipation with Comments on 'Anticipatory Anxiety.' " In *Psychoanalysis—A General Psychology: Essays in Honor of Heinz Hartman,* edited by Rudolph M. Loewenstein, *et al.,* pp. 315–36. New York: International Universities Press, 1966.

Spielman, Philip M. "Envy and Jealousy: "An Attempt at Clarification." *Psychoanalytic Quarterly* 40 (1971): 59–82.

Stein, Martin H. "The Marriage Bond." *Psychoanalytic Quarterly* 25 (1956): 238–59.

_____. "Self-Observation, Reality, and the Superego." In *Psycho-*

analysis—A General Psychology: Essays in Honor of Heinz Hart-mann, edited by Rudolph M. Loewenstein, *et al.*, pp. 257–313. New York: International Universities Press, 1966.

Tartakoff, Helen H. "The Normal Personality in Our Culture and the Nobel Prize Complex." In *Psychoanalysis—A General Psychology: Essays in Honor of Heinz Hartmann*, edited by Rudolph M. Loewenstein, *et al.*, pp. 222–49. New York: International Universities Press, 1966.

Tolpin, Paul H. "On the Regulation of Anxiety: Its Relation to 'The Timelessness of the Unconscious and Its Capacity for Hallucination.'" In *The Annual of Psychoanalysis: A Publication of the Chicago Institute for Psychoanalysis*, 2, 150–75. New York: International Universities Press, 1975.

Tonnies, Ferdinand. *Community & Society*. Translated and edited by Charles P. Loomis. Harper Torchbooks. New York: Harper and Row, 1963.

Weinshel, Edward M. "Some Psychoanalytic Considerations on Moods." *International Journal of Psychoanalysis* 51 (1970): 313–20.

Weinstein, Fred, and Platt, Gerald M. "The Coming Crisis in Psycho-History." *Journal of Modern History* 47 (1975): 202–81.

———. *Psychoanalytic Sociology: An Essay on the Interpretation of Historical Data and the Phenomena of Collective Behavior*. Baltimore: Johns Hopkins Press, 1973.

———. *The Wish to be Free: Society, Psyche, and Value Change*. Berkeley and Los Angeles: University of California Press, 1969.

Wixen, Burton H. "Object-Specific Superego Responses." *Journal of the American Psychoanalytic Association* 18 (1970): 831–40.

Index

335.974
T366m

54148